Stoic
Foundations

Stoic Foundations

THE CORNERSTONE WORKS OF STOICISM

—

BY MARCUS AURELIUS, SENECA, AND EPICTETUS

Translated by C. R. Haines, Richard Mott Gummere,
and William Abbott Oldfather

Introduction by Massimo Pigliucci

Go
hachette
BOOKS

Hachette Go, an imprint of Hachette Books
Hachette Book Group
1290 Avenue of the Americas
New York, NY 10104
HachetteGo.com
Facebook.com/HachetteGo
Instagram.com/HachetteGo

First Edition: November, 2023

Published by Hachette Go, an imprint of Hachette Book Group, Inc. The Hachette Go name and logo is a trademark of the Hachette Book Group.

The Hachette Speakers Bureau provides a wide range of authors for speaking events. To find out more, go to hachettespeakersbureau.com or email HachetteSpeakers@hbgusa.com.

Hachette Go books may be purchased in bulk for business, educational, or promotional use. For information, please contact your local bookseller or Hachette Book Group Special Markets Department at: special.markets@hbgusa.com.

The publisher is not responsible for websites (or their content) that are not owned by the publisher.

Print book interior design by Bart Dawson.

Library of Congress Cataloging-in-Publication Data has been applied for.

ISBNs: 978-0-306-83473-8 (trade paperback), 978-0-306-83475-2 (ebook)

Printed in the United States of America

LSC-C

Printing 1, 2023

Contents

———

Stoicism, a Very Brief Introduction

By Massimo Pigliucci

———

IMAGINE BEING TRANSPORTED BACK TO THE FOURTH CENTURY BCE. Athens is still the cultural capital of the Mediterranean world, though it has lost its political preeminence after the end of the Peloponnesian War against Sparta and the subsequent Macedonian conquest of all of Greece.

A fellow by the name of Zeno of Citium (modern-day Cyprus) is a wealthy merchant on his way by ship to the Athenian port of Piraeus with a precious cargo of purple dye. A big storm breaks out, and the ship sinks with all its wares. Zeno survives and makes it to shore. Once in Athens, he goes to a local bookshop where he hears the owner reading some passages aloud from the *Memorabilia*, a book by Xenophon about the life of Socrates.

Zeno is struck by the notion of living life as a philosopher and asks the bookseller where he can find one of these strange fellows. The shop owner points to a guy passing by and says, "There goes one. Follow him." The guy in question is Crates of Thebes, a philosopher belonging to the controversial school of the Cynics, people who gave up all their properties and relations to serve as examples of virtue to their fellow citizens. They also engaged in a lot of in-your-face behavior, flaunting social conventions and living in the streets. Hence their name: *kynikos* in Greek means dog-like, and it was not meant as a compliment.

Zeno does follow Crates and becomes his student, thus beginning over a decade of intense study of practical philosophy with teachers from a wide range of schools, including Platonism. Finally, around 301 BCE, Zeno feels ready to begin teaching philosophy to others. He chooses to do so in a public space, the Stoa Poikile, or painted porch, on the north side of the agora, Athens's major marketplace. The idea was that philosophy ought to benefit anyone who might be interested, and it should therefore be taught in the open, not in secluded schools like Plato's Academy, Aristotle's Lyceum, or Epicurus' Garden.

The new philosophy of Stoicism—named after the Stoa—was born. It quickly spread throughout the Mediterranean and became one of the dominant schools during the Hellenistic period (323 to 31 BCE) and then the Roman Empire. The three Roman authors you are about to read—Seneca the Younger, Epictetus, and Marcus Aurelius—were Stoics, and their collective writings represent the large majority of what has survived from that school until our time, two millennia later.

But what exactly *is* Stoicism? And why should we care about it in a century of advanced science and artificial intelligence? What good could Stoicism possibly do for us denizens of the twenty-first century?

At bottom, Stoicism is a philosophy of life, meaning a framework for living our life in the best way possible, for guiding us through our choices, and—most importantly—for becoming the most excellent human beings we can be.

There are two fundamental ideas on which Stoic philosophy is based: (i) we should live "in agreement with nature," as Zeno himself put it; and (ii) we should think of ourselves as *kosmopolitês*, that is, citizens of the world. Let's look at these two pillars of Stoicism, how they are deeply intertwined, and how they can help us develop both better selves and a better world to live in.

To be in agreement with nature means to take seriously what sort of animal human beings are and act accordingly. Consider first a non-human example. If you invite me over for dinner and I bring you a cactus as a present, you are now in charge of the cactus's well-being. What do you do? You inform yourself about the nature of cactuses. In doing so you'll discover that they are desert plants, which means that they need relatively little water (too much is going to kill them!) and a lot of light. To live in agreement with nature for a cactus means exactly that: little water, much light (and a few other things).

When it comes to human beings, the Stoics thought that the two most important and distinctive aspects of our species are that we are highly social animals and that we are capable of reason. Today we would say that's how evolution has made us. It follows that a good human life is one in which we act pro-socially while using our minds to solve problems.

Which brings us to cosmopolitanism. Reason and observation tell us that all human beings are fundamentally the same. Regardless of their gender, ethnicity, or culture, we all want the same things (love, recognition, material support, and so on), and we all fear the same things (pain, suffering, death). We are, in other terms, all members of the same worldwide family of humanity, the cosmopolis. What follows from that is that we ought to be helpful to one another, no matter who those others are and where they come from.

Think of the implications of living pro-socially and reasonably within a worldwide community. There would be no wars, all conflicts would be resolved on the basis of reason and evidence, and there would be no artificial national boundaries. That is exactly the view articulated by Zeno of Citium in a book he wrote titled *The Republic*. We are certainly still very far from that ideal goal, and yet evidence from the study of history tells us that human communities have steadily increased in size—from small bands of mostly related individuals to large nation states; that we have constantly struggled to find new ways to resolve our differences without recourse to violence; and that we are trying to consider a global perspective by way of institutions like the United Nations, the World Health Organization, and many others.

Indeed, the sort of problems we face, from pandemics (literally: an epidemic affecting everyone, everywhere) to climate change, are global in nature and therefore require a global perspective to be effectively tackled. They also require the use of reason, as the alternative is increased violence and disruption. In other words, the world really needs Stoicism.

But how do we practice Stoic philosophy on a day-to-day basis? There are a number of ways, but perhaps the simplest one is to use the four cardinal virtues as a moral compass to be deployed every time we make a decision, big or small as it may be.

A virtue is simply a character trait, or a behavioral tendency. Let's say you have a friend who you think of as generous. What do you mean by that? Well, to be generous means that, other things being equal, your friend *acts* generously, that is, she invests time, effort, and resources to help other people.

The Stoics recognized a number of worthwhile virtues that we can cultivate, but four were essential: mindfulness (*phronêsis*), justice (*dikaiosynê*), courage (*andreia*), and temperance (*sôphrosynê*). Stoic mindfulness is the knowledge of what is good, of what is bad, and of how to achieve the first and steer clear from the latter. Justice means behaving fairly toward others, treating them with respect and dignity. Courage is the notion that we should do the right thing even when it costs us personally. And temperance is about self-control and moderation, doing things in right measure.

The Stoic approach consists in asking yourself whether what you are about to do is in accordance with the four cardinal virtues. If it is, go ahead and do it. If it isn't, abstain. For instance, should I intervene if I see a coworker being harassed by my boss? Mindfulness tells me that intervention, broadly speaking, is the right thing to do; justice concurs because I will ensure that my coworker is treated fairly and with dignity; it will require courage because I could face retaliation from my boss; and temperance says that the best course of action is to step in firmly but calmly, no violence being necessary. Try it out. Live like a Stoic for a week or a month and see how it feels. I am betting that you and your loved ones will soon see improvements in the way you handle the challenges and setbacks of life.

And you couldn't possibly ask for better guides to your practice than the three authors you are about to read. Seneca's *Letters* are an informal curriculum in Stoic philosophy that the first century Roman statesman and philosopher wrote for the benefit of his friend Lucilius. Epictetus's manual, the *Enchiridion*, is a short but practical guide to the Stoic life. And the emperor Marcus Aurelius's *Meditations*, though written as a personal philosophical diary of reflection and self-improvement, brim with wisdom and empathy for fellow human beings, thus dismantling the stereotype of Stoicism as the philosophy of the stiff upper lip.

As Seneca himself wrote, one sure way to get guidance on how to live a good life and become a better human being is to regularly spend time with the best of what humanity has produced over the course of centuries. These three books certainly make any such list. Their authors may become your lifelong companions, and their writings will change your life for the better, beginning now.

Publisher's Note on Translations

———

THE THREE TRANSLATIONS INCLUDED IN *STOIC FOUNDATIONS* HAVE been selected because they are both accessible and readable, while having stood the test of time.

In the case of Haines's translation of *Meditations*, the text has been lightly modernized to make it more readable and accessible for modern readers, primarily by trading the informal second person (thee and thou) in favor of the more modern "you" and "your." Gummere's translation of Seneca and Oldfather's translation of the *Enchiridion* remain largely untouched, with only occasional substitutions for confusing or archaic diction and modern spellings.

Meditations

—

MARCUS AURELIUS

Translated by C. R. Haines

That which is done well enough is done quickly enough.

Caesar Augustus

Contents

_____

BOOK I

———

1 FROM MY GRANDFATHER VERUS, A KINDLY DISPOSITION AND sweetness of temper.

2. From what I heard of my Father and my memory of him, modesty, and manliness.

3. From my Mother, the fear of God, and generosity; and abstention not only from doing ill but even from the very thought of doing it; and furthermore to live the simple life, far removed from the habits of the rich.

4. From my Grandfather's Father, to dispense with attendance at public schools, and to enjoy good teachers at home, and to recognize that on such things money should be eagerly spent.

5. From my Tutor, not to side with the Green Jacket or the Blue at the races, or to back the Light-Shield Champion or the Heavy-Shield in the lists; not to shirk toil, and to have few wants, and to do my own work, and mind my own concerns; and to turn a deaf ear to slander.

6. From Diognetus, not to be taken up with trifles; and not to give credence to the statements of miracle-mongers and wizards about incantations and the exorcizing of demons, and such-like marvels; and not to keep quails, nor to be excited about such things: not to resent plain speaking; and to become familiar with philosophy and be a hearer first of Baccheius, then of Tandasis and Marcianus; and to write dialogues as a boy; and to set my heart on a pallet-bed and a pelt and whatever else tallied with the Greek regimen.

7. From Rusticus, to become aware of the fact that I needed amendment and training for my character; and not to be led aside into an argumentative sophistry; nor compose treatises on speculative subjects, or deliver little homilies, or pose ostentatiously as the moral athlete or unselfish man; and to eschew rhetoric, poetry, and fine language; and not to go about the house in my robes, nor commit any such breach of good taste; and to write letters without affectation, like his own letter written to my mother from Sinuessa; to show oneself ready to be reconciled to those who have lost their temper and trespassed against one, and ready to meet them halfway as soon as ever they seem to be willing to retrace their steps; to read with minute care and not to be content with a superficial bird's-eye view; nor to be too quick in agreeing with every voluble talker; and to make the acquaintance of the Memoirs of Epictetus, which he supplied me with out of his own library.

Look to nothing else . . . save Reason alone

8. From Apollonius, self-reliance and an unequivocal determination not to leave anything to chance; and to look to nothing else even for a moment save Reason alone; and to remain ever the same, in the throes of pain, on the loss of a child, during a lingering illness; and to see plainly from a living example that one and the same man can be very vehement and yet gentle: not to be impatient in instructing others; and to see in him a man who obviously counted as the least among his gifts his practical experience and facility in imparting philosophic truths; and to learn in accepting seeming favors from friends not to give up our independence for such things nor take them callously as a matter of course.

9. From Sextus, kindliness, and the example of a household patriarchally governed; and the conception of life in accordance with Nature; and dignity without affectation; and an intuitive consideration for friends; and a toleration of the unlearned and the unreasoning.

And his tactful treatment of all his friends, so that simply to be with him was more delightful than any flattery, while at the same time those who enjoyed this privilege looked up to him with the utmost reverence; and the grasp and method which he showed in discovering and marshalling the essential axioms of life.

And never to exhibit any symptom of anger or any other passion, but to be at the same time utterly impervious to all passions and full of natural affection; and to praise without noisy obtrusiveness, and to possess great learning but make no parade of it.

10. From Alexander the Grammarian, not to be captious; nor in a carping spirit find fault with those who import into their conversation any expression which is barbarous or ungrammatical or mispronounced, but tactfully to bring in the very expression, that ought to have been used, by way of answer, or as it were in joint support of the assertion, or as a joint consideration of the thing itself and not of the language, or by some such graceful reminder.

11. From Fronto, to note the envy, the subtlety, and the dissimulation which are habitual to a tyrant; and that, as a general rule, those among us who rank as patricians are somewhat wanting in natural affection.

12. From Alexander the Platonist, not to say to anyone often or without necessity, nor write in a letter, I am too busy, nor in this fashion constantly plead urgent affairs as an excuse for evading the obligations entailed upon us by our relations toward those around us.

13. From Catulus, not to disregard a friend's expostulation even when it is unreasonable, but to try to bring him back to his usual friendliness; and to speak with wholehearted goodwill of one's teachers, as it is recorded that Domitius did of Athenodotus; and to be genuinely fond of one's children.

14. From my "brother" Severus, love of family, love of truth, love of justice, and (thanks to him!) to know Thrasea, Helvidius, Cato, Dion, Brutus; and the conception of a state with one law for all, based upon individual equality and freedom of speech, and of a sovereignty which prizes above all things the liberty of the subject; and furthermore from him also

to set a well-balanced and unvarying value on philosophy; and readiness to do others a kindness, and eager generosity, and optimism, and confidence in the love of friends; and perfect openness in the case of those that came in for his censure; and the absence of any need for his friends to surmise what he did or did not wish, so plain was it.

15. From Maximus, self-mastery and stability of purpose; and cheeriness in sickness as well as in all other circumstances; and a character justly proportioned of sweetness and gravity; and to perform without grumbling the task that lies to one's hand.

And the confidence of every one in him that what he said was also what he thought, and that what he did was done with no ill intent. And not to show surprise, and not to be daunted; never to be hurried, or hold back, or be at a loss, or downcast, or smile a forced smile, or, again, be ill-tempered or suspicious.

And beneficence and placability and veracity; and to give the impression of a man who cannot deviate from the right way rather than of one who is kept in it; and that no one could have thought himself looked down upon by him, or could go so far as to imagine himself a better man than he; and to keep pleasantry within due bounds.

16. From my Father, mildness, and an unshakable adherence to decisions deliberately come to; and no empty vanity in respect to so-called honors; and a love of work and thoroughness; and a readiness to hear any suggestions for the common good; and an inflexible determination to give every man his due; and to know by experience when is the time to insist and when to desist; and to suppress all passion for boys.

And his public spirit, and his not at all requiring his friends to sup with him or necessarily attend him abroad, and their always finding him the same when any urgent affairs had kept them away; and the spirit of thorough investigation which he showed in the meetings of his Council, and his perseverance; nay his never desisting prematurely from an enquiry on the strength of off-hand impressions; and his faculty for keeping his friends and never being bored with them or infatuated about them; and his self-reliance in every emergency, and his good humor; and his habit of looking ahead and making provision for the smallest details without any heroics.

And his restricting in his reign public acclamations and every sort of adulation; and his unsleeping attention to the needs of the empire, and his wise stewardship of its resources, and his patient tolerance of the censure that all this entailed; and his freedom from superstition with respect to the gods and from hunting for popularity with respect to men by pandering to their desires or by courting the mob: his soberness in all things and steadfastness; and the absence in him of all vulgar tastes and any craze for novelty.

And the example that he gave of utilizing without pride, and at the same without any apology, all the lavish gifts of Fortune that contribute toward the comfort of life, so as to enjoy them when present as a matter of course, and, when absent, not to miss them: and no one could charge him with sophistry, flippancy, or pedantry; but he was a man mature, complete, deaf to flattery, able to preside over his own affairs and those of others.

Besides this also was his high appreciation of all true philosophers without any upbraiding of the others, and at the same time without any undue subservience to them; then again his easiness of access and his graciousness that yet had nothing fulsome about it; and his reasonable attention to his bodily requirements, not as one too fond of life, or vain of his outward appearance, nor yet as one who neglected it, but so as by his own carefulness to need but very seldom the skill of the leech or medicines and outward applications.

But most of all a readiness to acknowledge without jealousy the claims of those who were endowed with any especial gift, such as eloquence or knowledge of law or ethics or any other subject, and to give them active support, that each might gain the honor to which his individual eminence entitled him; and his loyalty to constitutional precedent without any parade of the fact that it was according to precedent.

Furthermore he was not prone to change or vacillation, but attached to the same places and the same things; and after his spasms of violent headache he would come back at once to his usual employments with renewed vigor; and his secrets were not many but very few and at very rare intervals, and then only political secrets; and he showed good sense and moderation in his management of public spectacles, and in the construction of public works, and in congiaria and the like, as a man who had an eye to what had to be done and not to the credit to be gained thereby.

He did not bathe at all hours; he did not build for the love of building; he gave no thought to his food, or to the texture and color of his clothes, or the comeliness of his slaves. His robe came up from Lorium, his country-seat in the plains, and Lanuvium supplied his wants for the most part. Think of how he dealt with the customs' officer at Tusculum when the latter apologized, and it was a type of his usual conduct.

There was nothing rude in him, nor yet overbearing or violent nor carried, as the phrase goes, "to the sweating state"; but everything was considered separately, as by a man of ample leisure, calmly, methodically, manfully, consistently. One might apply to him what is told of Socrates, that he was able to abstain from or enjoy those things that many are not strong enough to refrain from and too much inclined to enjoy. But to have the strength to persist in the one case and be abstemious in the other is characteristic of a man who has a perfect and indomitable soul, as was seen in the illness of Maxim us.

17. From the gods, to have good grandfathers, good parents, a good sister, good teachers, good companions, kinsmen, friends—nearly all of them; and that I fell into no trespass against any of them, and yet I had a disposition that way inclined, such as might have led me into something of the sort, had it so chanced; but by the grace of God there was no such coincidence of circumstances as was likely to put me to the test.

And that I was not brought up any longer with my grandfather's concubine, and that I kept unstained the flower of my youth; and that I did not make trial of my manhood before the due time, but even postponed it.

That I was subordinated to a ruler and a father capable of ridding me of all conceit, and of bringing me to recognize that it is possible to live in a Court and yet do without bodyguards and gorgeous garments and linkmen and statues and the like pomp; and that it is in such a man's power to reduce himself very nearly to the condition of a private individual and yet not on this account to be more paltry or more remiss in dealing with what the interests of the state require to be done in imperial fashion.

That it was my lot to have such a brother, capable by his character of stimulating me to watchful care over myself, and at the same time delighting me by his deference and affection: that my children have not been devoid of intelligence nor physically deformed. That I did not make more progress in rhetoric and poetry and my other studies, in which I should perhaps have been engrossed, had I felt myself making good way in them. That I lost no time in promoting my tutors to such posts of honor as they seemed to desire, and that I did not put them off with the hope that I would do this later on since they were still young. That I got to know Apollonius, Rusticus, Maximus.

That I had clear and frequent conceptions as to the true meaning of a life according to Nature, so that as far as the gods were concerned and their blessings and assistance and intention, there was nothing to prevent me from beginning at once to live in accordance with Nature, though I still come short of this ideal by my own fault, and by not attending to the reminders, nay, almost the instructions, of the gods.

That my body holds out so long in such a life as mine; that I did not touch Benedicta or Theodotus, but that even afterward, when I did give way to amatory passions, I was cured of them; that, though often offended with Rusticus, I never went so far as to do anything for which I should have been sorry; that my mother, though she was to die young, yet spent her last years with me.

That as often as I had the inclination to help anyone, who was in pecuniary distress or needing any other assistance, I was never told that there was no money available for the purpose; and that I was never under any similar need of accepting help from another. That I have been blessed with a wife so docile, so affectionate, so unaffected; that I had no lack of suitable tutors for my children.

That by the agency of dreams I was given antidotes both of other kinds and against the spitting of blood and vertigo; and there is that response also at Caieta, "as you shall use it." And that, when I had set my heart on philosophy, I did not fall into the hands of a sophist, nor sat down at the authors desk, or became a solver of syllogisms, nor busied myself with physical phenomena. For all the above the gods as helpers and good fortune need.

Written among the Quadi on the Gran.

BOOK II

———

1 Say to yourself at daybreak: I shall come across the busy-body, the thankless, the overbearing, the treacherous, the envious, the unneighborly. All this has befallen them because they know not good from evil. But I, in that I have comprehended the nature of the Good that it is beautiful, and the nature of Evil that it is ugly, and the nature of the wrong-doer himself that it is akin to me, not as partaker of the same blood and seed but of intelligence and a morsel of the Divine, can neither be injured by any of them—for no one can involve me in what is debasing— nor can I be wroth with my kinsman and hate him. For we have come into being for cooperation, as have the feet, the hands, the eyelids, the rows of upper and lower teeth. Therefore to thwart one another is against Nature; and we do thwart one another by showing resentment and aversion.

2. This that I am, whatever it be, is mere flesh and a little breath and the ruling Reason. Away with your books! Be no longer drawn aside by them: it is not allowed. But as one already dying disdain the flesh: it is nothing but gore and bones and a network compact of nerves and veins and arteries. Look at the breath too, what sort of thing it is; air: and not even that always the same,

> **This that I am, whatever it be, is mere flesh and a little breath and the ruling Reason**

but every minute belched forth and again gulped down. Then, thirdly, there is the ruling Reason. Put your thought thus: you are an old man; let this be a thrall no longer, no more a puppet pulled aside by every selfish impulse; nor let it grumble any longer at what is allotted to it in the present or dread it in the future.

3. Full of Providence are the works of the gods, nor are Fortune's works independent of Nature or of the woven texture and interlacement of all that is under the control of Providence. Thence are all things derived; but Necessity too plays its part and the Welfare of the whole Universe of which you are a portion. But good for every part of Nature is that which the Nature of the Whole brings about, and which goes to preserve it. Now it is the changes not only of the elements but of the things compounded of them that preserve the Universe. Let these reflections suffice you, if you hold them as principles. But away with your thirst for books, that you may die not murmuring but with a good grace, truly and from your heart grateful to the gods.

4. Call to mind how long you defer these things, and how many times you have received from the gods grace of the appointed day and you use it not. Yet now, if never before, you should realize of what Universe you are a part, and as an emanation from what Controller of that Universe you subsist; and that a limit has been set to your time, which if you use not to let daylight into your soul, it will be gone—and you!—and never again shall the chance be yours.

5. Every hour make up your mind sturdily as a Roman and a man to do what you have in hand with scrupulous and unaffected dignity and love of your kind and independence and justice; and to give yourself rest from all other impressions. And you will give yourself this, if you execute every act of your life as though it were your last, divesting yourself of all aimlessness and all passionate antipathy to the convictions of reason, and all hypocrisy and self-love and dissatisfaction with your allotted share. You see how few are the things, by mastering which a man may lead a life of tranquility and godlikeness; for the gods also will ask no more from him who keeps these precepts.

6. Wrong yourself, wrong yourself, O my Soul! But the time for honoring yourself will have gone by; for a man has but one life, and this for you is well-nigh closed, and yet you do not hold yourself in reverence, but set your well-being in the souls of others.

7. Do those things draw you at all away, which befall you from without? Make then leisure for yourself for the learning of some good thing more, and cease being carried aside hither and thither. But therewith must you take heed of the other error. For they too are triflers, who by their activities have worn themselves out in life without even having an aim whereto they can direct every impulse, aye and even every thought.

8. Not easily is a man found to be unhappy by reason of his not regarding what is going on in another man's soul; but those who do not attend closely to the motions of their own souls must inevitably be unhappy.

9. This must always be borne in mind, what is the Nature of the whole Universe, and what mine, and how this stands in relation to that, being too what sort of a part of what sort of a whole; and that no one can prevent you from doing and saying always what is in keeping with the Nature of which you are a part.

> Those who do not attend closely to the motions of their own souls must inevitably be unhappy

10. Theophrastus in his comparison of wrongdoings—for, speaking in a somewhat popular way, such comparison may be made—says in the true philosophical spirit that the offences which are due to lust are more heinous than those which are due to anger. For the man who is moved with anger seems to turn his back upon reason with some pain and unconscious compunction; but he who does wrong from lust, being mastered by pleasure, seems in some sort to be more incontinent and more unmanly in his wrong-doing. Rightly then, and not unworthily of a philosopher, he said

that the wrongdoing which is allied with pleasure calls for a severer condemnation than that which is allied with pain; and, speaking generally, that the one wrong-doer is more like a man, who, being sinned against first, has been driven by pain to be angry, while the other, being led by lust to do some act, has of his own motion been impelled to do evil.

11. Let your every deed and word and thought be those of a man who can depart from life this moment, but to go away from among men, if there are gods, is nothing dreadful; for they would not involve you in evil. But if indeed there are no gods, or if they do not concern themselves with the affairs of men, what boots it for me to live in a Universe empty of gods or empty of Providence? Nay, but there are gods, and they do concern themselves with human things; and they have put it wholly in man's power not to fall into evils that are truly such. And had there been any evil in what lies beyond, for this too would they have made provision, that it should be in every man's power not to fall into it. But how can that make a man's life worse which does not make the man worse? Yet the Nature of the Whole could not have been guilty of an oversight from ignorance or, while cognizant of these things, through lack of power to guard against or amend them; nor could it have gone so far amiss either from inability or unskillfulness, as to allow good and evil to fall without any discrimination alike upon the evil and the good. Still it is a fact that death and life, honor and dishonor, pain and pleasure, riches and penury, do among men one and all betide the Good and the Evil alike, being in themselves neither honorable nor shameful. Consequently they are neither good nor evil.

Death and life, honor and dishonor, pain and pleasure, riches and penury… are neither good nor evil

12. How quickly all things vanish away, in the Universe their actual bodies, and the remembrance of them in Eternity, and of

what character are all objects of sense, and particularly those that entice us with pleasure or terrify us with pain or are acclaimed by vanity—how worthless and despicable and unclean and ephemeral and dead!—this is for our faculty of intelligence to apprehend; as also what they really are whose conceptions and whose voices award renown; what it is to die, and that if a man look at death in itself, and with the analysis of reason strip it of its phantom terrors, no longer will he conceive it to be aught but a function of Nature,—but if a man be frightened by a function of Nature, he is childish; and this is not only Nature's function but her welfare;—and how man is in touch with God and with what part of himself, and in what disposition of this portion of the man.

13. Nothing can be more miserable than the man who goes through the whole round of things, and, as the poet says, pries into the things beneath the earth, and would fain guess the thoughts in his neighbor's heart, while having no conception that he needs but to associate himself with the divine genius in his bosom, and to serve it truly. And service of it is to keep it pure from passion and aimlessness and discontent with anything that proceeds from gods or men. For that which proceeds from the gods is worthy of reverence in that it is excellent; and that which proceeds from men, of love, in that they are akin, and, at times and in a manner, of compassion, in that they are ignorant of good and evil—a defect this no less than the loss of power to distinguish between white and black.

14. Even if your life is to last three thousand years or for the matter of that thirty thousand, yet bear

> **No man can part with either the past or the future. For how can a man be deprived of what he does not possess?... For it is but the present that a man can be deprived of**

in mind that no one ever parts with any other life than the one he is now living, nor lives any other than that which he now parts with. The longest life, then, and the shortest amount to the same. For the present time is of equal duration for all, while that which we lose is not ours; and consequently what is parted with is obviously a mere moment. No man can part with either the past or the future. For how can a man be deprived of what he does not possess? These two things, then, must needs be remembered: the one, that all things from time everlasting have been cast in the same mold and repeated cycle after cycle, and so it makes no difference whether a man see the same things recur through a hundred years or two hundred, or through eternity: the other, that the longest liver and he whose time to die comes soonest part with no more the one than the other. For it is but the present that a man can be deprived of, if, as is the fact, it is this alone that he has, and what he has not a man cannot part with.

15. Remember that everything is but what we think it. For obvious indeed is the saying fathered on Monimus the Cynic, obvious too the utility of what was said, if one accepts the gist of it as far as it is true.

16. The soul of man does wrong to itself then most of all, when it makes itself, as far as it can do so, a boil, as it were a malignant growth in the Universe. For to grumble at anything that happens is a rebellion against Nature, in some part of which are bound up the natures of all other things. And the soul wrongs itself then again, when it turns away from any man or even opposes him with intent to do him harm, as is the case with those who are angry. It does wrong to itself, thirdly, when it is overcome by pleasure or pain. Fourthly, when it assumes a mask, and in act or word is insincere or untruthful. Fifthly, when it directs some act or desire of its own toward no mark, and expends its energy on any thing whatever aimlessly and unadvisedly, whereas even the most trifling things should be done with reference to the end in view. Now the end for rational beings is to submit themselves to the reason and law of that archetypal city and polity—the Universe.

17. Of the life of man the duration is but a point, its substance streaming away, its perception dim, the fabric of the entire body prone to decay, and the soul a vortex, and fortune incalculable, and fame uncertain. In a word all the things of the body are as a river, and the things of the soul as a dream and a vapor; and life is a warfare and a pilgrim's sojourn, and fame after death is only forgetfulness. What then is it that can help us on our way? One thing and one alone—Philosophy; and this consists in keeping the divine "genius" within pure and unwronged, lord of all pleasures and pains, doing nothing aimlessly or with deliberate falsehood and hypocrisy, independent of another's action or inaction; and furthermore welcoming what happens and is allotted, as issuing from the same source, whatever it be, from which the man himself has issued; and above all waiting for death with a good grace as being but a setting free of the elements of which every thing living is made up. But if there be nothing terrible in each thing being continuously changed into another thing, why should a man look askance at the change and dissolution of all things? For it is in the way of Nature, and in the way of Nature there can be no evil.

Written at Carnuntum.

Now Haimburg in Hungary.

> Things of the soul as a dream and a vapor; and life is a warfare and a pilgrim's sojourn, and fame after death is only forgetfulness

BOOK III

———

1 WE OUGHT NOT TO THINK ONLY UPON THE FACT THAT OUR LIFE each day is waning away, what is left of it being ever less, but this also should be a subject for thought, that even if life be prolonged, yet is it uncertain whether the mind will remain equally fitted in the future for the understanding of facts and for that contemplation which strains after the knowledge of things divine and human. For if a man has entered upon his dotage, there will still be his the power of breathing, and digestion, and thought, and desire, and all such-like faculties; but the full use of himself, the accurate appreciation of the items of duty, the nice discrimination of what presents itself to the senses, and a clear judgment on the question whether it is time for him to end his own life, and all such decisions, as above all require well-trained powers of reasoning—these are already flickering out in him. It needs, then, that we should press onward, not only because we come each moment nearer to death, but also because our insight into facts and our close touch of them is gradually ceasing even before we die.

2. Such things as this also we ought to note with care, that the accessories too of natural operations have a charm and attractiveness of their own. For instance, when bread is in the baking, some of the parts split open, and these very fissures, though in a sense thwarting the bread maker's design, have an appropriateness of their own and in a peculiar way stimulate the desire for food. Again when figs are at their ripest, they gape open; and in olives that are ready to fall their very approach to over-ripeness gives a

20

peculiar beauty to the fruit. And the full ears of corn bending downward, and the lion's beetling brows, and the foam dripping from the jaws of the wild-boar, and many other things, though, if looked at apart from their setting, they are far from being comely, yet, as resultants from the operations of Nature, lend them an added charm and entice our admiration.

And so, if a man has sensibility and a deeper insight into the workings of the Universe, scarcely anything, though it exist only as a secondary consequence to something else, but will seem to him to form in its own peculiar way a pleasing adjunct to the whole. And he will look on the actual gaping jaws of wild beasts with no less pleasure than the representations of them by artists and modelers; and he will be able to see in the aged of either sex a mature prime and comely ripeness, and gaze with chaste eyes upon the alluring loveliness of the young. And many such things there are which do not appeal to everyone, but will come home to him alone who is genuinely intimate with Nature and her works.

3. Hippocrates, after healing many a sick man, fell sick himself and died. Many a death have Chaldaeans foretold, and then their own fate has overtaken them also. Alexander, Pompeius, and Gaius Caesar times without number utterly destroyed whole cities, and cut to pieces many myriads of horse and foot on the field of battle, yet the day came when they too departed this life. Heraclitus, after endless speculations on the destruction of the world by fire, came to be filled internally with water, and died beplastered with cowdung. And lice caused the death of Democritus, and other vermin of Socrates.

What of this? You have gone aboard, you have set sail, you have touched land; go ashore; if indeed for another life, there is nothing even there void of gods; but if to a state of non-sensation, you will cease being at the mercy of pleasure and pain and lackeying the bodily vessel which is so much baser than that which ministers to it. For the one is intelligence and a divine "genius," the other dust and putrescence.

4. Fritter not away what is left of your life in thoughts about others, unless you can bring these thoughts into relation with some common interest. For verily you cut yourself off from other work, that is, by thinking

what so and so is doing and why, what he is saying, having what in mind, contriving what, and all the many like things such as whirl you aside from keeping close watch over your own ruling Reason.

Fritter not away what is left of your life in thoughts about others

We ought therefore to eschew the aimless and the unprofitable in the chain of our thoughts, still more all that is over-curious and ill-natured, and a man should accustom himself to think only of those things about which, if one were to ask on a sudden, What is now in your thoughts? you could quite frankly answer at once, This or that; so that your answer should immediately make manifest that all that is in you is simple and kindly and worthy of a living being that is social and has no thought for pleasures or for the entire range of sensual images, or for any rivalry, envy, suspicion, or anything else, whereat you would blush to admit that you had it in your mind.

For in truth such a man, one who no longer puts off being reckoned now, if never before, among the best, is in some sort a priest and minister of the gods, putting to use also that which, enthroned within him, keeps the man unstained by pleasures, invulnerable to all pain, beyond the touch of any wrong, proof against all evil, a champion in the highest of championships—that of never being overthrown by any passion—dyed in grain with justice, welcoming with all his soul everything that befalls and is allotted him, and seldom, nor yet without a great and a general necessity, concerning himself with the words or deeds or thoughts of another. For it is only the things which relate to himself that he brings within the scope of his activities, and he never ceases to ponder over what is being spun for him as his share in the fabric of the Universe, and he sees to it that the former are worthy, and is assured that the latter is good. For the fate which is allotted to each man is swept along with him in the Universe as well as sweeps him along with it.

And he bears in mind that all that is rational is akin, and that it is in man's nature to care for all men, and that we should not embrace the opinion of all, but of those alone who live in conscious agreement with Nature. But what sort of men they, whose life is not after this pattern, are at home and abroad, by night and in the day, in what vices they wallow and with whom—of this he is ever mindful. Consequently he takes no account of praise from such men, who in fact cannot even win their own approval.

5. Do nothing unwillingly nor selfishly nor without examination nor against the grain. Dress not your thought in too fine a garb. Be not a man of superfluous words or superfluous deeds. Moreover let the god that is in you be lord of a living creature, that is manly, and of full age, and concerned with statecraft, and a Roman, and a ruler, who has taken his post as one who awaits the signal of recall from life in all readiness, needing no oath nor any man as his voucher. Be the cheery face and independence of help from without and independence of such ease as others can give. It needs then to stand, and not be set, upright.

> **Do nothing unwillingly nor selfishly nor without examination nor against the grain**

6. If indeed you find in the life of man a better thing than justice, than truth, than temperance, than manliness, and, in a word, than your mind's satisfaction with itself in things wherein it shows you acting according to the true dictates of reason, and with destiny in what is allotted you apart from your choice—if, I say, you see anything better than this, turn to it with all your soul and take your fill of the best, as you find it.

But if there appears nothing better than the very deity enthroned in you, which has brought into subjection to itself all individual desires, which scrutinizes the thoughts, and, in the words of Socrates, has withdrawn itself from all the enticements of the senses, and brought itself into subjection to the gods, and cherishes a fellow-feeling for men—if you find everything else pettier and of less account than this, give place to nothing else, to which if you are but once plucked aside, and incline thereto, never more will you be able without distraction to give paramount honor to that good which is your own peculiar heritage. For it is not right that any extraneous thing at all, such as the praise of the many, or office, or wealth, or indulgence in pleasure, should avail against that good which is identical with reason and a civic spirit. All these things, even if they seem for a little to fit smoothly into our lives, on a sudden overpower us and sweep us away.

But do you, I say, simply and freely choose the better and hold fast to it. But that is the better which is to my interest. If it is to your interest as a rational creature, hold that fast; but if as a mere animal, declare it boldly and maintain your judgment without arrogance. Only see to it that you have made your inquiry without error.

7. Prize not anything as being to your interest that will ever force you to break your word, to surrender your honor, to hate, suspect, or curse anyone, to play the hypocrite, to lust after anything that needs walls and curtains, For he that has chosen before all else his own intelligence and good "genius," and to be a devotee of its supreme worth, does not strike a tragic attitude or whine, nor will he ask for either a wilderness or a concourse of men; above all he will live neither chasing anything nor shunning it. And he recks not at all whether he is to have his soul overlaid with his body for a longer or a shorter span of time, for even if he must take his departure at once, he will go as willingly as if he were to discharge any other function that can be discharged with decency and orderliness, making sure through life of this one thing, that his thoughts should not in any case assume a character out of keeping with a rational and civic creature.

8. In the mind of the man that has been chastened and thoroughly cleansed you will find no foul abscess or gangrene or hidden sore. Nor is his life cut short, when the day of destiny overtakes him, as we might say of a tragedian's part, who leaves the stage before finishing his speech and playing out the piece. Furthermore there is nothing there slavish or affected, no

dependence on others or severance from them, no sense of accountability or skulking to avoid it.

9. Hold sacred your capacity for forming opinions, with that it rests wholly that your ruling Reason should never admit any opinion out of harmony with Nature, and with the constitution of a rational creature. This ensures due deliberation and fellowship with mankind and fealty to the gods.

> **Hold sacred your capacity for forming opinions**

10. Jettison everything else, then, and lay hold of these things only, few as they are; and remember withal that it is only this present, a moment of time, that a man lives: all the rest either has been lived or may never be. Little indeed, then, is a man's life, and little the nook of earth whereon he lives, and little even the longest after-fame, and that too handed on through a succession of manikins, each one of them very soon to be dead, with no knowledge even of themselves, let alone of a man who has died long since.

11. To the stand-bys mentioned add yet another, that a definition or delineation should be made of every object that presents itself, so that we may see what sort of thing it is in its essence stripped of its adjuncts, a separate whole taken as such, and tell over with ourselves both its particular designation and the names of the elements that compose it and into which it will be disintegrated.

For nothing is so conducive to greatness of mind as the ability to examine systematically and honestly everything that meets us in life, and to regard these things always in such a way as to form a conception of the kind of Universe they belong to, and of the use which the thing in question subserves in it; what value it has for the whole Universe and what for man, citizen as he is of the highest state, of which all other states are but as households; what it actually is, and compounded of what elements, and likely to last how long—namely this that now gives me the impression in question; and what virtue it calls for from me, such as gentleness, manly courage, truth, fidelity, guilelessness, independence, and the rest.

In each case therefore must you say: This has come from God; and this is due to the conjunction of fate and the contexture of the world's web and some such coincidence and chance; while that comes from a clansman and a kinsman and a neighbor, albeit one who is ignorant of what is really in accordance with his nature. But I am not ignorant, therefore I treat him kindly and justly, in accordance with the natural law of neighborliness; at the same time, of things that are neither good nor bad, my aim is to hit their true worth.

12. If in obedience to right reason you do the thing that your hand finds to do earnestly, manfully, graciously, and in no sense as a by-work, and keep that divine "genius" of yours in its virgin state, just as if even now you were called upon to restore it to the Giver—if you grapple this to you, looking for nothing, shrinking from nothing, but content with a present sphere of activity such as Nature allows, and with chivalrous truth in every word and utterance of your tongue, you will be happy in your life. And there is no one that is able to prevent this.

13. Just as physicians always keep their lancets and instruments ready to their hands for emergency operations, so also do you keep your axioms ready for the diagnosis of things human and divine, and for the performing of every act, even the pettiest, with the fullest consciousness of the mutual ties between these two. For you will never carry out well any human duty unless you correlate it to the divine, nor the reverse.

14. Go astray no more; for you are not likely to read your little Memoranda, or the Acts of the Romans and the Greeks of Old Time, and the extracts from their writings which you were laying up against your old age. Haste then to the consummation and, casting away all empty hopes, if you care for your welfare, come to your own rescue, while it is allowed you.

15. They know not how full of meaning are—to thieve, to sow, to buy, to be at peace, to see what needs doing, and this is not a matter for the eye but for another sort of sight.

16. Body, Soul, Intelligence: for the body sensations, for the soul desires, for the intelligence axioms. To receive impressions by way of the senses is not denied even to cattle; to be as puppets pulled by the strings

of desire is common to wild beasts and to pathics and to a Phalaris and a Nero. Yet to have the intelligence a guide to what they deem their duty is an attribute of those also who do not believe in gods and those who fail their country in its need and those who do their deeds behind closed doors.

If then all else is the common property of the classes mentioned, there is left as the characteristic of the good man to delight in and to welcome what befalls and what is being spun for him by destiny; and not to sully the divine "genius" that is enthroned in his bosom, nor yet to perplex it with a multitude of impressions, but to maintain it to the end in a gracious serenity, in orderly obedience to God, uttering no word that is not true and doing no deed that is not just. But if all men disbelieve in his living a simple and modest and cheerful life, he is not angry with any of them, nor swerves from the path which leads to his life's goal, whither he must go pure, peaceful, ready for release, needing no force to bring him into accord with his lot.

If you care for your welfare, come to your own rescue

BOOK IV

——

1 THAT WHICH HOLDS THE MASTERY WITHIN US, WHEN IT IS IN accordance with Nature, is so disposed toward what befalls, that it can always adapt itself with ease to what is possible and granted us. For it is wedded to no definite material, but, though in the pursuit of its high aims it works under reservations, yet it converts into material for itself any obstacle that it meets with, just as fire when it gets the mastery of what is thrown in upon it. A little flame would have been stifled by it, but the blazing fire instantly assimilates what is cast upon it and, consuming it, leaps the higher in consequence.

2. Take no act in hand aimlessly or otherwise than in accordance with the true principles perfective of the are.

3. Men seek out retreats for themselves in the country, by the seaside, on the mountains, and you too are wont to long above all for such things. But all this is unphilosophical to the last degree, when you can at a moment's notice retire into yourself. For nowhere can a man find a retreat more full of peace or more free from care than his own soul—above all if he have that within him, a steadfast look at which and he is at once in all good ease, and by good ease I mean nothing other than good order. Make use then of this retirement continually and regenerate yourself. Let your axioms be short and elemental, such as when set before you will at once rid you of all trouble, and send you away with no discontent at those things to which you are returning.

Why with what are you discontented? The wickedness of men? Take this conclusion to heart, that rational creatures have been made for one another; that forbearance is part of justice; that wrong-doing is involuntary; and think how many ere now, after passing their lives in implacable enmity, suspicion, hatred, and at daggers drawn with one another, have been laid out and burnt to ashes—think of this, I say, and at last stay your fretting. But are you discontented with your share in the whole? Recall the alternative: Either Providence or Atoms! and the abundant proofs there are that the Universe is as it were a state. But is it the affections of the body that shall still lay hold on you? Remember that the Intelligence, when it has once abstracted itself and learned its own power, has nothing to do with the motions smooth or rough of the vital breath. Remember too of all that you have heard and subscribed to about pleasure and pain.

Nowhere can a man find a retreat more full of peace or more free from care than his own soul

But will that paltry thing, Fame, pluck you aside? Look at the swift approach of complete forgetfulness, and the void of infinite time on this side of us and on that, and the empty echo of acclamation, and the fickleness and uncritical judgment of those who claim to speak well of us, and the narrowness of the arena to which all this is confined. For the whole earth is but a point, and how tiny a corner of it is this the place of our sojourning! and how many therein and of what sort are the men who shall praise you!

From now therefore remember the retreat into this little plot that is yourself. Above all distract not yourself, be not too eager, but be your own master, and look upon life as a man, as a human being, as a citizen, as a mortal creature. But among the principles readiest to your hand, upon which you will pore, let there be these two. One, that objective things do not lay hold of the soul, but stand quiescent without; while disturbances are but the outcome of that opinion which is within us. A second, that all this visible world changes in a moment, and will be no more; and continually remember the changes of how many things you have already been a witness. "The Universe—mutation: Life—opinion."

4. If the intellectual capacity is common to us all, common too is the reason, which makes us rational creatures. If so, that reason also is common which tells us to do or not to do. If so, law also is common. If so, we are citizens. If so, we are fellow-members of an organized community. If so, the Universe is as it were a state—for of what other single polity can the whole race of mankind be said to be fellow-members?—and from it, this common State, we get the intellectual, the rational, and the legal instinct, or whence do we get them? For just as the earthy part has been portioned off for me from some earth, and the watery from another element, and the aerial from some source, and the hot and fiery from some source of its own—for nothing comes from the non-existent, any more than it disappears into nothingness—so also the intellect has undoubtedly come from somewhere.

> **Death like birth is a secret of Nature … and not at all a thing in fact for any to be ashamed of**

5. Death like birth is a secret of Nature—a combination of the same elements, a breaking up into the same—and not at all a thing in fact for any to be ashamed of, for it is not out of keeping with an intellectual creature or the reason of his equipment.

6. Given such men, it was in the nature of the case inevitable that their conduct should be of this kind. To wish it otherwise, is to wish that the fig-tree had no acrid juice. As a general conclusion call this to mind, that within a very short time both you and he will be dead, and a little later not even your names will be left behind you.

7. Erase the opinion, I am harmed, and at once the feeling of being harmed disappears; erase the feeling, and the harm disappears at once.

8. That which does not make a man himself worse than before cannot make his life worse either, nor injure it whether from without or within.

9. The nature of the general good could not but have acted so.

10. Note that all that befalls do so justly. Keep close watch and you will find this true, I do not say, as a matter of sequence merely but as a matter of justice also, and as would be expected from One whose dispensation is based on desert. Keep close watch, then, as you have begun, and whatsoever you do, do it as only a good man should in the strictest sense of that word. In every sphere of activity safeguard this.

> **Erase the opinion, I am harmed, and at once the feeling of being harmed disappears**

11. Harbor no such opinions as he holds who does you violence, or as he would have you hold. See things in all their naked reality.

12. You shouldest have these two readinesses always at hand; the one which prompts you to do only what your reason in its royal and law-making capacity shall suggest for the good of mankind; the other to change your mind, if one be near to set you right, and convert you from some vain conceit. But this conversion should be the outcome of a persuasion in every case that the thing is just or to the common interest—and some such cause should be the only one—not because it is seemingly pleasant or popular.

13. Have you reason? I have. Why then not use it? For if this performs its part, what else would you have?

14. You have subsisted as part of the Whole. You will vanish into that which begat you, or rather you will be taken again into its Seminal Reason by a process of change.

15. Many little pellets of frankincense fall upon the same altar, some are cast on it sooner, some later: but it makes no difference.

16. Ere ten days are past, you will rank as a god with them that hold you now a wild-beast or an ape, if you but turn back to your axioms and your reverence of reason.

17. Behave not as though you had ten thousand years to live. Your doom hangs over you. While you live, while you may, become good.

18. What richness of leisure doth he gain who has no eye for his neighbor's words or deeds or thoughts, but only for his own doings, that they be just and righteous! It is not for the good man to peer about into the blackness of another's heart, but to "run straight for the goal with never a glance aside."

While you live, while you may, become good

19. He whose heart flutters for after-fame does not reflect that very soon every one of those who remember him, and he himself, will be dead, and their successors again after them, until at last the entire recollection of the man will be extinct, handed on as it is by links that flare up and are quenched. But put the case that those who are to remember are even immortal, and the remembrance immortal, what then is that to you? To the dead man, I need scarcely say, the praise is nothing, but what is it to the living, except, indeed, in a subsidiary way? For you reject the bounty of nature unseasonably in the present, and cling to what others shall say of you hereafter.

20. Everything, which has any sort of beauty of its own, is beautiful of itself, and looks no further than itself, not counting praise as part of itself. For indeed that which is praised is made neither better nor worse thereby. This is true also of the things that in common parlance are called beautiful, such as material things and works of are. Does, then, the truly beautiful need anything beyond? Nay, no more than law, than truth, than kindness, than modesty. Which of these owes its beauty to being praised, or loses it by being blamed? What! Does an emerald forfeit its excellence by not being praised? Does gold, ivory, purple, a lyre, a poniard, a floweret, a shrub?

21. If souls outlive their bodies, how does the air contain them from times beyond ken? How does the earth contain the bodies of those who have been buried in it for such endless ages? For just as on earth the change of these bodies, after continuance for a certain indefinite time, followed by dissolution, makes room for other dead bodies, so souls, when transferred into the air, after lasting for a certain time, suffer change and are diffused and become fire, being taken again into the Seminal Reason of the Whole, and so allow room for those that subsequently take up their abode there. This would be the answer one would give on the assumption that souls outlive their bodies.

But not only must the multitude of bodies thus constantly being buried be taken into account, but also that of the creatures devoured daily by ourselves and the other animals. How great is the number consumed and thus in a way buried in the bodies of those who feed upon them! And yet room is made for them all by their conversion into blood, by their transmutation into air or fire.

Where in this case lies the way of search for the truth? In a separation of the Material from the Causal.

22. Be not whirled aside; but in every impulse fulfill the claims of justice, and in every impression safeguard certainty.

23. All that is in tune with you, O Universe, is in tune with me! Nothing that is in due time for you is too early or too late for me! All that your seasons bring, O Nature, is fruit for me! All things come from you, subsist in you, go back to you. There is one who says Dear City of Cecrops! Will you not say O dear City of Zeus?

24. If you would be tranquil in heart, says the Sage, do not many things. Is not this a better maxim? do but what is needful, and what the reason of a living creature born for a civic life demands, and as it demands. For this brings the tranquility which comes of doing few things no less than of doing them well. For nine-tenths of our words and deeds being unnecessary, if a man retrench there, he will have more abundant leisure and fret the less. Wherefore forget not on every occasion to ask yourself, Is this one of the unnecessary things? But we must retrench not only actions

but thoughts which are unnecessary, for then neither will superfluous actions follow.

25. Try living the life of the good man who is more than content with what is allotted to him out of the whole, and is satisfied with his own acts as just and his own disposition as kindly: see how that answers.

26. Have you looked on that side of the picture? Look now on this! Fret not yourself; study to be simple. Does a man do wrong? The wrong rests with him. Has something befallen you? It is well. Everything that befalls was from the beginning destined and spun for you as your share out of the Whole. To sum up, life is short. Make profit of the present by right reasoning and justice. In your relaxation be sober.

27. Either there is a well-arranged Order of things, or a maze, indeed, but not without a plan. Or can a sort of order subsist in you, while in the Universe there is no order, and that too when all things, though separated and dispersed, are still in sympathetic connection?

28. A black character, an unmanly character, an obstinate character, inhuman, animal, childish, stupid, counterfeit, cringing, mercenary, tyrannical.

29. If he is an alien in the Universe who has no cognizance of the things that are in it, no less is he an alien who has no cognizance of what is happening in it. He is an exile, who exiles himself from civic reason; blind, he who will not see with the eyes of his understanding; a beggar, he who is dependent on another, and cannot draw from his own resources all that his life requires; an boil on the Universe, he who renounces, and severs himself from, the reason of our common Nature, because he is ill pleased at what happens—for the same Nature brings this into being, that also brought you; a limb cut off from the community, he who cuts off his own soul from the soul of all rational things, which is but one.

30. One philosopher goes without a shirt, a second without a book, a third yonder half-naked: says he, I am starving for bread, yet cleave I fast to Reason; and I too: I get no fruit of my learning, yet cleave I to her.

31. Cherish the art, though humble, that you have learned, and take your rest therein; and pass through the remainder of your days as one

that with his whole soul has given all that is his in trust to the gods, and has made of himself neither a tyrant nor a slave to any man.

32. Think by way of illustration upon the times of Vespasian, and you will see all these things: mankind marrying, rearing children, sickening, dying, warring, making holiday, trafficking, tilling, flattering others, vaunting themselves, suspecting, scheming, praying for the death of others, murmuring at their own lot, loving, hoarding, coveting a consulate, coveting a kingdom. Not a vestige of that life of theirs is left anywhere any longer.

Change the scene again to the times of Trajan. Again it is all the same; that life too is dead. In like manner contemplate all the other records of past time and of entire nations, and see how many after all their high-strung efforts sank down so soon in death and were resolved into the elements. But above all must you dwell in thought upon those whom you have yourself known, who, following after vanity, neglected to do the things that accorded with their own constitution and, cleaving steadfastly thereto, to be content with them. And here it is essential to remember that a due sense of value and proportion should regulate the care bestowed on every action. For thus will you never give over in disgust, if you busy not yourself beyond what is right with the lesser things.

33. Expressions once in use are now obsolete. So also the names of those much be-sung heroes of old are in some sense obsolete, Camillus, Caeso, Volesus, Dentatus, and a little later Scipio and Cato, then also Augustus, and then Hadrianus and Antoninus. For all things quickly fade away and become legendary, and soon absolute oblivion encairns them. And here I speak of those who made an extraordinary blaze in the world. For the rest, as soon as the breath is out of their bodies, it is, Out of sight, out of mind. But what, when all is said, is even everlasting remembrance? Wholly vanity. What then is it that calls for our devotion? This one thing: justice in thought, in act unselfishness and a tongue that cannot lie and a disposition ready to welcome all that befalls as unavoidable, as familiar, as issuing from a like origin and fountain-head.

34. Offer yourself whole-heartedly to Clotho, letting her spin your thread to serve what purpose soever she will.

35. Ephemeral all of them, the rememberer as well as the remembered!

36. Unceasingly contemplate the generation of all things through change, and accustom yourself to the thought that the Nature of the Universe delights above all in changing the things that exist and making new ones of the same pattern. For in a manner everything that exists is the seed of that which shall come out of it. But you imagine that only to be seed that is deposited in the earth or the womb, a view beyond measure unphilosophical.

Ephemeral all of them, the rememberer as well as the remembered

37. A moment and you will be dead; and not even yet are you simple, nor unperturbed, nor free from all suspicion that you can be injured by externals, nor gracious to all, nor convinced that wisdom and just dealing are but one.

38. Consider narrowly their ruling Reason, and see what wise men avoid and what they seek after.

39. Harm to you cannot depend on another's ruling Reason, nor yet on any vagary or phase of your environment. On what then? On the power that is your of judging what is evil. Let this, then, pass no judgment, and all is well. Even if its closest associate, the poor body, be cut, be burnt, fester, gangrene, yet let the part which forms a judgment about these things hold its peace, that is, let it assume nothing to be either good or bad, which can befall a good man or a bad indifferently. For that which befalls alike the man who lives by the rule and the man who lives contrary to the rule of Nature, is neither in accordance with Nature nor contrary to it.

40. Cease not to think of the Universe as one living Being, possessed of a single Substance and a single Soul; and how all things trace back to its single sentience; and how it does all things by a single impulse; and how all existing things are joint causes of all things that come into existence;

and how intertwined in the fabric is the thread and how closely woven the web.

41. You are a little soul bearing up a corpse, as Epictetus said.

42. Nothing is evil to that which is subject to change, even as there is no good for that which exists as the result of change.

43. As a river consisting of all things that come into being, aye, a rushing torrent, is Time. No sooner is a thing sighted than it is carried past, and lo, another is passing, and it too will be carried away.

44. Everything that happens is as usual and familiar, as the rose in spring and the fruit in summer. The same applies to disease and death and slander and treachery and all that gladdens the foolish or saddens them.

45. That which comes after always has a close relationship to what has gone before. For it is not like some enumeration of items separately taken and following a mere hard and fast sequence, but there is a rational connection; and just as existing things have been combined in a harmonious order, so also all that comes into being bears the stamp not of a mere succession but of a wonderful relationship.

> **You are a little soul bearing up a corpse**

46. Always bear in mind what Heraclitus said: The death of earth is to pass into water, and the death of water to pass into air, and of air to pass into fire, and so back again. Bear in mind too the wayfarer who forgets the trend of his way, and that men are at variance with the one thing with which they are in the most unbroken communion, the Reason that administers the whole Universe; and that what they encounter every day, this they deem strange; and that we must not act and speak like men asleep,—for in fact even in sleep we seem to act and speak;—and that there should be nothing of the children from parents style, that is, no mere perfunctory what our fathers have told us.

47. Just as, if a God had told you, You will die tomorrow or in any case the day after, you would no longer count it of any consequence whether it were the day after tomorrow or tomorrow, unless you are in the last degree mean-spirited, for how little is the difference!—so also

deem it but a trifling thing that you shouldest die after ever so many years rather than tomorrow.

48. Cease not to bear in mind how many physicians are dead after puckering up their brows so often over their patients; and how many astrologers after making a great parade of predicting the death of others; and how many philosophers after endless disquisitions on death and immortality; how many great captains after butchering thousands; how many tyrants after exercising with revolting insolence their power of life and death, as though themselves immortal; and how many entire cities are, if I may use the expression, dead, Helice and Pompeii and Herculaneum, and others without number.

Turn also to all, one after another, that come within your own knowledge. One closed a friend's eyes and was then himself laid out, and the friend who closed his, he too was laid out—and all this in a few short years. In a word, fail not to note how short-lived are all mortal things, and how paltry—yesterday a little mucus, tomorrow a mummy or burnt ash. Pass then through this tiny span of time in accordance with Nature, and come to your journey's end with a good grace, just as an olive falls when it is fully ripe, praising the earth that bare it and grateful to the tree that gave it growth.

49. Be like a headland of rock on which the waves break incessantly; but it stands fast and around it the seething of the waters sinks to rest.

> **Be like a headland of rock on which the waves break incessantly; but it stands fast**

Ah, unlucky am I, that this has befallen me! Nay, but rather, lucky am I that, though this has befallen me, yet am I still unhurt, neither crushed by the present nor dreading the future. For something of the kind could have befallen everyone, but everyone would not have remained unhurt in spite of it. Why then count that rather a misfortune than this a good fortune? And in any case do you reckon that a misfortune for a man which is not a miscarriage from his nature? And would you have that to be an aberration from a man's nature, which does not contravene the will of his nature! What then? This will you have learned to know. Does what has befallen you hinder you one whit from being just, high-minded, chaste, sensible, deliberate, straightforward, modest, free, and from possessing all the other qualities, the presence of which enables a man's nature to come fully into its own? Forget not in future, when anything would lead you to feel hurt, to take your stand upon this axiom: This is no misfortune, but to bear it nobly is good fortune.

50. An unphilosophical but none the less an effective help to the contemning of death is to tell over the names of those who have clung long and tenaciously to life. How are they better off than those who were cut off before their time? After all, they lie buried somewhere at last, Cadicianus, Fabius, Julianus, Lepidus, and any others like them, who after carrying many to their graves were at last carried to their own. Small, in any point of view, is the difference in length, and that too lived out to the dregs amid what great cares and with what sort of companions and in what kind of a body! Count it then of no consequence. For look at the yawning gulf of Time behind you, and before you at another Infinity to come. In this Eternity the life of a baby of three days and the life of a Nestor of three centuries are as one.

51. Run ever the short way; and the short way is the way of Nature, that leads to all that is most sound in speech and act. For a resolve such as this is a release from troubles and strife, from all mental reservation and affectation.

BOOK V

—

1 AT DAYBREAK, WHEN LOATH TO RISE, HAVE THIS THOUGHT READY in your mind: I am rising for a man's work. Am I then still peevish that I am going to do that for which I was born and for the sake of which I came into the world? Or was I made for this, that I should nuzzle under the bed-clothes and keep myself warm? But this is pleasanter. Have you been made then for pleasure? In a word, I ask you, to be acted upon or to act? Consider each tiny plant, each little bird, the ant, the spider, the bee, how they go about their own work and do each his part for the building up of an orderly Universe. Do you then refuse to do the work of a man?

Do you not hasten to do what Nature bids you. But some rest, too, is necessary. I do not deny it. Howbeit Nature has set limits to this, and no less so to eating and drinking. Yet you exceed these limits and exceed sufficiency. But in acts it is no longer so; there you come short of the possibility.

For you love not yourself, else surely had you loved your nature also and to do her will. But others who love their own are wear themselves to a shadow with their labors over it, forgetting to wash or take food. But

> **Am I then still peevish that I am going to do that for which I was born and for the sake of which I came into the world?**

40

you hold your own nature in less honor than the chaser of metal his art of chasing, than the dancer his dancing, than the miser his moneybags, than the popularity-hunter his little applause. And these, when they are exceptionally in earnest, are ready to forgo food and sleep, so that they forward the things in which they are interested. But do you deem the acts of a social being of less worth and less deserving of attention?

2. How easy a thing it is to put away and blot out every impression that is disturbing or alien, and to be at once in perfect peace.

3. Deem no word or deed that is in accord with Nature to be unworthy of you, and be not plucked aside by the consequent censure of others or what they say, but if a thing is good to do or say, judge not yourself unworthy of it. For those others have their own ruling Reason and follow their own bent. Do not you turn your eyes aside, but keep to the straight path, following your own and the universal Nature; and the path of these twain is one.

4. I fare forth through all that Nature wills until the day when I shall sink down and rest from my labors, breathing forth my last breath into the air whence I daily draw it in, and falling upon that earth, whence also my father gathered the seed, and my mother the blood, and my nurse the milk; whence daily for so many years I am fed and watered; which bears me as I tread it under foot and make full use of it in a thousand ways.

5. Sharpness of wit men cannot praise you for. Granted! Yet there are many other qualities of which you cannot say: I had not that by nature. Well then, display those which are wholly in your power, sterling sincerity, dignity, endurance of toil, abstinence from pleasure. Grumble not at your lot, be content with little, be kindly, independent, frugal, serious, high-minded. Do you not see how many virtues it is in your power to display now, in respect of which you can plead no natural incapacity or incompatibility, and yet you are content still with a lower standard? Or are you forced to be discontented, to be grasping, to flatter, to inveigh against the body, to play the toady and the braggart, and to be so unstable in your soul, because you have no natural gifts? By the gods, No! but long ere now could you have shaken yourself free from all this and have lain under the

imputation only, if it must be so, of being somewhat slow and dull of apprehension. And this too you must amend with training and not ignore your dullness or be in love with it.

6. One man, when he has done another a kindness, is ready also to reckon on a return. A second is not ready to do this, but yet in his heart of hearts ranks the other as a debtor, and he is conscious of what he has done But a third is in a manner not conscious of it, but is like the vine that has borne a cluster of grapes, and when it has once borne its due fruit looks for no reward beyond, as it is with a steed when it has run its course, a hound when it has singled out the trail, a bee when she has made her comb. And so a man when he has done one thing well, does not cry it abroad, but betakes himself to a second, as a vine to bear afresh her clusters in due season.

A man then must be of those who act thus as it were unconsciously? Yes; but he must be conscious of the fact, for it is, we are told, the peculiar characteristic of the man of true neighborly instincts to be aware that he puts such instincts into practice. And by heaven to wish that his neighbor also should be aware of it. What you sayest is true; but you misconceive what is now said: consequently you will be one of those whom I mentioned before, for in fact they are led astray by a certain plausibility of reasoning. But if you think it worthwhile to understand what has been said, fear not that you will be led thereby to neglect any social act.

7. A prayer of the Athenians: Rain, Rain, O dear Zeus, upon the corn-land of the Athenians and their meads. Either pray not at all, or in this simple and frank fashion.

8. We have all heard, Aesculapius has prescribed for so and so riding exercise, or cold baths, or walking barefoot. Precisely so it may be said that the Universal Nature has prescribed for so and so sickness or maim or loss or what not of the same kind. For, in the former case, prescribed has some such meaning as this: He ordained this for so and so as conducive to his health; while in the latter what befalls each man has been ordained in some way as conducive to his destiny. For we say that things fall to us, as the masons too say that the huge squared stones in walls and pyramids fall into their places, adjusting themselves harmoniously to one

another in a sort of structural unity. For, in fine, there is one harmony of all things, and just as from all bodies the Universe is made up into such a body as it is, so from all causes is Destiny made up into such a Cause. This is recognized by the most unthinking, for they say: Fate brought this on him. So then this was brought on this man, and this prescribed for this man. Let us then accept our fate, as we accept the prescriptions of Aesculapius. And in fact in these, too, there are many "bitter pills," but we welcome them in hope of health.

Take much the same view of the accomplishment and consummation of what Nature approves as of your health, and so welcome whatever happens, should it even be somewhat distasteful, because it contributes to the health of the Universe and the well-faring and well-doing of Zeus himself. For he had not brought this on a man, unless it had brought welfare to the Whole. For take any nature you will, it never brings upon that which is under its control anything that does not conduce to its interests.

For two reasons then it behooves you to acquiesce in what befalls: one, that it was for you it took place, and was prescribed for you, and had reference in some sort to you, being a thread of destiny spun from the first for you from the most ancient causes; the other, that even what befalls each individual is the cause of the well-faring, of the consummation and by heaven of the very permanence of that which controls the Universe. For the perfection of the Whole is impaired, if you cut off ever so little of the coherence and continuance of the Causes no less than of the parts. And you cut them off, as far as lies with you, and bring them to an end, when you murmur.

Love the course to which you return

9. Do not feel qualms or despondency or discomfiture if you do not invariably succeed in acting from right principles; but when you are foiled, come back again to them, and rejoice if on the whole your conduct is worthy of a man, and love the course to which you return. Come not back to Philosophy as to a schoolmaster, but as the sore-eyed to their sponges and their white of egg, as this patient

to his plaster and that to his fomentations. Thus will you rest satisfied with
Reason, yet make no parade of obeying her. And forget not that Philosophy
wishes but what your nature wishes, whereas your wish was for something
else that accords not with Nature. Yes, for it would have been the acme of
delight. Ah, is not that the very reason why pleasure trips us up? Nay, see
if these be not more delightful still: high-mindedness, independence, simplicity, tenderness of heart, sanctity of life. Why what is more delightful
than wisdom herself, when you think how sure and smooth in all its workings is the faculty of understanding and knowledge?

10. Things are in a sense so wrapped up in mystery that not a few philosophers, and they no ordinary ones, have concluded that they are wholly
beyond our comprehension: nay, even the Stoics themselves find them hard
to comprehend. Indeed every assent we give to the impressions of our senses
is liable to error, for where is the man who never errs? Pass on then to the
objective things themselves, how transitory they are, how worthless, the
property, quite possibly, of a boy-minion, a harlot, or a brigand. After that
turn to the characters of your associates, even the most refined of whom it
is difficult to put up with, let alone the fact that a man has enough to do to
endure himself.

What then there can be amid such murk and nastiness, and in so ceaseless an ebbing of substance and of time, of movement and things moved,
that deserves to be greatly valued or to excite our ambition in the least, I
cannot even conceive. On the contrary, a man should take heart of grace
to await his natural dissolution, and without any chafing at delay comfort
himself with these twin thoughts alone: the one, that nothing will befall
me that is not in accord with the Nature of the Universe; the other, that it
is in my power to do nothing contrary to the God and the "genius" within
me. For no one can force me to disobey that.

11. To what use then am I putting my soul? Never fail to ask yourself
this question and to cross-examine yourself thus: What relation have I to
this part of me which they call the ruling Reason? And whose Soul anyhow
have I got now? The Soul of a child? Of a youth? Of a woman? Of a tyrant?
Of a domestic animal? Of a wild beast?

12. What are counted as good things in the estimation of the many you can gather even from this. For if a man fix his mind upon certain things as really and unquestionably good, such as wisdom, temperance, justice, manliness, with this preconception in his mind he could no longer bear to listen to the poet's, By reason of his wealth of goods—; for it would not apply. But, if a man first fix his mind upon the things which appear good to the multitude, he will listen and readily accept as aptly added the quotation from the Comic Poet. In this way even the multitude have a perception of the difference. For otherwise this jest would not offend and be repudiated, while we accept it as appropriately and wittily said of wealth and of the advantages which wait upon luxury and popularity. Go on, then, and ask whether we should prize and count as good those things, with which first fixed in our mind we might germanely quote of their possessor, that for his very wealth of goods he has no place to ease himself in.

13. I am made up of the Causal and the Material, and neither of these disappears into nothing, just as neither did it come into existence out of nothing. So shall my every part by change be told off to form some part of the Universe, and that again be changed into another part of it, and so on to infinity. It was by such process of change that I too came into being and my parents, and so backwards into a second infinity. And the statement is quite legitimate, even if the Universe be arranged according to completed cycles.

14. Reason and the art of reasoning are in themselves and in their own proper acts self-sufficing faculties. Starting from a principle peculiar to them, they journey on to the end set before them. Wherefore such actions are termed right acts, as signifying that they follow the right way.

15. Call none of those things a man's that do not fall to him as man. They cannot be claimed of a man; man's nature does not guarantee them; they are no consummations of that nature. Consequently neither is the end for which man lives placed in these things, nor yet that which is perfective of the end, namely The Good. Moreover, if any of these things did fall to a man, it would not fall to him to scorn them and set his face against them, nor would a man be commendable who showed himself still lacking in

these things, nor yet would he be a good man who came short of himself in any of them, if so be these things were good. But as it is, the more a man can cut himself free, or even be set free, from these and other such things with equanimity, by so much the more is he good.

16. The character of your mind will be such as is the character of your frequent thoughts, for the soul takes its dye from the thoughts. Dye her then with a continuous succession of such thoughts as these: Where life is possible, there it is possible also to live well.—But the life is life in a Court. Well, in a Court too it is possible to live well. And again: A thing is drawn toward that for the sake of which it has been made, and its end lies in that toward which it is drawn and, where its end lies, there lie also its interest and its good. The Good, then, for a rational creature is fellowship with others. For it has been made clear long ago that we were constituted for fellowship. Or was it not obvious that the lower were for the sake of the higher and the higher for the sake of one another? And living things are higher than lifeless, and those that have reason than those that have life only.

17. To crave impossibilities is lunacy; but it is impossible for the wicked to act otherwise.

18. Nothing befalls anyone that he is not fitted by nature to bear. Others experience the same things as you, but either from ignorance that anything has befallen them, or to manifest their greatness of mind, they stand firm and get no hurt. A strange thing indeed that ignorance and vanity should prove stronger than wisdom!

Where life is possible, there it is possible also to live well

19. Things of themselves cannot take the least hold of the Soul, nor have any access to her, nor deflect or move her; but the Soul alone deflects and moves herself, and whatever judgments she deems it right to form, in conformity with them she fashions for herself the things that submit themselves to her from without.

20. In one respect a man is of very close concern to us, in so far as we must do him good and forbear; but in so far as any stand in the way of

those acts which concern us closely, then man becomes for me as much one of things indifferent as the sun, as the wind, as a wild-beast. Though a man may in some sort fetter my activity, yet on my own initiative and mental attitude no fetters can be put because of the power they possess of conditional action and of adaptation to circumstances. For everything that stands in the way of its activity is adapted and transmuted by the mind into a furtherance of it, and that which is a check on this action is converted into a help to it, and that which is a hindrance in our path goes but to make it easier.

21. Prize the most excellent thing in the Universe; and this is that which utilizes all things and controls all things. Prize in like manner the most excellent thing in yourself; and this is that which is akin to the other. For this, which utilizes all else is in you too, and by it your life is governed.

22. That which is not hurtful to the community cannot hurt the individual. Test every case of apparent hurt by this rule: if the community be not hurt by this, neither am I hurt; but if the community be hurt, there is no need to be angry with him that has done the hurt, but to inquire, In what has he seen amiss?

23. Think often on the swiftness with which the things that exist and that are coming into existence are swept past us and carried out of sight. For all substance is as a river in ceaseless flow, its activities ever changing and its causes subject to countless variations, and scarcely anything stable; and ever beside us is this infinity of the past and yawning abyss of the future, wherein all things are disappearing. Is he not senseless who in such an environment puffs himself up, or is distracted, or frets as over a trouble lasting and far-reaching?

24. Keep in memory the universal Substance, of which you are a tiny part; and universal Time, of which a brief, nay an almost momentary, span has been allotted you; and Destiny, in which how fractional your share?

25. Another does me some wrong? He shall see to it. His disposition is his own, his activities are his own. What the universal Nature wills me to have now, that I now have, and what my nature wills me now to do, that I do.

26. Let the ruling and master Reason of your soul be proof against any motions in the flesh smooth or rough. Let it not mingle itself with them, but isolate and restrict those tendencies to their true spheres. But when in virtue of that other sympathetic connection these tendencies grow up into the mind as is to be expected in a single organism, then must you not go about to resist the sensation, natural as it is, but see that your ruling Reason adds no opinion of its own as to whether such is good or bad.

27. Walk with the gods! And he does walk with the gods, who lets them see his soul invariably satisfied with its lot and carrying out the will of that "genius" a particle of himself, which Zeus has given to every man as his captain and guide—and this is none other than each man's intelligence and reason.

28. If a man's armpits are unpleasant, are you angry with him? If he has foul breath? What would be the use? The man has such a mouth, he has such armpits. Some such effluvium was bound to come from such a source. But the man has sense, you say, with a little attention he could see how he offends. I congratulate you! Well, you too have sense. By a rational attitude, then, in yourself evoke a rational attitude in him, enlighten him, admonish him. If he listen, you will cure him, and have no need of anger.

Neither tragedian nor harlot.

29. You can live on earth as you purpose to live when departed. But if men will not have it so, then is it time for you even to go out of life, yet not as one who is treated ill. 'Tis smoky and I go away. Why think it a great matter? But while no such cause drives me forth, I remain a free man, and none shall prevent me from doing what I will, and I will what is in accordance with the nature of a rational and social creature.

30. The intelligence of the Universe is social. It has at any rate made the lower things for the sake of the higher, and it adapted the higher to one another. You see how it has subordinated, coordinated, and given each its due lot and brought the more excellent things into mutual accord.

31. How have you borne yourself heretofore toward gods, parents, brethen, wife, children, teachers, tutors, friends, relations, household? Can you say truly of them all to this day,

Doing to no man wrong, nor speaking aught that is evil?

And call to mind all that you have passed through, all you have found strength to bear; that the story of your life is now full-told and your service is ending; and how many beautiful sights you have seen, how many pleasures and pains you have disregarded, forgone what ambitions, and repaid with kindness how much unkindness.

32. Why do unskilled and ignorant souls confound him who has skill and has knowledge? What soul, then, has skill and knowledge? Even that which knows beginning and end, and the reason that informs all Substance, and governs the Whole from ordered cycle to cycle through all eternity.

33. But a little while and you will be burnt ashes or a few dry bones, and possibly a name, possibly not a name even. And a name is but sound and a far off echo. And all that we prize so highly in our lives is empty and corrupt and paltry, and we but as puppies snapping at each other, as quarrelsome children now laughing and anon in tears. But faith and modesty and justice and truth.

Up from the wide-wayed Earth have winged their flight to Olympus.

> ## A name is but sound and a far off echo

What then keeps you here?—if indeed sensible objects are ever changing and unstable, and our faculties are so feeble and so easily misled; and the poor soul itself is an exhalation from blood; and to be well-thought of in such a world mere vanity. What then remains? To wait with a good grace for the end, whether it be extinction or translation. But till our time for that be come, what suffices? What but to reverence the gods and to praise them, to do good unto men and to bear with them and forbear, but for all else that comes within the compass of this poor flesh and breath, to remember that it is not your nor under your control?

34. You have it in your power that the current of your life be ever fair, if also 'tis your to make fair way, if also in ordered way to think and act. The Soul of God and the souls of men and of every rational creature have these

two characteristics in common: to suffer no let or hindrance from another, and to find their good in a condition and practice of justice, and to confine their propension to this.

35. If this be no vice of mine nor the outcome of any vice of mine, and if the common interest does not suffer, why concern myself about it? And how can the common interest suffer?

36. Be not carried incontinently away by sense-impressions, but rally to the fight as you can and as is due. If there be failure in things indifferent, yet think not there is any great harm done; for that is an evil habit. But as the greybeard (in the play) taking his leave reclaimed his foster-child's top, not forgetting that it was but a top, so do you here also. Since indeed you are found haranguing at the campaigns, O Man, have you forgotten what this really means? Aye, but people will have it. Must you too be a fool in consequence?

Time was that wheresoever forsaken I was a man well-portioned; but that man well-portioned is he that has given himself a good portion; and good portions are good tendencies of the soul, good impulses, good actions.

BOOK VI

1 THE UNIVERSAL SUBSTANCE IS DOCILE AND DUCTILE; AND THE Reason that controls it has no motive in itself to do wrong. For it has no wrongness and does no wrong, nor is anything harmed by it. But all things come into being and fulfill their purpose as it directs.

2. Make no difference in doing your duty whether you are shivering or warm, drowsy or sleep-satisfied, defamed or extolled, dying or anything else. For the act of dying too is one of the acts of life. So it is enough in this also to get the work in hand done well.

3. Look within. Let not the special quality or worth of anything escape you.

4. All objective things will soon be changed and either etherialized into the Universal Substance, if that indeed be one, or dispersed abroad.

5. The controlling Reason knows its own bent and its work and the medium it works in.

6. The best way of avenging yourself is not to do likewise.

7. Delight in this one thing and take your rest therein—from social act to go on to social act, keeping all your thoughts on God.

8. The ruling Reason can arouse and deflect itself, make itself whatever it will, and invest everything that befalls with such a semblance as it wills.

9. In accordance with the Nature of the Universe is accomplished each several thing. For surely this cannot be in accordance with any other nature, that either envelops it from without, or is enveloped by it within, or exists in external detachment outside it.

10. Either a medley and a tangled web and a dispersion abroad, or a unity and a plan and a Providence. If the former, why should I even wish to abide in such a random welter and chaos? Why care for anything else than to turn again to the dust at last. Why be disquieted? For, do what I will, the dispersion must overtake me. But if the latter, I bow in reverence, my feet are on the rock, and I put my trust in the Power that rules.

11. When forced, as it seems, by your environment to be utterly disquieted, return with all speed into your self, staying in discord no longer than you must. By constant recurrence to the harmony, you will gain more command over it.

12. Had you at once a stepmother and a mother you would pay due service to the former, and yet your constant recourse would be to your mother. So have you now the court and philosophy for stepmother and mother. Cease not then to come to the latter and take your rest in her, whereby will both your court life seem more tolerable to you, and you to your court life.

13. As in the case of meat and similar eatables the thought strikes us, this is the dead body of a fish, this of a fowl or pig; and again that this wine is merely the juice of a grape-cluster, and this purple-edged robe is nothing but sheep's wool steeped in the blood of a shellfish; or, of sexual intercourse, that it is merely internal attrition and the spasmodic excretion of mucus—such, I say, as are these impressions that get to grips with the actual things and enter into the heart of them, so as to see them as they really are, thus should it be your life through, and where things look to be above measure convincing, laying them quite bare, behold their paltriness and strip off their conventional prestige. For conceit is a past master in fallacies and, when you flatter yourself most that you are engaged in worthy tasks, then are you most of all deluded by it. At any rate, see what Crates has to say about none other than Xenocrates.

14. Objects admired by the common sort come chiefly under things of the most general kind, which are held together by physical coherence, such as stones and wood, or by a natural unity, such as figs, vines, olives; and those which are admired by persons of a somewhat higher capacity may be

classed as things which are held together by a conscious life, such as flocks and herds; and those which are admired by persons still more refined, as things held together by a rational soul; I do not mean rational as part of the Universal Reason, but in the sense of master of an art or expert in some other way, or merely in so far as to own a host of slaves. But he that prizes a soul which is rational, universal, and civic, no longer turns after anything else, but rather than everything besides keeps his own soul, in itself and in its activity, rational and social, and to this end works conjointly with all that is akin to him.

> **You flatter yourself most that you are engaged in worthy tasks**

15. Some things are hastening to be, others to be no more, while of those that haste into being some part is already extinct. Fluxes and changes perpetually renew the world, just as the unbroken march of time makes ever new the infinity of ages. In this river of change, which of the things which swirl past him, whereon no firm foothold is possible, should a man prize so highly? As well fall in love with a sparrow that flits past and in a moment is gone from our eyes. In fact a man's life itself is but as an exhalation from blood and an inhalation from the air. For just as it is to draw in the air once into our lungs and give it back again, as we do every moment, so is it to give back thither, whence you did draw it first, your faculty of breathing which you received at your birth yesterday or the day before.

16. Neither is it an inner respiration, such as that of plants, that we should prize, nor the breathing which we have in common with cattle and wild animals, nor the impressions we receive through our senses, nor that we are pulled by our impulses like marionettes, nor our gregarious instincts, nor our need of nutriment; for that is on a par with the rejection of the waste products of our food.

What then is to be prized? The clapping of hands? No. Then not the clapping of tongues either. For the acclamations of the multitude are but a clapping of tongues. So overboard goes that poor thing Fame also. What is left to be prized? This methinks: to limit our action or inaction to the needs of our own constitution, an end that all occupations and arts set before themselves. For the aim of every art is that the thing constituted should be adapted to the work for which it has been constituted. It is so with the vine-dresser who looks after the vines, the colt-trainer, and the keeper of the kennel. And this is the end which the care of children and the methods of teaching have in view. There then is the thing to be prized!

> The acclamations of the multitude are but a clapping of tongues

This once fairly made your own, you will not seek to gain for yourself any of the other things as well. Will you not cease prizing many other things also? Then you will neither be free nor sufficient unto yourself nor unmoved by passion. For you must needs be full of envy and jealousy, be suspicious of those that can rob you of such things, and scheme against those who possess what you prize. In fine, a man who needs any of those things cannot but be in complete turmoil, and in many cases find fault even with the gods. But by reverencing and prizing your own mind, you will make yourself pleasing in your own sight, in accord with mankind, and in harmony with the gods, that is, grateful to them for all that they dispense and have ordained.

17. Up, down, round and round sweep the elements along. But the motion of virtue is in none of these ways. It is something more divine, and going forward on a mysterious path fares well upon its way.

18. What a way to act! Men are wary of commending their contemporaries and associates, while they themselves set great store by the commendation of posterity, whom they have never seen or shall see. But this is next door to taking it amiss that your predecessors also did not commend you.

19. Because you find a thing difficult for yourself to accomplish do not conceive it to be impracticable for others; but whatever is possible for a man and in keeping with his nature consider also attainable by yourself.

20. Suppose that a competitor in the ring has gashed us with his nails and butted us violently with his head, we do not protest or take it amiss or suspect our opponent in future of foul play. Still we do keep an eye on him, not indeed as an enemy, or from suspicion of him, but with good-humored avoidance. Act much in the same way in all the other parts of life. Let us make many allowances for our fellow-athletes as it were. Avoidance is always possible, as I have said, without suspicion or hatred.

21. If any one can prove and bring home to me that a conception or act of mine is wrong, I will amend it, and be thankful. For I seek the truth, whereby no one was ever harmed. But he is harmed who persists in his own self-deception and ignorance.

22. I do my own duty; other things do not distract me. For they are either inanimate or irrational, or such as have gone astray and know not the road.

23. Conduct yourself with magnanimity and freedom toward irrational creatures and, generally, toward circumstances and objective things, for you have reason and they have none. But men have reason, therefore treat them as fellow creatures. And in all cases call upon the gods, and do not concern yourself with the question, How long shall I do this? Three hours are enough so spent.

24. Death reduced to the same condition Alexander the Macedonian and his muleteer, for either

> I seek the truth, whereby no one was ever harmed. But he is harmed who persists in his own self-deception and ignorance

they were taken back into the same Seminal Reason of the Universe or scattered alike into the atoms.

25. Bear in mind how many things happen to each one of us with respect to our bodies as well as our souls in the same momentary space of time, so will you cease to wonder that many more things—not to say all the things that come into existence in that One and Whole which in fact we call the Universe—subsist in it at one time.

26. If one inquires of you, How is the name Antoninus written? will you with vehemence enunciate each constituent letter? What then? If your listeners lose their temper, will you lose yours? Would you not go on gently to enumerate each letter? So recollect that in life too every duty is the sum of separate items. Of these you must take heed, and carry through methodically what is set before you, in no wise troubled or showing counter-irritation against those who are irritated with you.

27. How intolerant it is not to permit men to cherish an impulse toward what is in their eyes congenial and advantageous! Yet in a sense you withhold from them the right to do this, when you resent their wrong-doing. For they are undoubtedly drawn to what they deem congenial and advantageous. But they are mistaken. Well, then, teach and enlighten them without any resentment.

28. Death is a release from the impressions of sense, and from impulses that make us their puppets, from the vagaries of the mind, and the hard service of the flesh.

29. It is a disgrace for the soul to be the first to succumb in that life in which the body does not succumb,

30. See you be not Caesarified, nor take that dye, for there is the possibility. So keep yourself a simple and good man, uncorrupt, dignified, plain, a friend of justice, god-fearing, gracious, affectionate, manful in doing your duty. Strive to be always such as Philosophy minded to make you. Revere the gods, save mankind. Life is short. This only is the harvest of earthly existence, a righteous disposition and social acts.

Do all things as a disciple of Antoninus. Think of his constancy in every act rationally undertaken, his invariable equability, his piety, his

serenity of countenance, his sweetness of disposition, his contempt for
the bubble of fame, and his zeal for getting a true grasp of affairs. How
he would never on any account dismiss a
thing until he had first thoroughly scruti-
nized and clearly conceived it; how he put
up with those who found fault with him
unfairly, finding no fault with them in
return; how he was never in a hurry; how
he gave no ear to slander, and with what
nicety he tested dispositions and acts; was

Revere the gods, save mankind. Life is short

no imputer of blame, and no craven, not a suspicious man, nor a sophist,
what little sufficed him whether for lodging or bed, dress, food, or attendance; how fond he was of work, and how long-suffering; how he would
remain the whole day at the same occupation, owing to his spartan diet
not even requiring to relieve nature except at the customary time; and
how loyal he was to his friends and always the same; and his forbearance
toward those who openly opposed his views, and his pleasure when anyone
pointed out something better; and how god-fearing he was and yet not
given to superstition. Take heed to all this, that your last hour come upon
you as much at peace with your conscience as he was.

31. Be sober once more and call back your senses, and being roused
again from sleep and realizing that they were but dreams that beset you,
now awake again, look at these realities as you did at those your dreams.

32. I consist of body and soul. To the body indeed all things are indifferent, for it cannot concern itself with them. But to the mind only those
things are indifferent which are not its own activities; and all those things
that are its own activities are in its own power. Howbeit, of these it is only
concerned with the present; for as to its activities in the past and the future,
these two rank at once among things indifferent.

33. For hand or foot to feel pain is no violation of nature, so long as the
foot does its own appointed work, and the hand its own. Similarly pain for
a man, as man, is no unnatural thing so long as he does a man's appointed
work. But, if not unnatural, then is it not an evil either.

34. The pleasures of the brigand, the pathic, the parricide, the tyrant—just think what they are!

35. Do you not see how the mechanic craftsman, though to some extent willing to humor the non-expert, yet holds fast none the less to the principles of his handicraft, and cannot endure to depart from them. Is it not strange that the architect and the physician should hold the rationale of their respective arts in higher reverence than a man his own reason, which he has in common with the gods?

36. Asia, Europe, corners of the Universe: the whole Ocean a drop in the Universe: Athos but a little clod therein: all the present a point in Eternity:—everything on a tiny scale, so easily changed, so quickly vanished.

All things come from that one source, from that ruling Reason of the Universe, either under a primary impulse from it or by way of consequence. And therefore the gape of the lion's jaws and poison and all noxious things, such as thorns and mire, are but after-results of the grand and the beautiful. Look not then on these as alien to that which you reverence, but turn your thoughts to the one source of all things.

37. He, who sees what now is, has seen all that ever has been from times everlasting, and that shall be to eternity; for all things are of one lineage and one likeness.

38. Meditate often on the intimate union and mutual interdependence of all things in the Universe. For in a manner all things are mutually intertwined, and thus all things have a liking for one another. For these things are consequent one on another by reason of their contracting and expanding motion, the sympathy that breathes through them, and the unity of all substance.

39. Fit yourself to the environment that is your portion, and love the men among whom your lot is thrown, but whole-heartedly.

40. Every implement, tool, or vessel is well if it does the work for which it is made, and yet in their case the maker is not at hand. But in the things which owe their organic unity to Nature, the Power that made is within them and abides there. Wherefore also must you reverence it the

more, and realize that if you keep and conduct yourself ever according to its will, all is to your mind. So also to its mind are the things of the Universe.

41. If you regard anything not in your own choice as good or evil for yourself, it is inevitable that, on the incidence of such an evil or the miscarriage of such a good, you should upbraid the gods, aye, and hate men as the actual or supposed cause of the one or the other; and in fact many are the wrongdoings we commit by setting a value on such things. But if we discriminate as good and evil only the things in our power, there is no occasion left for accusing the gods or taking the stand of an enemy toward men.

42. We are all fellow-workers toward the fulfilment of one object, some of us knowingly and intelligently, others blindly; just as Heraclitus, I think, says that even when they sleep men are workers and fellow-agents in all that goes on in the world. One is a co-agent in this, another in that, and in abundant measure also he that murmurs and seeks to hinder or prevent what occurs. For the Universe had need of such men also. It remains then for you to decide with whom you are ranging yourself. For He who controls the Universe will in any case put you to a good use and admit you to a place among his fellow-workers and coadjutors. But see that you fill no such place as the paltry and ridiculous line in the play which Chrysippus mentions.

43. Does the sun take upon himself to discharge the functions of the rain? or Asclepius of the Fruit-bearer? And what of each particular star? Do they not differ in glory yet co-operate to one end?

44. If the gods have taken counsel about me and the things to befall me, doubtless they have taken good counsel. For it is not easy even to imagine a god without wisdom. And what motive could they have impelling them to do me evil? For what advantage could thereby accrue to them or to the Universe which is their special care? But if the gods have taken no counsel for me individually, yet they have in any case done so for the interests of the Universe, and I am bound to welcome and make the best of those things also that befall as a necessary corollary to those interests. But if so be they

take counsel about nothing at all—an impious belief—in good truth let us have no more of sacrifices and prayers and oaths, nor do any other of these things every one of which is a recognition of the gods as if they were at our side and dwelling among us—but if so be, I say, they do not take counsel about any of our concerns, it is still in my power to take counsel about myself, and it is for me to consider my own interest. And that is to every man's interest which is agreeable to his own constitution and nature. But my nature is rational and civic; my city and country, as Antoninus, is Rome; as a man, the world. The things then that are of advantage to these communities, these, and no other, are good for me.

45. All that befalls the Individual is to the interest of the Whole also. So far, so good. But further careful observation will show you that, as a general rule, what is to the interest of one man is also to the interest of other men. But in this case the word interest must be taken in a more general sense as it applies to intermediate things.

All that befalls the Individual is to the interest of the Whole

46. As the shows in the amphitheater and such places grate upon you as being an everlasting repetition of the same sight, and the similarity makes the spectacle pall, such must be the effect of the whole of life. For everything up and down is ever the same and the result of the same things. How long then?

47. Never lose sight of the fact that men of all kinds, of all sorts of vocations and of every race under heaven, are dead; and so carry your thought down even to Philistion and Phoebus and Origanion. Now turn to all other folk. We must pass at last to the same borne whither so many wonderful orators have gone, so many grave philosophers, Heraclitus, Pythagoras, Socrates: so many heroes of old time, and so many warriors, so many tyrants of later days: and besides them, Eudoxus, Hipparchus, Archimedes, and other acute natures, men of large minds, lovers of toil, men of versatile powers, men of strong will, mockers, like Menippus and many another

such, of man's perishable and transitory life itself. About all these reflect that they have long since been in their graves. What terrible thing then is this for them? What pray for those whose very names are unknown? One thing on earth is worth much—to live out our lives in truth and justice, and in charity with liars and unjust men.

48. When you would cheer your heart, think upon the good qualities of your associates; as for instance, this one's energy, that one's modesty, the generosity of a third, and some other trait of a fourth. For nothing is so cheering as the images of the virtues mirrored in the characters of those who live with us, and presenting themselves in as great a throng as possible. Have these images then ever before your eyes.

49. You are not aggrieved, are you, at being so many pounds in weight and not three hundred? Then why be aggrieved if you have only so many years to live and no more? For as you are contented with the amount of matter allotted you, so be content also with the time.

50. Try persuasion first, but even though men would say you nay, act when the principles of justice so direct. Should any one however withstand you by force, take refuge in being well-content and unhurt, and utilize the obstacle for the display of some other virtue. Recollect that the impulse you had was conditioned by circumstances, and your aim was not to do impossibilities. What then was it? To feel some such impulse as you did in that you are successful. That which alone was in the sphere of our choice is realized.

51. The lover of glory conceives his own good to consist in another's action, the lover of pleasure in his own feelings, but the possessor of understanding in his own actions.

> **One thing on earth is worth much—to live out our lives in truth and justice, and in charity with liars and unjust men**

52. We need not form any opinion about the thing in question or be harassed in soul, for Nature gives the thing itself no power to compel our judgments.

53. Train yourself to pay careful attention to what is being said by another and as far as possible enter into his soul.

54. That which is not in the interests of the hive cannot be in the interests of the bee.

55. If the sailors spoke ill of a steersman or the sick of a physician, what else would they have in mind but how the man should best effect the safety of the crew or the health of his patients?

56. How many have already left the world who came into it with me!

57. To the jaundiced honey tastes bitter; and the victim of hydrophobia has a horror of water; and to little children their ball is a treasure. Why then be angry? Or do you think that error is a less potent factor than bile in the jaundiced and virus in the victim of rabies?

58. From living according to the reason of your nature no one can prevent you: contrary to the reason of the Universal Nature nothing shall befall you.

59. The persons men wish to please, the objects they wish to gain, the means they employ—think of the character of all these! How soon will Time hide all things! How many a thing has it already hidden!

BOOK VII

———

1 WHAT IS VICE? A FAMILIAR SIGHT ENOUGH. SO IN EVERYTHING that befalls have the thought ready: This is a familiar sight. Look up, look down, everywhere you will find the same things, whereof histories ancient, medieval, and modern are full; and full of them at this day are cities and houses. There is no new thing under the sun. Everything is familiar, everything fleeting.

2. How else can your axioms be made dead than by the extinction of the ideas that answer to them? And these it lies with you ever to kindle anew into flame. I am competent to form the true conception of a thing. If so, why am I harassed? What is outside the scope of my mind has absolutely no concern with my mind. Learn this lesson and you stand erect.

You can begin a new life! See but things afresh as you used to see them; for in this consists the new life.

3. Empty love of pageantry, stage-plays, flocks and herds, sham-fights, a bone thrown to lap-dogs, crumbs cast in a fish-pond, painful travail of ants and their bearing of burdens, scurrying of scared little mice, puppets moved by strings: amid such environment therefore you must take your place graciously and not "snorting defiance," nay you must keep abreast of the fact that everyone is worth just so much as those things are worth in which he is interested.

Everything is familiar, everything fleeting

4. In conversation keep abreast of what is being said, and, in every effort, of what is being done. In the latter see from the first to what end it has reference, and in the former be careful to catch the meaning.

5. Is my mind competent for this or not? If competent, I apply it to the task as an instrument given me by the Universal Nature. If not competent, I either withdraw from the work in favor of someone who can accomplish it better, unless for other reasons duty forbids; or I do the best I can, taking to assist me any one that can utilize my ruling Reason to effect what is at the moment seasonable and useful for the common welfare. For in whatsoever I do either by myself or with another I must direct my energies to this alone, that it shall conduce to the common interest and be in harmony with it.

6. How many much-lauded heroes have already been given as a prey unto forgetfulness, and how many that lauded them have long ago disappeared!

Blush not to be helped

7. Blush not to be helped; for you are bound to carry out the task that is laid upon you as a soldier to storm the breach. What then, if for very lameness you cannot mount the ramparts unaided, but can do this with another's help?

8. Be not disquieted about the future. If you must come thither, you will come armed with the same reason which you apply now to the present.

9. All things are mutually intertwined, and the tie is sacred, and scarcely anything is alien the one to the other. For all things have been ranged side by side, and together help to order one ordered Universe. For there is both one Universe, made up of all things, and one God immanent in all things, and one Substance, and one Law, one Reason common to all intelligent creatures, and one Truth: if indeed there is also one perfecting of living creatures that have the same origin and share the same reason.

10. A very little while and all that is material is lost to sight in the Substance of the Universe, a little while and all Cause is taken back into the

Reason of the Universe, a little while and the remembrance of everything is entombed in Eternity.

11. To the rational creature the same act is at once according to nature and according to reason.

12. Upright, or made upright.

13. The principle which obtains where limbs and body unite to form one organism, holds good also for rational things with their separate individualities, constituted as they are to work in conjunction. But the perception of this shall come more home to you, if you say to yourself, I am a limb of the organized body of rational things. But if you say you are but a part, not yet do you love mankind from the heart, nor yet does well-doing delight you for its own sake. You practice it still as a bare duty, not yet as a boon to yourself.

14. Let any external thing, that will, be incident to whatever is able to feel this incidence. For that which feels can, if it please, complain. But I, if I do not consider what has befallen me to be an evil, am still unhurt. And I can refuse so to consider it.

15. Let any say or do what he will, I cannot but for my part be good. So might the emerald—or gold or purple—never tire of repeating, Whatever any one shall do or say, I cannot but be an emerald and keep my color.

16. The ruling Reason is never the disturber of its own peace, never, for instance, hurries itself into lust. But if another can cause it fear or pain, let it do so. For it will not let its own assumptions lead it into such aberrations.

Let the body take thought for itself, if it may, that it suffer no hurt and, if it do so suffer, let it proclaim the fact. But the soul that has the faculty of fear, the faculty of pain, and alone can assume that these exist, can never suffer; for it is not given to making any such admission.

In itself the ruling Reason wants for nothing unless it creates its own needs, and in like manner nothing can disturb it, nothing impede it, unless the disturbance or impediment come from itself.

17. Well-being is a good Being, or a ruling Reason that is good. Why then do you appear, O Imagination? Leave, in God's name, as you earnest,

for I desire you not! But you are come according to your ancient wont. I bear you no malice; only depart from me!

18. Does a man shrink from change? Why, what can come into being save by change? What be nearer or dearer to the Nature of the Universe? Can you take a hot bath unless the wood for the furnace suffer a change? Could you be fed, if your food suffered no change, and can any of the needs of life be provided for apart from change? See you not that a personal change is similar, and similarly necessary to the Nature of the Universe?

19. Through the universal Substance as through a rushing torrent all bodies pass on their way, united with the Whole in nature and activity, as our members are with one another.

How many a Chrysippus, how many a Socrates, how many an Epictetus has Time already devoured! Whatsoever man you have to do with and whatsoever thing, let the same thought strike you.

20. I am concerned about one thing only, that I of myself do not what man's constitution does not will, or wills not now, or in a way that it wills not.

21. A little while and you will have forgotten everything, a little while and everything will have forgotten you.

22. It is a man's especial privilege to love even those who stumble. And this love follows as soon as you reflect that they are of kin to you and that they do wrong involuntarily and through ignorance, and that within a little while both they and you will be dead; and this, above all, that the man has done you no hurt; for he has not made your ruling Reason worse than it was before.

It is a man's especial privilege to love even those who stumble

23. The Nature of the Whole out of the Substance of the Whole, as out of wax, molds at one time a horse, and breaking up the mold kneads the material up again into a tree, then into a man, and then into something else; and every one of these

subsists but for a moment. It is no more a hardship for the coffer to be broken up than it was for it to be fitted together.

24. An angry scowl on the face is beyond measure unnatural, and when it is often seen there, all comeliness begins at once to die away, and in the end is so utterly extinguished that it can never be rekindled at all. From this very fact try to reach the conclusion that it is contrary to reason. The consciousness of wrong-doing once lost, what motive is left for living any more?

25. Everything that you see will the Nature that controls the Universe change, no one knows how soon, and out of its substance make other compounds, and again others out of theirs, that the world may ever renew its youth.

26. Does a man do you wrong? Go to and mark what notion of good and evil was his that did the wrong. Once perceive that and you will feel compassion, not surprise or anger. For you have still yourself either the same notion of good and evil as he or another not unlike. You needs must forgive him then. But if your notions of good and evil are no longer such, all the more easily will you be gracious to him that sees awry.

27. Dream not of that which you have not as though already yours, but of what you have pick out the choicest blessings, and do not forget in respect of them how eagerly you would have coveted them, had they not been yours. Albeit beware that you do not inure yourself, by reason of this your delight in them, to prize them so highly as to be distressed if at any time they are lost to you.

28. Gather yourself into yourself. It is characteristic of the rational Ruling Faculty to be satisfied with its own righteous dealing and the peace which that brings.

29. Efface imagination! Cease to be pulled as a puppet by your passions. Isolate the present. Recognize what befalls either you or another. Dissect and analyze all that comes under your ken into the Causal and the Material. Meditate on your last hour. Let the wrong your neighbor does you rest with him that did the wrong.

30. Do your utmost to keep up with what is said. Let your mind enter into the things that are done and the things that are doing them.

31. Make your face to shine with simplicity and modesty and disregard of all that lies between virtue and vice. Love human-kind. Follow God. Says the Sage: All things by Law, but in very truth only elements. But it suffices to remember that all things are by law: there you have it briefly enough.

32. Of Death: Either dispersion if atoms; or, if a single Whole, either extinction or a change of state.

33. Of Pain: When unbearable it destroys us, when lasting, it is bearable, and the mind safeguards its own calm by withdrawing itself, and the ruling Reason takes no hurt. As to the parts that are impaired by the pain, let them say their say about it as they can.

34. Of Glory: Look at the minds of its votaries, their characteristics, ambitions, antipathies. Remember too that, as the sands of the sea drifting one upon the other bury the earlier deposits, so in life the earlier things are very soon hidden under what comes after.

35. [From Plato.] Do you think that the life of man can seem any great matter to him who has true grandeur of soul and a comprehensive outlook on all Time and all Substance? "It cannot seem so," said he. Will such a man then deem death a terrible thing? "Not in the least."

36. [From Antisthenes.] 'Tis royal to do well and be ill spoken of.

37. It is a shame that while the countenance is subject to the mind, taking its cast and livery from it, the mind cannot take its cast and its livery from itself.

'Tis royal to do well and be ill spoken of

38. It nought availeth to be angry with things,
For they reck not of it.

39. Unto the deathless gods and to us give cause for rejoicing.

40. Our lives are reaped like the ripe ears of corn, and as one falls, another still is born.

41. Though me and both my sons the gods have spurned, for this too there is reason.

42. For justice and good luck shall bide with me.

43. No chorus of loud dirges, no hysteria.

44. [Citations from Plato]:

I might fairly answer such a questioner: You are mistaken if you think that a man, who is worth anything at all, ought to let considerations of life and death weigh with him rather than in all that he does consider but this, whether it is just or unjust and the work of a good man or a bad.

45. This, O men of Athens, is the true state of the case: Wherever a man has stationed himself, deeming it the best for him, or has been stationed by his commander, there methinks he ought to stay and run every risk, taking into account neither death nor anything else save dishonor.

46. But, my good sir, see whether nobility and goodness do not mean something other than to save and be saved; for surely a man worthy of the name must waive aside the question of the duration of life however extended, and must not cling basely to life, but leaving these things in the hands of God pin his faith to the women's adage, "his destiny no man can flee," and thereafter consider in what way he may best live for such time as he has to live.

47. Watch the stars in their courses as one that runneth about with them therein; and think constantly upon the reciprocal changes of the elements, for thoughts on these things cleanse away the mire of our earthly life.

48. Noble is this saying of Plato's. Moreover he who discourses of men should, as if from some vantage-point above, take a bird's-eye view of the things of earth, in its gatherings, armies, husbandry, its marriages and separations, its births and deaths, the din of the law-court and the silence of the desert, barbarous races manifold, its feasts and mourning and markets, the medley of it all and its orderly conjunction of contraries.

49. Pass in review the far-off things of the past and its succession of sovereignties without number. You can look forward and see the future

also. For it will most surely be of the same character, and it cannot but carry on the rhythm of existing things. Consequently it is all one, whether we witness human life for forty years or ten thousand. For what more will you see?

50. All that is earth-born gravitates earthwards,

Dust unto dust; and all that from ether Grows, speeds swiftly hack again heavenward; that is, either there is a breaking up of the closely-linked atoms or, what is much the same, a scattering of the impassive elements.

51. Again:

With meats and drinks and curious sorceries Side-track the stream, so be they may not die. When a storm from the gods beats down on our bark, At our oars then we needs must toil and complain not.

52. Better at wrestling, maybe, but not at showing public spirit or modesty, or being readier for every contingency or more gracious to our neighbor if he sees awry.

53. A work that can be accomplished in obedience to that reason which we share with the gods is attended with no fear. For no harm need be anticipated, where by an activity that follows the right road, and satisfies the demands of our constitution, we can ensure our own interest.

54. At all times and in all places it rests with you both to be content with your present lot as a worshipper of the gods, and to deal righteously with your present neighbors, and to labor lovingly at your present thoughts, that nothing unverified should steal into them.

55. Look not about you at the ruling Reason of others, but look with straight eyes at this, To what is Nature guiding you?—both the Nature of the Universe, by means of what befalls you and your nature by means of the acts you have to do. But everyone must do what follows from his own constitution; and all other things have been constituted for the sake of rational beings—just as in every other case the lower are for the sake of the higher—but the rational for their own sake.

Social obligation then is the leading feature in the constitution of man and, coming second to it, an uncompromising resistance to bodily inclinations. For it is the privilege of a rational and intelligent motion to isolate itself, and never to be overcome by the motions of sense or desire; for either kind is animal-like. But the motion of the Intelligence claims ever to have the preeminence and never to be mastered by them. And rightly so, for it is its nature to put all those to its own use. Thirdly, the rational constitution is free from precipitancy and cannot be misled. Let the ruling Reason then, clinging to these characteristics, accomplish a straight course and then it comes into its own.

56. As one that is dead, and his life till now lived and gone, you must live the rest of your days as so much to the good, and live according to Nature.

57. Love only what befalls you and is spun for you by fate. For what can be more befitting for you?

58. In every contingency keep before your eyes those who, when these same things befell them, were straightway aggrieved, estranged, rebellious. Where are they now? Nowhere! What then? Would you too be like them? Why not leave those alien deflections to what deflects and is deflected by them, and devote yourself wholly to the question how to turn these contingencies to the best advantage? For then will you make a noble use of them, and they shall be your raw material. Only in thought and will take heed to be beautiful to yourself in all that you do. And remember, in rejecting the one and using the other, that the thing which matters is the aim of the action.

Look within. Within is the fountain of Good

59. Look within. Within is the fountain of Good, ready always to well forth if you will alway delve.

60. The body too should be firmly set and suffer no distortion in movement or bearing. For what the mind effects in the face, by keeping it composed and well-favored, should be looked for similarly in the whole body. But all this must be secured without conscious effort.

61. The business of life is more akin to wrestling than dancing, for it requires of us to stand ready and unshakeable against every assault however unforeseen.

62. Continually reflect, who they are whose favorable testimony you desire, and what their ruling Reason; for thus will you not find fault with those who unintentionally offend, nor will you want their testimony, when you look into the inner springs of their opinions and desires.

63. Every soul, says Plato, is bereft of truth against its will. Therefore it is the same also with justice and temperance and loving kindness and every like quality. It is essential to keep this ever in mind, for it will make you gentler toward all.

64. Whenever you are in pain, have this reflection ready, that this is nothing to be ashamed of, nor can it make worse the mind that holds the helm. For it cannot impair it in so far as it is rational or in so far as it is social. In most pains, however, call to your rescue even Epicurus when he says that a pain is never unbearable or interminable, so that you remember its limitations and add nothing to it in imagination. Recollect this too that many of our every-day discomforts are really pain in disguise, such as drowsiness, a high temperature, want of appetite. When inclined to be vexed at any of these, say to yourself: I am giving in to pain.

65. See that you never have for the inhuman the feeling which the inhuman have for human kind.

66. How do we know that Telauges may not have excelled Socrates in character? For it is not enough that Socrates died a more glorious death, and disputed more deftly with the Sophists, and with more hardihood braved whole nights in the frost, and, when called upon to fetch the Salaminian, deemed it more spirited to disobey, and that he carried his head high as he walked—and about the truth of this one can easily judge—; but the point to elucidate is this: what sort of soul had Socrates, and could he rest satisfied with being just in his dealings with men and religious in his attitude toward the gods, neither resentful at the wickedness of others nor yet lackeying the ignorance of anyone, nor regarding as alien to himself

anything allotted to him from the Whole, nor bearing it as a burden intolerable, nor letting his intelligence be swayed sympathetically by the affections of the flesh?

67. Nature did not make so intimate a blend in the compound as not to allow a man to isolate himself and keep his own things in his own power. For it is very possible to be a godlike man and yet not to be recognized by any. Never forget this; nor that the happy life depends on the fewest possible things; nor because you have been baulked in the hope of becoming skilled in dialectics and physics, need you despair of being free and modest and unselfish and obedient to God.

68. You may live out your life with none to constrain you in the utmost peace of mind even though the whole world cry out against you what they will, even though beasts tear limb from limb this plastic clay that has encased you with its growth. For what in all this debars the mind from keeping itself in calmness, in a right judgment as to its environment, and in readiness to use all that is put at its disposal? so that the judgment can say to that which meets it: In essential substance you are this, whatever else the common fame would have you be. And the use can say to the object presented to it: You was I seeking. For the thing in hand is for me ever material for the exercise of rational and civic virtue, and in a word for the art of a man or of god. For everything that befalls is intimately connected with god or man, and is not new or difficult to deal with, but familiar and feasible.

69. This is the mark of a perfect character, to pass through each day as if it were the last, without agitation, without torpor, without pretense.

70. The gods—and they are immortal—do not take it amiss that for a time so long they must inevitably and always put up with worthless men who are what they are and so many; nay they even care for them in all manner of ways. But you, though destined to die so soon, cry off, and that too though you are one of the worthless ones yourself.

71. It is absurd not to eschew our own wickedness, which is possible, but to eschew that of others, which is not possible.

72. Whatever your rational and civic faculty discovers to be neither intelligent nor social, it judges with good reason to fall short of its own standard.

73. When you have done well to another and another has fared well at your hands, why go on like the foolish to look for a third thing besides, that is, the credit also of having done well or a return for the same?

74. No one wearies of benefits received; and to act by the law of Nature is its own benefit. Weary not then of being benefited therein, wherein you benefit others.

75. The Nature of the Whole felt impelled to the creation of a Universe; but now either all that comes into being does so by a natural sequence, or even the most paramount things, toward which the ruling Reason of the Universe feels an impulse of its own, are devoid of intelligence. Recollect this and you will face many an ill with more serenity.

BOOK VIII

1 THIS TOO SERVES AS A CORRECTIVE TO VAIN-GLORIOUSNESS, THAT you are no longer able to have lived your life wholly, or even from your youth up, as a philosopher. You can clearly perceive, and many others can see it too, that you are far from Philosophy. So then your life is a chaos, and no longer is it easy for you to win the credit of being a philosopher; and the facts of your life too war against it. If then your eyes have seen where the truth lies, care no more what men shall think of you, but be content if the rest of your life, whether long or short, be lived as your nature wills. Make sure then what that will is, and let nothing else draw you aside. For past experience tells you in how much you have gone astray, nor anywhere lighted upon the true life; no, not in the subtleties of logic, or in wealth or fame or enjoyment, or anywhere. Where then is it to be found? In doing that which is the quest of man's nature. How then shall a man do this? By having axioms as the source of his impulses and actions. What axioms? On the nature of Good and Evil, showing that nothing is for a man's good save what makes him just, temperate, manly, free; nor any thing for his ill that makes him not the reverse of these.

2. In every action ask yourself, How does this affect me? Shall I regret it? But a little and I am dead and all is past and gone. What more do I ask for, as long as my present work is that of a living creature, intelligent, social, and under one law with God?

3. What are Alexander and Gaius and Pompeius to Diogenes and Heraclitus and Socrates? For these latter had their eyes opened to things and

to the causes and the material substance of things, and their ruling Reason was their very own. But those—what a host of cares, what a world of slavery!

> You may burst yourself with rage, but they will go on doing the same things none the less

4. You may burst yourself with rage, but they will go on doing the same things none the less.

5. Firstly, fret not yourself, for all things are as the Nature of the Universe would have them, and within a little you will be nonexistent, and nowhere, like Hadrianus and Augustus. Secondly, look steadfastly at the thing, and see it as it is and, remembering that you must be a good man, and what the Nature of man calls for, do this without swerving, and speak as seems to you most just, only be it graciously, modestly, and without feigning.

6. The Nature of the Universe is charged with this task, to transfer yonder the things which are here, to interchange them, to take them hence and convey them thither. All things are but phases of change, but nothing new-fangled need be feared; all things are of the wonted type, nay, their distributions also are alike.

7. Every nature is content with itself when it speeds well on its way; and a rational nature speeds well on its way, when in its impressions it gives assent to nothing that is false or obscure, and directs its impulses toward none but social acts, and limits its inclinations and its aversions only to things that are in its power, and welcomes all that the Universal Nature allots it. For it is a part of that, as the nature of the leaf is of the plant-nature; with the difference however, that in the case of the plant the nature of the leaf is part of a nature void both of sentience and reason, and liable to be thwarted, while a man's nature is part of a nature unthwartable and intelligent and just, if indeed it divides up equally and in due measure to every one his quotas of time, substance, cause, activity,

circumstance. And consider, not whether you will find one thing in every case equal to one thing, but whether, collectively, the whole of this equal to the aggregate of that.

8. You cannot be a student. But you can refrain from insolence; but you can rise superior to pleasures and pains; but you can tread under your feet the love of glory; but you can forbear to be angry with the unfeeling and the thankless, aye and even care for them.

9. Let no one hear you any more grumbling at life in a Court, nay let not your own ears hear you.

10. Repentance is a sort of self-reproach at some useful thing passed by; but the good must needs be a useful thing, and ever to be cultivated by the true good man; but the true good man would never regret having passed a pleasure by. Pleasure therefore is neither a useful thing nor a good.

11. What of itself is the thing in question as individually constituted? What is the substance and material of it? What the causal part? What doeth it in the Universe? How long doth it subsist?

12. When you are loath to get up, call to mind that the due discharge of social duties is in accordance with your constitution and in accordance with man's nature, while even irrational animals share with us the faculty of sleep; but what is in accordance with the nature of the individual is more congenial, more closely akin to him, aye and more attractive.

13. Persistently and, if possible, in every case test your impressions by the rules of physics, ethics, logic.

14. Whatever man you meetest, put to yourself at once this question: What are this man's convictions about good and evil? For if they are such and such about pleasure and pain and what is productive of them, about good report and ill report, about death and life, it will be in no way strange or surprising to me if he does such and such things. So I will remember that he is constrained to act as he does.

15. Remember that, as it is monstrous to be surprised at a fig-tree bearing figs, so also is it to be surprised at the Universe bearing its own particular crop. Likewise it is monstrous for a physician or a steersman to be surprised that a patient has fever or that a contrary wind has sprung up.

16. Remember that neither a change of mind nor a willingness to be set right by others is inconsistent with true freedom of will. For yours alone is the active effort that effects its purpose in accordance with your impulse and judgment, aye and your intelligence also.

17. If the choice rests with you, why do the thing? If with another, whom do you blame? Atoms or gods? To do either would be crazy folly. No one is to blame. For if you can, set the offender right. Failing that, at least set the thing itself right. If that too be impracticable, what purpose is served by imputing blame? For without a purpose nothing should be done.

18. That which dies is not cast out of the Universe. As it remains here, it also suffers change here and is dissolved into its own constituents, which are the elements of the Universe and your own. Yes, and they too suffer change and murmur not.

19. Every thing, be it a horse, be it a vine, has come into being for some end. Why wonder? Helios himself will say: I exist to do some work; and so of all the other gods. For what then do you exist? For pleasure? Surely it is not to be thought of.

20. Nature has included in its aim in every case the ceasing to be no less than the beginning and the duration, just as the man who tosses up his ball. But what good does the ball gain while tossed upward, or harm as it comes down, or finally when it reaches the ground? Or what good accrues to the bubble while it coheres, or harm in its bursting? And the same holds good with the lamp-flame.

21. Turn it inside out and see what it is like, what it comes to be when old, when sickly, when carrion.

They endure but for a short season, both praiser and praised, remem-berer and remembered. All this too in a tiny corner of this continent, and not even there are all in accord, no nor a man with himself; and the whole earth is itself a point.

22. Fix your attention on the subject-matter or the act or the principle or the thing signified.

Rightly served! You would rather become a good man tomorrow than be one today.

23. Am I doing some thing? I do it with reference to the well-being of mankind. Does something befall me? I accept it with a reference to the gods and to the Source of all things from which issue, linked together, the things that come into being.

24. What bathing is when you think of it—oil, sweat, filth, greasy water, everything revolting—such is every part of life and every object we meet with.

25. Lucilla buried Verus, then Lucilla was buried; Secunda Maximus, then Secunda; Epitynchanus Diotimus, then Epitynchanus; Antoninus Faustina, then Antoninus. The same tale always: Celer buried Hadrianus and then Celer was buried. And those acute wits, men renowned for their prescience or their pride, where are they? Such acute wits, for instance, as Charax and Demetrius [the Platonist] and Eudaemon, and others like them. All creatures of a day, dead long ago!—some not remembered even for a while, others transformed into legends, and yet others from legends faded into nothingness! Bear then in mind that either this your composite self must be scattered abroad, or your vital breath be quenched, or be transferred and set elsewhere.

26. It brings gladness to a man to do a man's true work. And a man's true work is to show goodwill to his own kind, to disdain the motions of the senses, to diagnose specious impressions, to take a comprehensive view of the Nature of the Universe and all that is done at her bidding.

27. You have three relationships—the first to the vessel you are contained in; the second to the divine Cause wherefrom issue all things to all; and the third to those that dwell with you.

28. Pain is an evil either to the body—let the body then denounce it—or to the Soul; but the Soul can ensure her own fair weather and her own calm sea, and refuse to account it an evil. For every conviction and impulse and desire and aversion is from within, and nothing climbs in thither.

The Soul can ensure her own fair weather and her own calm sea

29. Efface your impressions, saying ever to yourself: Now lies it with me that this soul should harbor no wickedness nor lust nor any disturbing element at all; but that, seeing the true nature of all things, I should deal with each as is its due. Remember this power that Nature gives you.

30. Say your say in the Senate or to any person whatsoever becomingly and naturally. Use sound speech.

31. The court of Augustus—wife, daughter, descendants, ancestors, sister, Agrippa, kinsfolk, household, friends, Areius, Maecenas, physicians, diviners—dead, the whole court of them! Pass on then to other records and the death not of individuals but of a clan, as of the Pompeii. And that well-known epitaph, Last of his race—think over it and the anxiety shown by the man's ancestors that they might leave a successor. But after all someone must be the last of the line—here again the death of a whole race!

32. Act by act you must build up your life, and be content, if each act as far as may be fulfils its end. And there is never a man that can prevent it doing this. But there will be some impediment from without. There can be none to your behaving justly, soberly, wisely. But what if some other exercise of activity be hindered? Well, a cheerful acceptance of the hindrance and a tactful transition to what is allowed will enable another action to be substituted that will be in keeping with the built-up life of which we are speaking.

33. Accept without arrogance, surrender without reluctance.

34. You have seen a hand cut off or a foot, or a head severed from the trunk, and lying at some distance from the rest of the body. Just so does the man treat himself, as far as he may, who wills not what befalls and severs himself from mankind or acts unsocially. Say you have been torn away in some sort from the unity of Nature; for by the law of your birth you were a part; but now you have cut yourself off. Yet here comes in that exquisite provision, that you can return again to your unity. To no other part has God granted this, to come together again, when once separated and cleft asunder. Aye, behold His goodness, wherewith He has glorified man! For He has let it rest with a man that he be never rent away from the Whole,

and if he do rend himself away, to return again and grow on to the rest and take up his position again as part.

35. Just as the Nature of rational things has given each rational being almost all his other powers, so also have we received this one from it; that, as this Nature molds to its purpose whatever interference or opposition it meets, and gives it a place in the destined order of things, and makes it a part of itself, so also can the rational creature convert every hindrance into material for itself and utilize it for its own purposes.

36. Let not the mental picture of life as a whole confound you. Fill not your thoughts with what and how many ills may conceivably await you, but in every present case ask yourself: What is there in this experience so crushing, so insupportable? You will blush to confess. Remind yourself further that it is not the future nor the past but the present always that brings you its burden. But this is reduced to insignificance if you isolate it, and take your mind to task if it cannot hold out against this mere trifle.

37. Does Pantheia now watch by the urn of her lord, or Pergamus? What, does Chabrias or Diotimus by Hadrian's? Absurd! What then? Had they sat there till now, would the dead have been aware of it? and, if aware of it, would they have been pleased? and, if pleased, would that have made the mourners immortal? Was it not destined that these like others should become old women and old men and then die? What then, when they were dead, would be left for those whom they had mourned to do? It is all stench and foul corruption "in a sack of skin,"

38. Have you keenness of sight? Use it with judgment ever so wisely, as the saying goes.

39. In the constitution of the rational creature I see no virtue incompatible with justice, but incompatible with pleasure I see—continence.

40. Take away your opinion as to any imagined pain, and you yourself are set in surest safety. What is "yourself"? Reason. But I am not reason. Be it so. At all events let the Reason not cause itself pain, but if any part in you is amiss, let it form its own opinion about itself.

41. To the animal nature a thwarting of sense-perception is an evil, as is also to the same nature the thwarting of impulse. There is similarly

some other thing that can thwart the constitution of plants and is an evil to them. Thus then the thwarting of intelligence is an evil to the intelligent nature. Transfer the application of all this to yourself. Does pain, does pleasure take hold of you? The senses shall look to it. Were you impelled to a thing and were thwarted? If your impulse counts on an unconditional fulfilment, failure at once becomes an evil to you as a rational creature. But accept the universal limitation, and you have so far received no hurt nor even been thwarted. Indeed no one else is in a way to thwart the inner purposes of the mind. For it no fire can touch, nor steel, nor tyrant, nor obloquy, nor any thing soever: a sphere once formed continues round and true.

42. It were not right that I should pain myself for not even another have I ever knowingly pained.

43. One thing delights one, another thing another. To me it is a delight if I keep my ruling Reason sound, not looking askance at man or anything that befalls man, but regarding all things with kindly eyes, accepting and using everything for its intrinsic worth.

44. See you dower yourself with this present time. Those that yearn rather for after-fame do not realize that their successors are sure to be very much the same as the contemporaries whom they find such a burden, and no less mortal. What is it anyway to you if there be this or that far-off echo of their voices, or if they have this or that opinion about you?

45. Take me up and cast me where you will. For even there will I keep my "genius" gracious, that is, content if in itself and in its activity it follow the laws of its own constitution.

Is this worthwhile, that on its account my soul should be ill at ease and fall below itself, groveling, grasping, floundering, affrighted? What could make it worthwhile?

46. Nothing can befall a man that is not a contingency natural to man; nor befall an ox, that is not natural to oxen, nor a vine, that is not natural to a vine, nor to a stone that is not proper to it. If therefore only what is natural and customary befalls each, why be aggrieved? For the common Nature brings you nothing that you cannot bear.

47. When you are vexed at some external cross, it is not the thing itself that troubles you, but your judgment on it. And this you can annul in a moment. But if you are vexed at something in your own character, who can prevent you from rectifying the principle that is to blame? So also if you are vexed at not undertaking that which seems to you a sound act, why not rather undertake it than be vexed? But there is a lion in the path! Be not vexed then, for the blame of inaction rests not with you. But life is not worth living, this left undone. Depart then from life, dying with the same kindly feelings as he who effects his purpose, and accepting with a good grace the obstacles that thwart you.

48. Never forget that the ruling Reason shows itself unconquerable when, concentrated in itself, it is content with itself, so it do nothing that it does not will, even if it refuse from mere opposition and not from reason—much, more, then, if it judge of a thing on reasonable grounds and advisedly. Therefore the Mind, unmastered by passions, is a very citadel, for a man has no fortress more impregnable wherein to find refuge and be untaken for ever. He indeed who has not seen this is ignorant, but he that has seen it and takes not refuge therein is luckless.

49. Say no more to yourself than what the initial impressions report. This has been told you, that so and so speaks ill of you. This has been told you, but it has not been told you that you are harmed. I see that my child is ailing. I see it, but I do not see that he is in danger. Keep then ever to first impressions and supplement them not on your part from within, and nothing happens to you. And yet do supplement them with this, that you are familiar with every possible contingency in the world.

50. The cucumber is bitter. Toss it away. There are briars in the path. Turn aside. That suffices, and you need not to add Why are such things found in the world? For you would be a laughing stock to any student of nature; just as you would be laughed at by a carpenter and a cobbler if you took them to task because in their shops are seen sawdust and parings from what they are making. And yet they have space for the disposal of their fragments; while the Universal Nature has nothing outside herself; but the marvel of her craftsmanship is that, though she is

limited to herself, she transmutes into her own substance all that within her seems to be perishing and decrepit and useless, and again from these very things produces other new ones; whereby she shows that she neither wants any substance outside herself nor needs a corner where she may cast her decaying matter. Her own space, her own material, her own proper craftsmanship is all that she requires.

51. Be not dilatory in doing, nor confused in conversation, nor vague in thought; let not your soul be wholly concentrated in itself nor uncontrollably agitated; leave yourself leisure in your life.

They kill us, they cut us limb from limb, they hunt us with execrations! How does that prevent your mind being still pure, sane, sober, just? Imagine a man to stand by a crystal-clear spring of sweet water, and to rail at it; yet it fails not to bubble up with wholesome water. Throw in mud or even filth and it will quickly winnow them away and purge itself of them and take never a stain. How then possess yourself of a living fountain and no mere well? By guiding yourself carefully every hour into freedom with kindliness, simplicity, and modesty.

Leave yourself leisure in your life

52. He that knows not what the Universe is knows not where he is. He that knows not the end of its being knows not who he is or what the Universe is. But he that is wanting in the knowledge of any of these things could not tell what is the end of his own being. What then must we think of those that court or eschew the verdict of the clappers, who have no conception where or who they are?

53. Care you to be praised by a man who execrates himself thrice within the hour? Care you to win the approval of a man who wins not his own? Can he be said to win his own approval who regrets almost every thing he does?

54. Be no longer content merely to breathe in unison with the all-embracing air, but from this moment think also in unison with the all-embracing Intelligence. For that intelligent faculty is everywhere

diffused and offers itself on every side to him that can take it in no less than the aerial to him that can breathe.

55. Taken generically, wickedness does no harm to the Universe, and the particular wickedness does no harm to others. It is harmful to the one individual alone, and he has been given the option of being quit of it the first moment he pleases.

56. To my power of choice the power of choice of my neighbor is as much a matter of indifference as is his vital breath and his flesh. For however much we may have been made for one another, yet our ruling Reason is in each case master in its own house. Else might my neighbor's wickedness become my bane; and this was not God's will, that another might not have my unhappiness in his keeping.

57. The sun's light is diffused down, as it seems, yes, and in every direction, yet it does not diffuse itself away. For this diffusion is an extension. At any rate the beams of the Sun are called Extensions, because they have an extension in space. And what a ray is you may easily see, if you observe the sun's light entering through a narrow chink into a darkened room, for it extends straight on, and is as it were brought up against any solid body it encounters that cuts off the air beyond. There the ray comes to a standstill, neither slipping off nor sinking down. Such then should be the diffusion and circumfusion of the mind, never a diffusing away but extension, and it should never make a violent or uncontrollable impact against any obstacle it meets with, no, nor collapse, but stand firm and illuminate what receives it. For that which conducts it not on its way will deprive itself willfully of its beams.

58. Dread of death is a dread of non-sensation or new sensation. But either you will feel no sensation, and so no sensation of any evil; or a different kind of sensation will be yours, and so the life of a different creature, but still a life.

Mankind have been created for the sake of one another

59. Mankind have been created for the sake of one another. Either instruct therefore or endure.

60. One is the way of an arrow, another of the mind. Howbeit the mind, both when it cautiously examines its ground and when it is engaged in its enquiry, is none the less moving straight forward and toward its goal.

61. Enter into every man's ruling Reason, and give every one else an opportunity to enter into yours.

BOOK IX

———

1 INJUSTICE IS IMPIETY. FOR IN THAT THE NATURE OF THE UNIVERSE has fashioned rational creatures for the sake of one another with a view to mutual benefit based upon worth, but by no means for harm, the transgressor of her will acts with obvious impiety against the most venerable of Deities.

And the liar too acts impiously with respect to the same Goddess. For the Nature of the Universe is the Nature of the things that are. And the things that are have an intimate connection with all the things that have ever been. Moreover this Nature is named Truth, and is the primary cause of all that is true. The willing liar then is impious in so far as his deceit is a wrong-doing; and the unwilling liar too, for he is out of tune with the Nature of the Whole, and an element of disorder by being in conflict with the Nature of an orderly Universe; for he is in conflict who allows himself, as far as his conduct goes, to be carried into opposition to what is true. And whereas he had previously been endowed by nature with the means of distinguishing false from true, by neglecting to use them he has lost the power.

Again he acts impiously who seeks after pleasure as a good thing and eschews pain as an evil. For such a man must inevitably find frequent fault with the Universal Nature as unfair in its apportionments to the worthless and the worthy, since the worthless are often lapped in pleasures and possess the things that make for pleasure, while the worthy meet with pain

87

and the things that make for pain. Moreover he that dreads pain will some day be in dread of something that must be in the world. And there we have impiety at once. And he that hunts after pleasures will not hold his hand from injustice. And this is palpable impiety.

But those, who are of one mind with Nature and would walk in her ways, must hold a neutral attitude toward those things toward which the Universal Nature is neutral—for she would not be the Maker of both were she not neutral toward both. So he clearly acts with impiety who is not himself neutral toward pain and pleasure, death and life, good report and ill report, things which the Nature of the Universe treats with neutrality. And by the Universal Nature treating these with neutrality I mean that all things happen neutrally in a chain of sequence to things that come into being and to their after products by some primeval impulse of Providence, in accordance with which She was impelled by some primal impulse to this making of an ordered Universe, when She had conceived certain principles for all that was to be, and allocated the powers generative of substances and changes and successions such as we see.

2. It were more graceful doubtless for a man to depart from mankind untainted with falsehood and all dissimulation and luxury and arrogance; failing that, however, the "next best course" is to breathe out his life when his gorge has risen at these things. Or is it your choice to throw in your lot with vice, and does not even your taste of it yet persuade you to fly from the pestilence? For the corruption of the mind is a pest far worse than any such miasma and vitiation of the air which we breathe around us. The latter is a pestilence for living creatures and affects their life, the former for human beings and affects their humanity.

3. Despise not death, but welcome it, for Nature wills it like all else. For dissolution is but one of the processes of Nature, associated with your life's various seasons, such as to be young, to be old, to wax to our prime and to reach it, to grow teeth and beard and gray hairs, to beget, conceive and bring forth. A man then that has reasoned the matter out should not take up toward death the attitude of indifference, eagerness, or scorn, but await it as one of the processes of Nature. Look for the hour when your soul

shall emerge from this its sheath, as now you await the moment when the child she carries shall come forth from your wife's womb.

But if you desire a commonplace solace too that will appeal to the heart, nothing will enable you to meet death with equanimity better than to observe the environment you are leaving and the sort of characters with whom your soul shall no longer be mixed up. For while it is very far from right to fall foul of them, but rather even to care for and deal gently with them, yet it is well to remember that not from men of like principles with your will your release be. For this alone, if anything, could draw us back and bind us to life, if it were but permitted us to live with those who have possessed themselves of the same principles as ours. But now you see how you are driven by sheer weariness at the jarring discord of your life with them to say: Tarry not, O Death, lest per adventure I too forget myself.

4. He that does wrong, does wrong to himself. The unjust man is unjust to himself, for he makes himself bad.

5. There is often an injustice of omission as well as of commission.

6. The present assumption rightly apprehended, the present act socially enacted, the present disposition satisfied with all that befalls it from the Cause external to it—these will suffice.

> There is often an injustice of omission as well as of commission

7. Efface imagination. Restrain impulse. Quench desire. Keep the ruling Reason in your own power.

8. Among irrational creatures one life is distributed, and among the rational one intellectual soul has been parceled out. Just as also there is one earth for all the things that are of the earth; and one is the light whereby we see, and one the air we all breathe that have sight and life.

9. All that share in a common element have an affinity for their own kind. The trend of all that is earthy is to earth; fluids all run together; it is the same with the aerial; so that only interposing obstacles and force

can keep them apart. Fire indeed has a tendency to rise by reason of the elemental fire, but is so quick to be kindled in sympathy with all fire here below that every sort of matter, a whit drier than usual, is easily kindled owing to its having fewer constituents calculated to offer resistance to its kindling. So then all that shares in the Universal Intelligent Nature has as strong an affinity toward what is akin, aye even a stronger. For the measure of its superiority to all other things is the measure of its readiness to blend and coalesce with that which is akin to it.

At any rate to begin with among irrational creatures we find swarms and herds and bird colonies and, as it were, love associations. For already at that stage there are souls, and the bond of affinity shows itself in the higher form to a degree of intensity not found in plants or stones or timber. But among rational creatures are found political communities and friendships and households and gatherings, and in wars treaties and armistices. But in things still higher a sort of unity in separation even exists, as in the stars. Thus the ascent to the higher form is able to effect a sympathetic connection even among things which are separate.

See then what actually happens at the present time; for at the present time it is only the intelligent creatures that have forgotten their mutual affinity and attraction, and here alone there is no sign of like flowing to like. Yet flee as they will, they are nevertheless caught in the toils, for Nature will have her way. Watch closely and you will see 'tis so. Easier at any rate were it to find an earthly thing in touch with nothing earthly than a man wholly severed from mankind.

10. They all bear fruit—Man and God and the Universe: each in its due season bears. It matters nought that in customary parlance such a term is strictly applicable only to the vine and such things. Reason too has its fruit both for all and for itself, and there issue from it other things such as is Reason itself.

11. If you are able, convert the wrong-doer. If not, bear in mind that kindliness was given you to meet just such a case. The gods too are kindly to such persons and even co-operate with them for certain ends—for

health, to wit, and wealth and fame, so benignant are they. You too can be the same; or say who is there that prevents you.

12. Do your work not as a drudge, nor as desirous of pity or praise. Desire one thing only, to act or not to act as civic reason directs.

13. This day have I got me out of all trouble, or rather have cast out all trouble, for it was not from without, but within, in my own imagination.

14. All these are things of familiar experience; in their duration ephemeral, in their material sordid. Everything is now as it was in the days of those whom we have buried.

15. Objective things stand outside the door, keeping themselves to themselves, without knowledge of or message about themselves. What then has for us a message about them? The ruling Reason.

16. Not in being acted upon but in activity lies the evil and the good of the rational and civic creature, just as his virtue too and his vice lie in activity and not in being acted upon.

17. The stone that is thrown into the air is none the worse for falling down, or the better for being carried upward.

18. Find the way within into their ruling Reason, and you will see what these judges are whom you fear and what their judgment of themselves is worth.

19. Change is the universal experience. You are yourself undergoing a perpetual transformation and, in some sort, decay: aye and the whole Universe as well.

20. Another's wrong-doing should be left with him.

21. A cessation of activity, a quiescence from impulse and opinion and, as it were, their death, is no evil. Turn now to consider the stages of your life—childhood, boyhood, manhood, old age—each step in the ladder of change a death. Is there anything terrible here? Pass on now to your life under your grandfather, then under your mother, then under your father, and finding there many other alterations, changes, and cessations, ask yourself: Is there anything terrible here? No, nor any in the ending and quiescence and change of the whole of life.

22. Speed to the ruling Reason of yourself, and of the Universe, and of your neighbor: of your own, that you may make it just; of that of the Universe, that you may therewithal remember of what you are a part; of your neighbor, that you may learn whether it was ignorance with him or understanding, and reflect at the same time that it is akin to you.

23. As you yourself are a part perfective of a civic organism, let also your every act be a part perfective of civic life. Every act of yours then that has no relation direct or indirect to this social end, tears your life asunder and destroys its unity, and creates a schism, just as in a commonwealth does the man who, as far as in him lies, stands aloof from such a concord of his fellows.

24. Children's squabbles and make-believe, and little souls bearing up corpses—the Invocation of the Dead might strike one as a more vivid reality!

25. Go straight to that which makes a thing what it is, its formative cause, and, isolating it from the material, regard it so. Then mark off the utmost time for which the individual object so qualified is calculated to subsist.

26. By not being content with your ruling Reason doing the work for which it was constituted, you have borne unnumbered ills. Nay, 'tis enough!

27. When men blame or hate you or give utterance to some such feelings against you, turn to their souls, enter into them, and see what sort of men they are. You will perceive that you need not be concerned as to what they think of you. Yet must you feel kindly toward them, for Nature made them dear to you. The gods too lend them aid in diverse ways by dreams and oracles, to win those very things on which their hearts are set.

28. The same, upward, downward, from cycle to cycle are the revolutions of the Universe. And either the Universal Mind feels an impulse to act in each separate case—and if this be so, accept its impulsion—or it felt this impulse once for all, and all subsequent things follow by way of consequence; and what matters which it be, for if you like to put it so the

world is all atoms [or indivisible]. But as to the Whole, if God—all is well; if haphazard—be not you also haphazard.

Presently the earth will cover us all. It too will soon be changed, and the resulting product will go on from change to change, and so forever and ever. When a man thinks of these successive waves of change and transformation, and their rapidity, he will hold every mortal thing in scorn.

29. The World-Cause is as a torrent, it sweeps everything along. How negligible these manikins that busy themselves with civic matters and flatter themselves that they act therein as philosophers! Drivellers all! What then, O Man? Do what Nature asks of you now. Make the effort if it be given you to do so and look not about to see if any shall know it. Dream not of Utopias, but be content if the least thing go forward, and count the outcome of the matter in hand as a small thing. For who can alter another's conviction? Failing a change of conviction, we merely get men pretending to be persuaded and chafing like slaves under coercion. Go to now and tell me of Alexander and Philip and Demetrius of Phalerum. Whether they realized the will of Nature and schooled themselves thereto, is their concern. But if they played the tragedy-hero, no one has condemned me to copy them. Simple and modest is the work of Philosophy: lead me not astray into pomposity and pride.

30. Take a bird's-eye view of the world, its endless gatherings and endless ceremonials, voyaging manifold in storm and calm, and the vicissitudes of things coming into being, participating in being, ceasing to be. Reflect too on the life lived long ago by other men, and the life that shall be lived after you, and is now being lived in barbarous countries; and how many have never even heard your name, and how many will very soon forget it, and how many who now perhaps acclaim, will very soon blame you, and that neither memory nor fame nor anything else whatever is worth reckoning.

31. Freedom from perturbance in all that befalls from the external Cause, and justice in all that your own inner Cause prompts you to do; that is, impulse and action finding fulfilment in the actual performance of social duty as being in accordance with your nature.

32. It is in your power to rid yourself of many unnecessary troubles, for they exist wholly in your imagination. You will at once set your feet in a large room by embracing the whole Universe in your mind and including in your purview time everlasting, and by observing the rapid change in every part of everything, and the shortness of the span between birth and dissolution, and that the yawning immensity before birth is only matched by the infinity after our dissolution.

33. All that your eyes behold will soon perish and they, who live to see it perish, will in their turn perish no less quickly; and he who outlives all his contemporaries and he who dies before his time will be as one in the grave.

34. What is the ruling Reason of these men, and about what sort of objects have they been in earnest, and from what motives do they lavish their love and their honor! View with the mind's eye their poor little souls in their nakedness. What immense conceit this of theirs, when they fancy that there is bane in their blame or profit in their praises!

35. Loss and change, they are but one. Therein does the Universal Nature take pleasure, through whom are all things done now as they have been in like fashion from time everlasting; and to eternity shall other like things be. Why then do you say that all things have been evil and will remain evil to the end, and that no help has after all been found in gods so many as they be, to right these things, but that the fiat has gone forth that the Universe should be bound in an unbroken chain of ill?

Loss and change, they are but one

36. Seeds of decay in the underlying material of everything—water, dust, bones, reek! Again, marble but nodules of earth, and gold and silver but dross, garments merely hair-tufts, and purple only blood. And so with everything else. The soul too another like thing and liable to change from this to that.

37. Have done with this miserable way of life, this grumbling, this apism! Why fret? What is the novelty here? What amazes you? The Cause? Look fairly at it. What then, the Material? Look fairly at that. Apart from

these two, there is nothing. But in regard to the gods also now even at the eleventh hour show yourself more simple, more worthy.

Whether your experience of these things lasts three hundred years or three, it is all one.

38. If he did wrong, with him lies the evil. But maybe he did no wrong.

39. Either there is one intelligent source, from which as in one body all after things proceed—and the part ought not to grumble at what is done in the interests of the whole—or there are atoms, and nothing but a medley and a dispersion. Why then be harassed? Say to your ruling Reason: You are dead! You are corrupt! You have become a wild beast! You are a hypocrite! You are one of the herd! You play with them!

40. Either the gods have no power or they have power. If they have no power, why pray to them? But if they have power, why not rather pray that they should give you freedom from fear of any of these things and from lust for any of these things and from grief at any of these things [rather] than that they should grant this or refuse that. For obviously if they can assist men at all, they can assist them in this. But perhaps you will say: the gods have put this in my power. Then is it not better to use what is in your power like a free man than to concern yourself with what is not in your power like a slave and an abject? And who told you that the gods do not cooperate with us even in the things that are in our power? Begin at any rate with prayers for such things and you will see. One prays: How may I lie with that woman! You: How may I not lust to lie with her! Another: How may I be quit of that man! You: How may I not wish to be quit of him! Another: How may I not lose my little child! You: How may I not dread to lose him! In a word, give your prayers this turn, and see what comes of it.

41. Listen to Epicurus where he says: In my illness my talk was not of any bodily feelings, nor did I chatter about such things to those who came to see me, but I went on with my cardinal disquisitions on natural philosophy, dwelling especially on this point, how the mind, having perforce its share in such affections of the flesh, yet remains unperturbed, safeguarding its own proper good. Nor did I—he goes on—let the physicians ride the high horse as if they were doing grand things, but my life went on well

and happily. Imitate him then in sickness, if you are sick, and in any other emergency; for it is a commonplace of every sect not to renounce Philosophy whatever difficulties we encounter, nor to consent to babble as he does that is unenlightened in philosophy and nature; . . . devote yourself to your present work alone and your instrument for performing it.

42. When you are offended by shamelessness in any one, put this question at once to yourself: Can it be then that shameless men should not exist in the world? It cannot be. Then ask not for what cannot be. For this man in question also is one of the shameless ones that must needs exist in the world. Have the same reflection ready for the rogue, the deceiver, or any other wrongdoer whatever. For the remembrance that this class of men cannot but exist will bring with it kindlier feelings toward individuals of the class. Right useful too is it to think at once of this: What virtue has Nature given man as a foil to the wrong-doing in question? For as an antidote against the unfeeling man she has given gentleness, and against another man some other resource.

In any case it is in your power to teach the man that has gone astray the error of his ways. For every one that doth amiss misses his true mark and has gone astray. But what harm have you suffered? You will find that not one of the persons against whom you are exasperated has done anything capable of making your mind worse; but it is in your mind that the evil for you and the harmful have their whole existence.

Where is the harm or the strangeness in the boor acting—like a boor? See whether you are not yourself the more to blame in not expecting that he would act thus wrongly. For your reason too could have given you means for concluding that this would most likely be the case. Nevertheless all this is forgotten, and you are surprised at his wrongdoing.

But above all, when you find fault with a man for faithlessness and ingratitude, turn your thoughts to yourself. For evidently the fault is your own, whether you had faith that a man with such a character would keep faith with you, or if in bestowing a kindness you did not bestow it absolutely and as from the very doing of it having at once received the full complete fruit.

For when you have done a kindness, what more would you have? Is not this enough that you have done something in accordance with your nature? Seek you a recompense for it? As though the eye should claim a reward for seeing, or the feet for walking! For just as these latter were made for their special work, and by carrying this out according to their individual constitution they come fully into their own, so also man, formed as he is by nature for benefiting others, when he has acted as benefactor or as co-factor in any other way for the general benefit, has done what he was constituted for, and has what is his.

BOOK X

——

1 WILL YOU THEN, O MY SOUL, EVER AT LAST BE GOOD AND SIMPLE and single and naked, showing yourself more visible than the body that overlies you? Will you ever taste the sweets of a loving and a tender heart? Ever be fulfilled and self-sufficing, longing for nothing, lusting after nothing animate or inanimate, for the enjoyment of pleasures—not time wherein the longer to enjoy them, nor place or country or congenial climes or men nearer to your liking—but contented with your present state and delighted with your present everything, convincing yourself withal that all that is present for you is present from the gods, and that everything is and shall be well with you that is pleasing to them and that they shall hereafter grant for the conservation of that Perfect Being that is good and just and beautiful, the Begetter and Upholder of all things, that embraces and gathers them in, when they are dissolved, to generate therefrom other like things? Will you ever at last fit yourself so to be a fellow citizen with the gods and with men as never to find fault with them or incur their condemnation?

2. Observe what your nature asks of you, as one controlled by Nature alone, then do this and with a good grace, if your nature as a living creature is not to be made worse thereby. Next must you observe what your nature as a living creature asks of you. And this must you wholly accept, if your nature as a rational living creature be not made worse thereby. Now the rational is indisputably also the civic. Comply with these rules then and be not needlessly busy about anything.

3. All that befalls either so befalls as you are fitted by nature to bear it or as you are not fitted. If the former, take it not amiss, but bear it as you are fitted to do. If the latter, take not that amiss either, for when it has destroyed you, it will itself perish. Howbeit be assured that you are fitted by nature to bear everything which it rests with your own opinion about it to render bearable and tolerable, according as you think it your interest or your duty to do so.

4. If a man makes a slip, enlighten him with loving kindness, and show him wherein he has seen amiss. Failing that, blame yourself or not even yourself.

5. Whatever befalls you was set in train for you from everlasting, and the chain of causes was from eternity weaving into one fabric your existence and the coincidence of this event.

6. Whether there be atoms or a Nature, let it be postulated first, that I am a part of the whole Universe controlled by Nature; secondly, that I stand in some intimate connection with other kindred parts. For bearing this in mind, as I am a part, I shall not be displeased with anything allotted me from the Whole. For what is advantageous to the whole can in no wise be injurious to the part For the Whole contains nothing that is not advantageous to itself; and all natures have this in common, but the Universal Nature is endowed with the additional attribute of never being forced by any external cause to engender anything hurtful to itself.

As long then as I remember that I am a part of such a whole, I shall be well pleased with all that happens; and in so far as I am in intimate connection with the parts that are akin to myself, I shall be guilty of no unsocial act, but I shall devote my attention rather to the parts that are akin to myself, and direct every impulse of mine to the common interest and withhold it from the reverse of this. That being done, life must flow smoothly, as you may see the life flow smoothly of a citizen who goes steadily on in a course of action beneficial to his fellow-citizens and cheerfully accepts whatever is assigned him by the State.

7. The parts of the Whole—all that Nature has comprised in the Universe—must inevitably perish, taking "perish" to mean "be changed."

But if this process is by nature for them both evil and inevitable, the Whole could never do its work satisfactorily, its parts ever going as they do from change to change and being constituted to perish in diverse ways. Did Nature herself set her hand to bringing evil upon parts of herself and rendering them not only liable to fall into evil but of necessity fallen into it, or was she not aware that such was the case? Both alternatives are incredible.

But supposing that we even put Nature as an agent out of the question and explain that these things are "naturally" so, even then it would be absurd to assert that the parts of the whole are naturally subject to change, and at the same time to be astonished at a thing or take it amiss as though it befell contrary to nature, and that though things dissolve into the very constituents out of which they are composed. For either there is a scattering of the elements out of which I have been built up, or a transmutation of the solid into the earthly and of the spiritual into the aerial; so that these too are taken back into the Reason of the Universe, whether cycle by cycle it be consumed with fire or renew itself by everlasting permutations.

Aye and so then do not be under the impression that the solid and the spiritual date from the moment of birth. For it was but yesterday or the day before that all this took in its increment from the food eaten and the air breathed. It is then this, that it took in, which changes, not the product of your mother's womb. But granted that you are ever so closely bound up with that by your individuality, this, I take it, has no bearing upon the present argument.

8. Assuming for yourself the appellations, a good man, a modest man, a truthteller, wise of heart, sympathetic of heart, great of heart, take heed you be not new-named. And if you should forfeit these titles, make haste to get back to them. And bear in mind that wise of heart was meant to signify for you a discerning consideration of every object and a thoroughness of thought; sympathetic of heart, a willing acceptance of all that the Universal Nature allots you; great of heart an uplifting of our mental part above the motions smooth or rough of the flesh, above the love of empty fame, the fear of death, and all other like things. Only keep yourself entitled to these appellations, not itching to receive them from others, and you will be

a new man and enter on a new life. For to be still such as you have been till now, and to submit to the rendings and defilements of such a life, is worthy of a man that shows beyond measure a dull senselessness and a clinging to life, and is on a level with the wild-beast fighters that are half-devoured in the arena, who, though a mass of wounds and gore, beg to be kept till the next day, only to be thrown again, torn as they are, to the same teeth and talons.

Take ship then on these few attributions, and if you can abide therein, so abide as one who has migrated to some Isles of the Blest. But if you feel yourself adrift, and cannot win your way, betake yourself with a good heart to some nook where you will prevail, or even depart altogether from life, not in wrath but in simplicity, independence, and modesty, having at least done this one thing well in life, that you have quitted it thus. Howbeit, to keep these attributions in mind it will assist you greatly if you bear the gods in mind, and that it is not flattery they crave but for all rational things to be conformed to their likeness, and that man should do a man's work, as the fig tree does the work of a fig tree, the dog of a dog, and the bee of a bee.

9. Plays, warfare, cowardice, torpor, servility—these will day by day obliterate all those holy principles of yours which, as the student of Nature, you do conceive and accept. But you must regard and do everything in such a way that at one and the same time the present task may be carried through, and full play given to the faculty of pure thought, and that the self-confidence engendered by a knowledge of each individual thing be kept intact, unobtrusive yet unconcealed.

When will you find your delight in simplicity? When in dignity? When in the knowledge of each separate thing, what it is in its essence, what place it fills in the Universe, how long it is formed by Nature to subsist, what are its component parts, to whom it can pertain, and who can bestow and take it away?

When will you find your delight in simplicity?

10. A spider prides itself on capturing a fly; one man on catching a hare, another on netting a sprat, another on taking wild boars, another bears, another Sarmatians. Are not these brigands, if you test their principles?

11. Make your own a scientific system of enquiry into the mutual change of all things, and pay diligent heed to this branch of study and exercise yourself in it For nothing is so conducive to greatness of mind. Let a man do this and he divests himself of his body and, realizing that he must almost at once relinquish all these things and depart from among men, he gives himself up wholly to just dealing in all his actions, and to the Universal Nature in all that befalls him. What others may say or think about him or do against him he does not even let enter his mind, being well satisfied with these two things—justice in all present acts and contentment with his present lot. And he gives up all engrossing cares and ambitions, and has no other wish than to achieve the straight course through the Law and, by achieving it, to be a follower of God.

12. What need of surmise when it lies with you to decide what should be done, and if you can see your course, to take it with a good grace and not turn aside; but if you cannot see it, to hold back and take counsel of the best counsellors; and if any other obstacles arise therein, to go forward as your present means shall allow with careful deliberation holding to what is clearly just? For to succeed in this is the best thing of all, since in fact to fail in this would be the only failure.

Leisurely without being lethargic and cheerful as well as composed shall he be who follows Reason in everything.

13. Ask yourself as soon as you are roused from sleep: Will it make any difference to me if another does what is just and right? It will make none. Have you forgotten that those who play the wanton in their praise and blame of others, are such as they are in their beds, at their board; and what are the things that they do, the things that they avoid or pursue, and how they pilfer and plunder, not with hands and feet but with the most precious part of them, whereby a man calls into being at will faith, modesty, truth, law, and a good "genius"?

14. Says the well-schooled and humble heart to Nature that gives and takes back all we have; Give what you will, take back what you will. But he says it without any bravado of fortitude, in simple obedience and good will to her.

15. You have but a short time left to live. Live as on a mountain; for whether it be here or there, matters not provided that, wherever a man lives, he lives as a citizen of the World-City. Let men look upon you, cite you, as a man in very deed that lives according to Nature. If they cannot bear with you, let them slay you. For it were better so than to live their life.

16. Put an end once for all to this discussion of what a good man should be, and be one.

Put an end once for all to this discussion of what a good man should be, and be one

17. Continually picture to yourself Time as a whole, and Substance as a whole, and every individual thing, in respect of substance, as but a fig-seed and, in respect to time, as but a twist of the drill.

18. Regarding attentively every existing thing reflect that it is already disintegrating and changing, and as it were in a state of decomposition and dispersion, or that everything is by nature made but to die.

19. What are they like when eating, sleeping, coupling, evacuating, and the rest! What again when lording it over others, when puffed up with pride, when filled with resentment or rebuking others from a loftier plane! Yet but a moment ago they were lackeying how many and for what ends, and anon will be at their old trade.

20. What the Universal Nature brings to everything is for the benefit of that thing, and for its benefit then when she brings it.

21. The earth is in love with showers and the majestic sky is in love. And the Universe is in love with making whatever has to be. To the Universe

then I say: Together with you I will be in lore. Is it not a way we have of speaking, to say, This or that loves to be so?

22. Either your life is here and you are inured to it; or you go elsewhere and this with your own will; or you die and have served out your service. There is no other alternative. Take heart then.

23. Never lose sight of the fact that a man's land is such as I told you, and how all the conditions are the same here as on the top of a mountain or on the seashore or wherever you please. Quite apposite will you find to be the words of Plato: Compassed about (by the city wall as) by a sheep-fold on the mountain, and milking flocks.

24. What is my ruling Reason and what am I making of it now? To what use do I now put it? Is it devoid of intelligence? Is it divorced and severed from neighborliness? Does it so coalesce and blend with the flesh as to be swayed by it?

25. He that flies from his master is a runaway. But the Law is our master, and he that transgresses the Law is a runaway. Now he also, that is moved by grief or wrath or fear, is fain that something should not have happened or be happening or happen in the future of what has been ordained by that which controls the whole Universe, that is by the Law laying down all that falls to a man's lot. He then is a runaway who is moved by fear or grief or wrath.

26. A man passes seed into a womb and goes his way, and anon another cause takes it in hand and works upon it and perfects a babe—what a consummation from what a beginning! Again he passes food down the throat, and anon another cause taking up the work creates sensation and impulse and, in fine, life and strength and other things how many and how mysterious! Muse then on these things that are done in such secrecy, and detect the efficient force, just as we detect the descending and the ascending none the less clearly that it is not with our eyes.

27. Bear in mind continually how all such things as now exist existed also before our day and, be assured, will exist after us. Set before your eyes whole dramas and their staging, one like another, all that your own experience has shown you or you have learned from past history, for instance the

entire court of Hadrianus, the entire court of Antoninus, the entire court of Philip, of Alexander, of Croesus. For all those scenes were such as we see now, only the performers being different.

28. Picture to yourself every one that is grieved at any occurrence whatever or dissatisfied, as being like the pig which struggles and screams when sacrificed; like it too him who, alone upon his bed, bewails in silence the fetters of our fate; and that to the rational creature alone has it been granted to submit willingly to what happens, mere submission being imperative on all.

29. In every act of your pause at each step and ask yourself: Is death to be dreaded for the loss of this?

30. Does another's wrong doing shock you? Turn incontinently to yourself and remember what analogous wrong doing there is of your own, such as deeming money to be a good or pleasure or a little cheap fame and the like. For by marking this you will quickly forget your wrath, with this reflection too to aid you, that a man is under constraint; for what should he do? Or, if you are able, remove the constraint.

31. Let a glance at Satyron call up the image of Socraticus or Eutyches or Hymen, and a glance at Euphrates the image of Eutychion or Silvanus, and a glance at Alciphron Tropaeophorus, and at Severus Xenophon or Crito. Let a glance at yourself bring to mind one of the Caesars, and so by analogy in every case. Then let the thought strike you: Where are they now? Nowhere, or none can say where. For thus will you habitually look upon human things as mere smoke and as naught; and more than ever so, if you remember that what has once changed will exist no more throughout eternity. Why strive then and strain? Why not be content to pass this your short span of life in becoming fashion?

What material, what a field for your work do you forgo! For what are all these things but objects for the exercise of a reason that has surveyed with accuracy and due inquiry into its nature the whole sphere of life? Continue then until you have assimilated these truths also to yourself, as the vigorous digestion assimilates every food, or the blazing fire converts into warmth and radiance whatever is cast into it.

32. Give no one the right to say of you with truth that you are not a sincere, that you are not a good man, but let anyone that shall form any such an idea of you be as one that lies. All this rests with you. For who is there to hinder you from being good and sincere? Resolve then to live no longer if you be not such. For neither doth Reason in that case insist that you should.

33. Taking our "material" into account, what can be said or done in the soundest way? Be it what it may, it rests with you to do or say it. And let us have no pretense that you are being hindered.

Never will you cease murmuring until it be so with you that the utilizing, in a manner consistent with the constitution of man, of the material presented to you and cast in your way shall be to you what indulgence is to the sensual. For everything must be accounted enjoyment that it is in a man's power to put into practice in accordance with his own nature; and it is everywhere in his power.

A cylinder we know has no power given it of individual motion everywhere, nor has fire or water or any other thing controlled by Nature or by an irrational soul. For the interposing and impeding obstacles are many. But Intelligence and Reason make their way through every impediment just as their nature or their will prompts them. Setting before your eyes this ease wherewith the Reason can force its way through every obstacle, as fire upward, as a stone downward, as a cylinder down a slope, look for nothing beyond. For other hindrances either concern that veritable corpse, the body, or, apart from imagination and the surrender of Reason herself, cannot crush us or work any harm at all. Else indeed would their victim at once become bad.

In fact in the case of all other organisms, if any evil happen to any of them, the victim itself becomes the worse for it. But a man so circumstanced becomes, if I may so say, better and more praiseworthy by putting such contingencies to a right use. In fine, remember that nothing that harms not the city can harm him whom Nature has made a citizen; nor yet does that harm a city which harms not law. But not one of the so-called mischances harms law. What does not harm law, then, does no harm to citizen or city.

34. Even an obvious and quite brief aphorism can serve to warn him that is bitten with the true doctrines against giving way to grief and fear; as for instance,

Such are the races of men as the leaves that the wind scatters earthwards.

And your children too are little leaves. Leaves also they who make an outcry as if they ought to be listened to, and scatter their praises or, contrariwise, their curses, or blame and scoff in secret. Leaves too they that are to hand down our after-fame. For all these things

Burgeon again with the season of spring; soon the wind has cast them down, and the forest puts forth others in their stead. Transitoriness is the common lot of all things, yet there is none of these that you hunt not after or shun, as though it were everlasting. A little while and you will close your eyes; aye, and for him that bore you to the grave shall another presently raise the dirge.

35. The sound eye should see all there is to be seen, but should not say: I want what is green only. For that is characteristic of a disordered eye. And the sound hearing and smell should be equipped for all that is to be heard or smelled. And the sound digestion should act toward all nutriment as a mill toward the grist which it was formed to grind. So should the sound mind be ready for all that befalls. But the mind that says: Let my children be safe! Let all applaud my every act! is but as an eye that looks for green things or as teeth that look for soft things.

36. There is no one so fortunate as not to have one or two standing by his death-bed who will welcome the evil which is befalling him. Say he was a worthy man and a wise; will there not be some one at the very end to say in his heart, We can breathe again at last, freed from this schoolmaster, not that he was hard on any of us, but I was all along conscious that he tacitly condemned us? So much for the worthy, but in our own case how many other reasons can be found for which hundreds would be only too glad to be quit of us! Think then upon this when dying, and your passing from life

will be easier if you reason thus: I am leaving a life in which even my intimates for whom I have so greatly toiled, prayed, and thought, aye even they
wish me gone, expecting belike to gain thereby some further ease. Why
then should anyone cling to a longer sojourn here?

Howbeit go away with no less kindliness toward them on this account,
but maintaining your true characteristics be friendly and good natured
and gracious; nor again as though wrenched apart, but rather should your
withdrawal from them be as that gentle slipping away of soul from body
which we see when a man makes a peaceful end. For it was Nature that
knit and kneaded you with them, and now she parts the tie. I am parted as
from kinsfolk, not dragged forcibly away, but going unresistingly. For this
severance too is a process of Nature.

37. In every act of another habituate yourself as far as may be to put to
yourself the question: What end has the man in view? But begin with yourself, cross-examine yourself first.

38. Bear in mind that what pulls the strings is that Hidden Thing
within us: that makes our speech, that our life, that, one may say, makes
the man. Never in your mental picture of it include the vessel that overlies
it nor these organs that are appurtenances thereof. They are like the work-
man's adze, only differing from it in being naturally attached to the body.
Since indeed, severed from the Cause that bids them move and bids them
stay, these parts are as useless as is the shuttle of the weaver, the pen of the
writer, and the whip of the charioteer.

BOOK XI

1 THE PROPERTIES OF THE RATIONAL SOUL ARE THESE; IT SEES ITSELF, dissects itself, molds itself to its own will, itself reaps its own fruits—whereas the fruits of the vegetable kingdom and the corresponding produce of animals are reaped by others,—it wins to its own goal wherever the bounds of life be set. In dancing and acting and such-like arts, if any break occurs, the whole action is rendered imperfect; but the rational soul in every part and wheresoever taken shows the work set before it fulfilled and all-sufficient for itself, so that it can say: I have to the full what is my own.

More than this, it goes about the whole Universe and the void surrounding it and traces its plan, and stretches forth into the infinitude of Time, and comprehends the cyclical Regeneration of all things, and takes stock of it, and discerns that our children will see nothing fresh, just as our fathers too never saw anything more than we. So that in a manner the man of forty years, if he have a grain of sense, in view of this sameness has seen all that has been and shall be. Again a property of the Rational Soul is the love of our neighbor, and truthfulness, and modesty, and to prize nothing above itself,—a characteristic also of Law. In this way then the Reason that is right reason and the Reason that is justice are one.

2. You will think but meanly of charming song and dance and the pancratium, if you analyze the melodious utterance into its several notes and in the case of each ask yourself: Has this the mastery over me? For you will recoil from such a confession. So too with the dance, if you do the like for each movement and posture. The same holds good of the fight. In fine,

109

virtue and its sphere of action excepted, remember to turn to the component parts, and by analyzing them come to despise them. Bring the same practice to bear on the whole of life also.

3. What a soul is that which is ready to be released from the body at any requisite moment, and be quenched or dissipated or hold together! But the readiness must spring from a man's inner judgment, and not be the result of mere opposition [as is the case with the Christians]. It must be associated with deliberation and dignity and, if others too are to be convinced, with nothing like stage-heroics.

4. Have I done some social act? Well, I am amply rewarded. Keep this truth ever ready to turn to, and in no wise slacken your efforts.

5. What is your vocation? To be a good man. But how to be successful in this save by assured conceptions on the one hand of the Universal Nature and on the other of the special constitution of man?

6. Originally tragedies were brought on to remind us of real events, and that such things naturally occur, and that on life's greater stage you must not be vexed at things, which on the stage you find so attractive. For it is seen that these things must be gone through, and they too have to endure them, who cry Ah, Kithaeron! Aye, and the dramatic writers contain some serviceable sayings, for example this more especially:

What is your vocation? To be a good man

Though both my sons and me the gods have spurned, For this too there is reason;

and again:

It nought availeth to be wroth with things;

and this:

Our lives are reaped like the ripe ears of corn;

and how many more like them.

And after Tragedy the old Comedy was put on the stage, exercising an educative freedom of speech, and by its very directness of utterance giving us no unserviceable warning against unbridled arrogance. In somewhat similar vein Diogenes also took up this role. After this, consider for what purpose the Middle Comedy was introduced, and subsequently the New, which little by little degenerated into ingenious mimicry. For that some serviceable things are said even by the writers of these is recognized by all. But what end in view had this whole enterprise of such poetical and dramatic composition?

7. How clearly is it borne in on you that there is no other state of life so fitted to call for the exercise of Philosophy as this in which you now find yourself.

8. A branch cut off from its neighbor branch cannot but be cut off from the whole plant. In the very same way a man severed from one man has fallen away from the fellowship of all men. Now a branch is cut off by others, but a man separates himself from his neighbor by his own agency in hating him or turning his back upon him; and is unaware that he has thereby sundered himself from the whole civic community. But mark the gift of Zeus who established the law of fellowship. For it is in our power to grow again to the neighbor branch, and again become perfective of the whole. But such a schism constantly repeated makes it difficult for the seceding part to unite again and resume its former condition. And in general the branch that from the first has shared in the growth of the tree and lived with its life is not like that which has been cut off and afterwards grafted on to it, as the gardeners are apt to tell you. Be of one bush, but not of one mind.

Be of one bush, but not of one mind

9. As those who withstand your progress along the path of right reason will never be able to turn you aside from sound action, so let them not wrest you from a kindly attitude toward them; but keep a watch over yourself in both directions alike, not only in steadfastness of judgment and action but also in gentleness toward those who endeavor to stand in your path or be in some other way a thorn in your side. For in fact it is a sign of weakness to be wroth with them, no less than to shrink from action and be terrified into surrender. For they that do the one or the other are alike

deserters of their post, the one as a coward, the other as estranged from a natural kinsman and friend.

10. "Nature in no case cometh short of art." For indeed the arts are copiers of various natures. If this be so, the most consummate and comprehensive Nature of all cannot be outdone by the inventive skill of are. And in every art the lower things are done for the sake of the higher; and this must hold good of the Universal Nature also. Aye and thence is the origin of Justice, and in justice all the other virtues have their root, since justice will not be maintained if we either put a value on things indifferent, or are easily duped and prone to slip and prone to change.

11. If therefore the things, the following after and eschewing of which disturb you, come not to you, but you in a manner yourself seek them out, at all events keep your judgment at rest about them and they will remain quiescent, and you will not be seen following after or eschewing them.

In justice all the other virtues have their root

12. The soul is "a sphere truly shaped," when it neither projects itself toward anything outside nor shrinks together inwardly, neither expands nor contracts, but irradiates a light whereby it sees the reality of all things and the reality that is in itself.

13. What if a man think scorn of me? That will be his affair. But it will be mine not to be found doing or saying anything worthy of scorn. What if he hate me? That will be his affair. But I will be kindly and good natured to everyone, and ready to show even my enemy where he has seen amiss, not by way of rebuke nor with a parade of forbearance, but genuinely and chivalrously like the famous Phocion, unless indeed he was speaking ironically. For such should be the inner springs of a man's heart that the gods see him not wrathfully disposed at any thing or counting it a hardship. Why, what evil can happen to you if you yourself now do what is congenial to your nature, and welcome what the Universal Nature now deems well-timed, you who are a man intensely eager that what is for the common interest should by one means or another be brought about?

14. Thinking scorn of one another, they yet fawn on one another, and eager to outdo their rivals they grovel one to another.

15. How corrupt is the man, how counterfeit, who proclaims aloud: I have elected to deal straightforwardly with you! Man, what are you at? There is no need to give this out. The fact will instantly declare itself. It ought to be written on the forehead. There is a ring in the voice that betrays it at once, it flashes out at once from the eyes, just as the loved one can read at a glance every secret in his lover's looks. The simple and good man should in fact be like a man who has a strong smell about him, so that, as soon as ever he comes near, his neighbor is, willy-nilly, aware of it. A calculated simplicity is a stiletto. There is nothing more hateful than the friendship of the wolf for the lamb. Eschew that above all things. The good man, the kindly, the genuine, betrays these characteristics in his eyes and there is no hiding it.

16. Vested in the soul is the power of living ever the noblest of lives, let a man but be indifferent toward things indifferent. And he will be indifferent, if he examine every one of these things both in its component parts and as a whole, and bear in mind that none of them is the cause in us of any opinion about itself, nor obtrudes itself on us. They remain quiescent, and it is we who father these judgments about them and as it were inscribe them on our minds, though it lies with us not to inscribe them and, if they chance to steal in undetected, to erase them at once. Bear in mind too that we shall have but a little while to attend to such things and presently life will be at an end. But why complain of the perversity of things? If they are as Nature wills, delight in them and let them be no hardship to you. If they contravene Nature, seek then what is in accord with your nature and speed toward that, even though it bring no fame. For it is pardonable for every man to seek his own good.

17. Think whence each thing has come, of what it is built up, into what it changes, what it will be when changed, and that it cannot take any harm.

18. Firstly: Consider your relation to mankind and that we came into the world for the sake of one another; and taking another point of view,

that I have come into it to be set over men, as a ram over a flock or a bull over a herd. Stare at the beginning from this premise: If not atoms, then an all-controlling Nature. If the latter, then the lower are for the sake of the higher and the higher for one another.

Secondly: What sort of men they are at board and in bed and elsewhere. Above all how they are the self-made slaves of their principles, and how they pride themselves on the very acts in question.

Thirdly: That if they are acting rightly in this, there is no call for us to be angry. If not rightly, it is obviously against their will and through ignorance. For it is against his will that every soul is deprived, as of truth, so too of the power of dealing with each man as is his due. At any rate, such men resent being called unjust, unfeeling, avaricious, and in a word doers of wrong to their neighbors.

Fourthly: That you too do many a wrong thing yourself and are much as others are, and if you do refrain from certain wrong-doings, yet have you a disposition inclinable thereto even supposing that through cowardice or a regard for your good name or some such base consideration you do not actually commit them.

Fifthly: That you have not even proved that they are doing wrong, for many things are done even "by way of policy." Speaking generally a man must know many things before he can pronounce an adequate opinion on the acts of another.

Sixthly: When you are above measure angry or even out of patience, remember that man's life is momentary, and in a little while we shall all have been laid out.

Seventhly: That in reality it is not the acts men do that vex us—for they belong to the domain of their ruling Reason—but the opinions we form of those acts. Eradicate these, be ready to discard your conclusion that the act in question is a calamity, and your anger is at an end. How then eradicate these opinions? By realizing that no act of another debases us. For unless that alone which debases is an evil, you too must perforce do many a wrong thing and become a brigand or any sort of man.

Eighthly: Think how much more grievous are the consequences of our anger and vexation at such actions than are the acts themselves which arouse that anger and vexation.

Ninthly: That kindness is irresistible, be it but sincere and no mock smile or a mask assumed. For what can the most unconscionable of men do to you, if you persist in being kindly to him, and when a chance is given exhort him mildly and, at the very time when he is trying to do you harm, quietly teach him a better way thus: Nay, my child, we have been made for other things. I shall be in no wise harmed, but you are harming yourself, my child. Show him delicately and without any personal reference that this is so, and that even honeybees do not act thus nor any creatures of gregarious instincts. But you must do this not in irony or by way of rebuke, but with kindly affection and without any bitterness at heart, not as from a master's chair, nor yet to impress the bystanders, but as if he were indeed alone even though others are present.

Remember then of these nine heads, taking them as a gift from the Muses, and begin at last to be a man while life is yours. But beware of flattering men no less than being angry with them. For both these are non-social and conducive of harm. In temptations to anger a precept ready to your hand is this: to be angry is not manly, but a mild and gentle disposition, as it is more human, so it is more masculine. Such a man, and not he who gives way to anger and discontent, is endowed with strength and sinews and manly courage. For the nearer such a mind attains to a passive calm, the nearer is the man to strength. As grief is a weakness, so also is anger. In both it is a case of a wound and a surrender.

But take if you will as a tenth gift from Apollo, the Leader of the Muses, this, that to expect the bad not to do wrong is worthy of a madman; for that is to wish for impossibilities. But to acquiesce in their wronging others, while expecting them to refrain from wronging you, is unfeeling and despotic.

19. Against four perversions of the ruling Reason you should above all keep unceasing watch, and, once detected, wholly abjure them, saying in

each case to yourself: This thought is not necessary; this is destructive of human fellowship; this could be no genuine utterance from the heart.— And not to speak from the heart, what is it but a contradiction in terms?— The fourth case is that of self-reproach, for that is an admission that the divine part of you has been worsted by and acknowledges its inferiority to the body, the baser and mortal partner, and to its gross notions.

20. Your soul and all the fiery part that is blended with you, though by Nature ascensive, yet in submission to the system of the Universe are held fast here in your compound personality. And the entire earthly part too in you and the humid, although naturally descensive, are yet upraised and take up a station not their natural one. Thus indeed we find the elements also in subjection to the Whole and, when set anywhere, remaining there under constraint until the signal sound for their release again therefrom.

Is it not then a paradox that the intelligent part alone of you should be rebellious and quarrel with its station? Yet is no constraint laid upon it but only so much as is in accordance with its nature. Howbeit it does not comply and takes a contrary course. For every motion toward acts of injustice and licentiousness, toward anger and grief and fear, but betokens one who cuts himself adrift from Nature, Aye and when the ruling Reason in a man is vexed at anything that befalls, at that very moment it deserts its station. For it was not made for justice alone, but also for piety and the service of God. And in fact the latter are included under the idea of a true fellowship, and indeed are prior to the practice of justice.

21. He who has not ever in view one and the same goal of life cannot be throughout his life one and the same. Nor does that which is stated suffice, there needs to be added what that goal should be. For just as opinion as to all the things that in one way or another are held by the mass of men to be good is not uniform, but only as to certain things, such, that is, as affect the common benefit, so must we set before ourselves as our goal the common and civic benefit. For he who directs all his individual impulses toward this goal will render his actions homogeneous and thereby be ever consistent with himself.

22. Do not forget the story of the town mouse and the country mouse, and the excitement and trepidation of the latter.

23. Socrates used to nickname the opinions of the multitude Ghouls, bogies to terrify children.

24. The Spartans at their spectacles assigned to strangers seats in the shade, but themselves took their chance of seats anywhere.

25. Socrates refused the invitation of Perdiccas to his court, That I come not, said he, to a dishonored grave, meaning, that I be not treated with generosity and have no power to return it.

26. In the writings of the Ephesians was laid down the advice to have constantly in remembrance some one of the ancients who lived virtuously.

27. Look, said the Pythagoreans, at the sky in the morning, that we may have in remembrance those hosts of heaven that ever follow the same course and accomplish their work in the same way, and their orderly system, and their purity, and their nakedness; for there is no veil before a star.

28. Think of Socrates with the sheepskin wrapped round him, when Xanthippe had gone off with his coat, and what he said to his friends when they drew back in their embarrassment at seeing him thus dressed.

29. In reading and writing you must learn first to follow instruction before you can give it. Much more is this true of life.

30. "Tis not for you, a slave, to reason why.

31. . . . and within me my heart laughed.

32. Virtue they will upbraid and speak harsh words in her hearing.

33. Only a madman will look for figs in winter. No better is he who looks for a child when he may no longer have one.

34. A man while fondly kissing his child, says Epictetus, should whisper in his heart: "Tomorrow perhaps you will die." Ill-omened words these! Nay, said he, nothing is ill-omened that signifies a natural process. Or it is ill-omened also to talk of ears of corn being reaped.

35. The grape unripe, mellow, dried—in every stage we have a change, not into non-existence, but into the not now existent.

36. Hear Epictetus: no one can rob us of our free choice.

37. We must, says he, hit upon the true science of assent and in the sphere of our impulses pay good heed that they be subject to proper reservations; that they have in view our neighbors welfare, that they are proportionate to worth. And we must abstain wholly from inordinate desire and show avoidance in none of the things that are not in our control.

No one can rob us of our free choice

38. It is no casual matter, then, said he, that is at stake, but whether we are to be sane or no.

39. Socrates was wont to say: What would ye have? The souls of reasoning or unreasoning creatures? Of reasoning creatures. Of what kind of reasoning creatures? Sound or vicious? Sound. Why then not make a shift to get them? Because we have them already. Why then fight and wrangle?

BOOK XII

———

1 ALL THOSE THINGS, WHICH YOU PRAY TO ATTAIN BY A ROUNDABOUT way, you can have at once if you deny them not to yourself; that is to say, if you leave all the Past to itself and entrust the Future to Providence, and but direct the Present in the way of piety and justice: piety, that you may love your lot, for Nature brought it to you and you to it; justice, that you may speak the truth freely and without finesse, and have an eye to law and the due worth of things in all that you do; and let nothing stand in your way, not the wickedness of others, nor your own opinion, nor what men say, nor even the sensations of the flesh that has grown around you; for the part affected will see to that.

If then, when the time of your departure is near, abandoning all else you prize your ruling Reason alone and that which in you is divine, and dread the thought, not that you must one day cease to live, but that you should never yet have begun to live according to Nature, then will you be a man worthy of the Universe that begat you, and no longer an alien in your fatherland, no longer will you marvel at what happens every day as if it were unforeseen, and be dependent on this or that.

2. God sees the Ruling Parts of all men stripped of material vessels and husks and sloughs. For only with the Intellectual Part of Himself is He in touch with those emanations only which have welled forth and been drawn off from Himself into them. But if you also will accustom yourself to do this, you will free yourself from the most of your distracting care. For he

that has no eye for the flesh that envelopes him will not, I believe, waste his time with taking thought for raiment and lodging and popularity and such accessories and frippery.

3. You are formed of three things in combination—body, vital breath, intelligence. Of these the first two are indeed yours, in so far as you must have them in your keeping, but the third alone is in any true sense yours. Wherefore, if you cut off from yourself, that is from your mind, all that others do or say and all that yourself have done or said, and all that harasses you in the future, or whatever you are involved in independently of your will by the body which envelopes you and the breath that is twinned with it, and whatever the circumambient rotation outside of you sweeps along, so that your intellectual faculty, delivered from the contingencies of destiny, may live pure and undetached by itself, doing what is just, desiring what befalls it, speaking the truth—if, I say, you strip from this ruling Reason all that cleaves to it from the bodily influences and the things that lie beyond in time and the things that are past, and if you fashion yourself like the Empedoclean

Sphere to its circle true in its poise well-rounded rejoicing,

and school yourself to live that life only which is yours, namely the present, so will you be able to pass through the remnant of your days calmly, kindly, and at peace with your own "genius."

4. Often have I marveled how each one of us loves himself above all men, yet sets less store by his own opinion of himself than by that of everyone else. At any rate, if a God or some wise teacher should come to a man and charge him to admit no thought or design into his mind that he could not utter aloud as soon as conceived, he could not endure this ordinance, for a single day. So it is clear that we pay more deference to the opinion our neighbors will have of us than to our own.

5. How can the gods, after disposing all things well and with good will toward men, ever have overlooked this one thing, that some of mankind, and they especially good men, who have had as it were the closest

commerce with the Divine, and by devout conduct and acts of worship have been in the most intimate fellowship with it, should when once dead have no second existence but be wholly extinguished? But if indeed this be haply so, doubt not that they would have ordained it otherwise, had it needed to be otherwise. For had it been just, it would also have been feasible, and had it been in conformity with Nature, Nature would have brought it about. Therefore from its not being so, if indeed it is not so, be assured that it ought not to have been so. For even yourself can see that in this presumptuous inquiry of your you are reasoning with God. But we should not thus be arguing with the gods were they not infinitely good and just. But in that case they could not have overlooked anything being wrongly and irrationally neglected in their thorough Ordering of the Universe.

6. Practice that also wherein you have no expectation of success. For even the left hand, which for every other function is inefficient by reason of a want of practice, has yet a firmer grip of the bridle than the right. For it has had practice in this.

7. Reflect on the condition of body and soul befitting a man when overtaken by death, on the shortness of life, on the yawning gulf of the past and of the time to come, on the impotence of all matter.

8. Look at the principles of causation stripped of their husks; at the objective of actions; at what pain is, what pleasure, what death, what fame. See who is to blame for a man's inner unrest; how no one can be thwarted by another; that nothing is but what thinking makes it.

Nothing is but what thinking makes it

9. In our use of principles of conduct we should imitate the fighter not the gladiator. For the latter lays aside the blade which he uses, and takes it up again, but the other always has his hand and needs only to clench it.

10. See things as they really are, analyzing them into Matter, Cause, Objective.

11. What a capacity Man has to do only what God shall approve and to welcome all that God assigns him!

12. Find no fault with gods for what is the course of Nature, for they do no wrong voluntarily or involuntarily; nor with men, for they do none save involuntarily. Find fault then with none.

13. How ludicrous is he and out of place who marvels at anything that happens in life.

14. There must be either a predestined Necessity and inviolable plan, or a gracious Providence, or a chaos without design or director. If then there be an inevitable Necessity, why kick against the pricks? If a Providence that is ready to be gracious, render yourself worthy of divine succour. But if a chaos without guide, congratulate yourself that amid such a surging sea you have in yourself a guiding Reason. And if the surge sweep you away, let it sweep away the poor Flesh and Breath with their appurtenances: for the Intelligence it shall never sweep away.

15. What! shall the truth that is in you and the justice and the temperance be extinguished ere you are, whereas the light of a lamp shines forth and keeps its radiance until the flame be quenched?

16. Another has given you cause to think that he has done wrong: But how do I know that it is a wrong? And even if he be guilty, suppose that his own heart has condemned him, and so he is as one who wounds his own face?

Note that he who would not have the wicked do wrong is as one who would not have the fig-tree secrete acrid juice in its fruit, would not have babies cry, or the horse neigh, or have any other things be that must be. Why, what else can be expected from such a disposition? If then it chafes you, cure the disposition.

17. If not meet, do it not: if not true, say it not. For let your impulse be in your own power.

18. Ever look to the whole of a thing, what exactly that is which produces the impression on you, and unfold it, analyzing it into its causes, its matter, its objective, and into its lifespan within which it must needs cease to be.

19. Become conscious at last that you have in yourself something better and more god-like than that which causes the bodily passions and turns you into a mere marionette. What is my mind now occupied with? Fear? Suspicion? Concupiscence? Some other like thing?

20. Firstly, eschew action that is aimless and has no objective. Secondly, take as the only goal of conduct what is to the common interest.

21. Remember that you will very soon be no one and nowhere, and so with all that you now see and all who are now living. For by Nature's law all things must change, be transformed, and perish, that other things may in their turn come into being.

22. Remember that all is but as your opinion of it, and that is in your power. Efface your opinion then, as you may do at will, and lo, a great calm! Like a mariner that has turned the headland you find all at set-fair and a halcyon sea.

23. Any single form of activity, be it what it may, ceasing in its own due season, suffers no ill because it has ceased, nor does the agent suffer in that it has ceased to act. Similarly then if life, that sum total of all our acts, cease in its own good time, it suffers no ill from this very fact, nor is he in an ill plight who has brought this chain of acts to an end in its own due time. The due season and the terminus are fixed by Nature, at times even by our individual nature, as when in old age, but in any case by the Universal Nature, the constant change of whose parts keeps the whole Universe ever youthful and in its prime. All that is advantageous to the Whole is ever fair and in its bloom. The ending of life then is not only no evil to the individual—for it brings him no disgrace, if in fact it be both outside our choice and not inimical to the general benefit—but a good, since it is timely for the Universe, bears its share in it and is borne along with it. For then is he, who is borne along on the same path as God, and borne in his judgment toward the same things, indeed a man god-borne.

24. You must have these three rules ready for use. Firstly, not to do anything, that you do, aimlessly, or otherwise than as Justice herself would have acted; and to realize that all that befalls you from without is due either to Chance or to Providence, nor have you any call to blame Chance or to

impeach Providence. Secondly this: to think what each creature is from conception till it receives a living soul, and from its reception of a living soul till its giving back of the same, and out of what it is built up and into what it is dissolved. Thirdly, that if carried suddenly into mid-heaven you should look down upon human affairs and their infinite diversity, you will indeed despise them, seeing at the same time in one view how great is the host that peoples the air and the aether around you; and that, however often you were lifted up on high, you would see the same sights, everything identical in kind, everything fleeting. Besides, the vanity of it all!

25. Overboard with opinion and you are safe ashore. And who is there prevents you from throwing it overboard?

26. In taking umbrage at anything, you forget this, that everything happens in accordance with the Universal Nature; and this, that the wrong-doing is another's; and this furthermore, that all that happens, always did happen, and will happen so, and is at this moment happening everywhere. And you forget how strong is the kinship between man and mankind, for it is a community not of corpuscles, of seed or blood, but of intelligence. And you forget this too, that each man's intelligence is God and has emanated from Him; and this, that nothing is a man's very own, but that his babe, his body, his very soul came forth from Him; and this, that everything is but opinion; and this, that it is only the present moment that a man lives and the present moment only that he loses.

27. Let your mind dwell continually on those who have shown unmea-sured resentment at things, who have been conspicuous above others for honors or disasters or enmities or any sort of special lot. Then consider, Where is all that now? Smoke and dust and a legend or not a legend even. Take any instance of the kind—Fabius Catullinus in the country, Lusius Lupus in his gardens, Stertinius at Baiae, Tiberius in Capreae, and Velius Rufus—in fact a craze for any thing whatever arrogantly indulged. How worthless is everything so inordinately desired! How much more worthy of a philosopher is it for a man without any artifice to show himself in the sphere assigned to him just, temperate, and a follower of the gods. For the

conceit that is conceited of its freedom from conceit is the most insufferable of all.

28. If any ask, Where have you seen the gods or how have you satisfied yourself of their existence that you are so devout a worshipper? I answer: In the first place, they are even visible to the eyes. In the next, I have not seen my own soul either, yet I honor it. So then from the continual proofs of their power I am assured that gods also exist and I reverence them.

29. Salvation in life depends on our seeing everything in its entirety and and its reality, in its Matter and its Cause: on our doing what is just and speaking what is true with all our soul. What remains but to get delight of life by dovetailing one good act on to another so as not to leave the smallest gap between?

30. There is one Light of the Sun, even though its continuity be broken by walls, mountains, and countless other things. There is one common Substance, even though it be broken up into countless bodies individually characterized. There is one Soul, though it be broken up among countless natures and with individual limitations. There is one Intelligent Soul, though it seem to be divided. Of the things mentioned, however, all the other parts, such as Breath, are the material Substratum of things, devoid of sensation and the ties of mutual affinity—yet even they are knit together by the faculty of intelligence and the gravitation which draws them together. But the mind is peculiarly impelled toward what is akin to it, and coalesces with it, and there is no break in the feeling of social fellowship.

31. What do you ask for? Continued existence? But what of sensation? Of desire? Of growth? Or again of coming to an end? Of the use of speech? The exercise of thought? Which of these, think you, is a thing to long for? But if these things are each and all of no account, address yourself to a final endeavor to follow Reason and to follow God. But it militates against this to prize such things, and to grieve if death comes to deprive us of them.

32. How tiny a fragment of boundless and abysmal Time has been appointed to each man! For in a moment it is lost in eternity. And how tiny

a part of the Universal Substance! How tiny of the Universal Soul! And on how tiny a clod of the whole Earth do you crawl! Keeping all these things in mind, think nothing of moment save to do what your nature leads you to do, and to bear what the Universal Nature brings you.

33. How does the ruling Reason treat itself? That is the gist of the whole matter. All else, be it in your choice or not, is dead dust and smoke.

34. Most efficacious in instilling a contempt for death is the fact that those who count pleasure a good and pain an evil have nevertheless condemned it.

35. Not even death can bring terror to him who regards that alone as good which comes in due season, and to whom it is all one whether his acts in obedience to right reason are few or many, and a matter of indifference whether he look upon the world for a longer or a shorter time.

36. Man, you have been a citizen in this World-City, what matters it to you if for five years or a hundred? For under its laws equal treatment is meted out to all. What hardship then is there in being banished from the city, not by a tyrant or an unjust judge but by Nature who settled you in it? So might a praetor who commissions a comic actor, dismiss him from the stage. But I have not played my five acts, but only three. Very possibly, but in life three acts count as a full play. For he, that is responsible for your composition originally and your dissolution now, decides when it is complete. But you are responsible for neither. Depart then with a good grace, for he also that dismisses you is gracious.

Letters from a Stoic

SELECTIONS

—

SENECA

Translated by Richard Mott Gummere

Contents

———

LETTERS

I. ON SAVING TIME

———

GREETINGS FROM SENECA TO HIS FRIEND LUCILIUS.

Continue to act thus, my dear Lucilius—set yourself free for your own sake; gather and save your time, which till lately has been forced from you, or filched away, or has merely slipped from your hands. Make yourself believe the truth of my words—that certain moments are torn from us, that some are gently removed, and that others glide beyond our reach. The most disgraceful kind of loss, however, is that due to carelessness. Furthermore, if you will pay close heed to the problem, you will find that the largest portion of our life passes while we are doing ill, a goodly share while we are doing nothing, and the whole while we are doing that which is not to the purpose. What man can you show me who places any value on his time, who reckons the worth of each day, who understands that he is dying daily? For we are mistaken when we look forward to death; the major portion of death has already passed. Whatever years be behind us are in death's hands.

While we are postponing, life speeds by

Therefore, Lucilius, do as you write me that you are doing: hold every hour in your grasp. Lay hold of today's task, and you will not need to depend so much upon tomorrow's. While we are postponing, life speeds by. Nothing, Lucilius, is ours, except time. We were entrusted by nature with the ownership of this single thing, so fleeting and slippery that anyone who will can oust us from possession. What fools these mortals be! They allow the cheapest and most useless things, which can easily be replaced, to be charged in the reckoning, after they have acquired them; but they never regard themselves as in debt when they have received some of that precious commodity—time! And yet time is the one loan which even a grateful recipient cannot repay.

You may desire to know how I, who preach to you so freely, am practicing. I confess frankly: my expense account balances, as you would expect from one who is free-handed but careful. I cannot boast that I waste nothing, but I can at least tell you what I am wasting, and the cause and manner of the loss; I can give you the reasons why I am a poor man. My situation, however, is the same as that of many who are reduced to slender means through no fault of their own: every one forgives them, but no one comes to their rescue.

What is the state of things, then? It is this: I do not regard a man as poor, if the little which remains is enough for him. I advise you, however, to keep what is really yours; and you cannot begin too early. For, as our ancestors believed, it is too late to spare when you reach the dregs of the cask. Of that which remains at the bottom, the amount is slight, and the quality is vile. Farewell.

III. ON TRUE AND FALSE FRIENDSHIP

———

YOU HAVE SENT A LETTER TO ME THROUGH THE HAND OF A "FRIEND" of yours, as you call him. And in your very next sentence you warn me not to discuss with him all the matters that concern you, saying that even you yourself are not accustomed to do this; in other words, you have in the same letter affirmed and denied that he is your friend. Now if you used this word of ours in the popular sense, and called him "friend" in the same way in which we speak of all candidates for election as "honorable gentlemen," and as we greet all men whom we meet casually, if their names slip us for the moment, with the salutation "my dear sir,"—so be it. But if you consider any man a friend whom you do not trust as you trust yourself, you are mightily mistaken and you do not sufficiently understand what true friendship means. Indeed, I would have you discuss everything with a friend; but first of all discuss the man himself. When friendship is settled, you must trust; before friendship is formed, you must pass judgment. Those persons indeed put last first and confound their duties, who, violating the rules of Theophrastus, judge a man after they have made him their friend, instead of making him their friend after they have judged him. Ponder for a long time whether you shall admit a given person to your friendship; but when you have decided to admit him, welcome him with all your heart and soul. Speak as boldly with him as with yourself. As to yourself, although you should live in such a way that you trust your own self with nothing which you could not entrust even to your enemy, yet, since certain matters occur which convention keeps secret, you should share with a friend at least all your worries and reflections. Regard him as loyal, and you will make him loyal. Some, for example, fearing to be deceived, have taught men to deceive; by their suspicions they have given their friend the right to do wrong. Why need I keep back any words in the presence of my friend? Why should I not regard myself as alone when in his company?

Ponder for a long time whether you shall admit a given person to your friendship; but when you have decided to admit him, welcome him with all your heart and soul

There is a class of men who communicate, to anyone whom they meet, matters which should be revealed to friends alone, and unload upon the chance listener whatever irks them. Others, again, fear to confide in their closest intimates; and if it were possible, they would not trust even themselves, burying their secrets deep in their hearts. But we should do neither. It is equally faulty to trust everyone and to trust no one. Yet the former fault is, I should say, the more ingenuous, the latter the more safe. In like manner you should rebuke these two kinds of men,—both those who always lack repose, and those who are always in repose. For love of bustle is not industry,—it is only the restlessness of a hunted mind. And true repose does not consist in condemning all motion as merely vexation; that kind of repose is slackness and inertia. Therefore, you should note the following saying, taken from my reading in Pomponius: "Some men shrink into dark corners, to such a degree that they see darkly by day." No, men should combine these tendencies, and he who reposes should act and he who acts should take repose. Discuss the problem with Nature; she will tell you that she has created both day and night. Farewell.

For love of bustle is not industry,—it is only the restlessness of a hunted mind

IV. ON THE TERRORS
OF DEATH

———

KEEP ON AS YOU HAVE BEGUN, AND MAKE ALL POSSIBLE HASTE, SO that you may have longer enjoyment of an improved mind, one that is at peace with itself. Doubtless you will derive enjoyment during the time when you are improving your mind and setting it at peace with itself; but quite different is the pleasure which comes from contemplation when one's mind is so cleansed from every stain that it shines. You remember, of course, what joy you felt when you laid aside the garments of boyhood and donned the man's toga, and were escorted to the forum; nevertheless, you may look for a still greater joy when you have laid aside the mind of boyhood and when wisdom has enrolled you among men. For it is not boyhood that still stays with us, but something worse,—boyishness. And this condition is all the more serious because we possess the authority of old age, together with the follies of boyhood, yea, even the follies of infancy. Boys fear trifles, children fear shadows, we fear both.

All you need to do is to advance; you will thus understand that some things are less to be dreaded, precisely because they inspire us with great fear. No evil is great which is the last evil of all. Death arrives; it would be a thing to dread, if it could remain with you. But death must either not come at all, or else must come and pass away.

"It is difficult, however," you say, "to bring the mind to a point where it can scorn life." But do you not see what trifling reasons impel men to scorn life? One hangs himself before the door of his mistress; another hurls himself from the housetop that he may no longer be compelled to bear the taunts of a bad-tempered master; a third, to be saved from arrest after running away, drives a sword into his vitals. Do you not suppose that virtue will be as efficacious as excessive fear? No man can have a peaceful life who thinks too much about lengthening it, or believes that living through many consulships is a great blessing. Rehearse this thought every day, that you may be able to depart from life contentedly; for many men clutch and cling to life, even as those who are carried down a rushing stream clutch and cling to briars and sharp rocks.

Most men ebb and flow in wretchedness between the fear of death and the hardships of life; they are unwilling to live, and yet they do not know how to die. For this reason, make life as a whole agreeable to yourself by banishing all worry about it. No good thing renders its possessor happy, unless his mind is reconciled to the possibility of loss; nothing, however, is lost with less discomfort than that which, when lost, cannot be missed. Therefore, encourage and toughen your spirit against the mishaps that afflict even the most powerful. For example, the fate of Pompey was settled by a boy and an eunuch, that of Crassus by a cruel and insolent Parthian. Gaius Caesar ordered Lepidus to bare his neck for the axe of the tribune Dexter; and he himself offered his own throat to Chaerea. No man has ever been so far advanced by Fortune that she did not threaten him as greatly as she had previously indulged him. Do not trust her seeming calm; in a moment the sea is moved to its depths. The very day the ships have made a brave show in the games, they are engulfed. Reflect that a highwayman or an enemy may cut your throat; and, though he is not your master, every slave wields the power of life and death over you. Therefore I declare to you: he is lord of your life that scorns his own. Think of those who have perished through plots in their own home, slain either openly or by guile; you will realize that just as many have been killed by angry slaves as by angry kings. What matter, therefore, how powerful he be whom you fear, when every one possesses the power which inspires your fear? "But," you will say, "if you should chance to fall into the hands of the enemy, the conqueror will command that you be led away,"—yes, whither you are already being led. Why do you voluntarily deceive yourself and require to be told now for the first time what fate it is that you have long been labouring under? Take my word for it: since the day you were born you are being led thither. We must ponder this thought, and thoughts of the like nature, if we desire to be calm as we await that last hour, the fear of which makes all previous hours uneasy.

But I must end my letter. Let me share with you the saying which pleased me today. It, too, is culled from another man's Garden: "Poverty brought into conformity with the law of nature, is great wealth." Do you know what limits that law of nature ordains for us? Merely to avert hunger, thirst, and cold. In order to banish hunger and thirst, it is not necessary for you to pay court at the doors of the purse-proud, or to submit to the stern frown, or to the kindness that humiliates; nor is it necessary for you to scour the seas, or go campaigning; nature's needs are easily provided and ready to hand. It is the superfluous things for which men sweat—the superfluous things that wear our togas threadbare, that force us to grow old in camp, that dash us upon foreign shores. That which is enough is ready to our hands. He who has made a fair compact with poverty is rich. Farewell.

VII. ON CROWDS

——

D O YOU ASK ME WHAT YOU SHOULD REGARD AS ESPECIALLY TO BE avoided? I say, crowds; for as yet you cannot trust yourself to them with safety. I shall admit my own weakness, at any rate; for I never bring back home the same character that I took abroad with me. Something of that which I have forced to be calm within me is disturbed; some of the foes that I have routed return again. Just as the sick man, who has been weak for a long time, is in such a condition that he cannot be taken out of the house without suffering a relapse, so we ourselves are affected when our souls are recovering from a lingering disease. To consort with the crowd is harmful; there is no person who does not make some vice attractive to us, or stamp it upon us, or taint us unconsciously therewith. Certainly, the greater the mob with which we mingle, the greater the danger.

But nothing is so damaging to good character as the habit of lounging at the games; for then it is that vice steals subtly upon one through the avenue of pleasure. What do you think I mean? I mean that I come home more greedy, more ambitious, more voluptuous, and even more cruel and inhuman, because I have been among human beings. By chance I attended a mid-day exhibition, expecting some fun, wit, and relaxation—an exhibition at which men's eyes have respite from the slaughter of their fellow men. But it was quite the reverse. The previous combats were the essence of compassion; but now all the trifling is put aside and it is pure murder. The men have no defensive armor. They are exposed to blows at all points, and no one ever strikes in vain. Many persons prefer this program to the usual pairs and to the bouts "by request." Of course they do; there is no helmet or shield to deflect the weapon. What is the need of defensive armor, or of skill? All these mean delaying death. In the morning they throw men to the lions and the bears; at noon, they throw them to the spectators. The spectators demand that the slayer shall face the man who is to slay him in his turn; and they always reserve the latest conqueror for another butchering. The outcome of every fight is death, and the means are fire and sword. This sort of thing goes on while the arena is empty. You may retort: "But he was a highway robber; he killed a man!" And what of it? Granted that, as a murderer, he deserved this punishment, what crime have you committed, poor fellow, that you should deserve to sit and see this show? In the morning they cried "Kill him! Lash him! Burn him! Why does he meet the sword in so cowardly a way? Why does he strike so feebly? Why doesn't he die game? Whip him to meet his wounds! Let them receive blow for blow, with chests bare and exposed to the stroke!" And when the games stop for the intermission, they announce: "A little throatcutting in the meantime, so that there may still be something going on!"

Come now; do you not understand even this truth, that a bad example reacts on the agent? Thank the immortal gods that you are teaching cruelty to a person who cannot learn to be cruel. The young character, which cannot hold fast to righteousness, must be rescued from the mob; it is too easy to side with the majority. Even Socrates, Cato, and Laelius might have been shaken in their moral strength by a crowd that was unlike them; so true it is that none of us, no matter how much he cultivates his abilities, can withstand the shock of faults that approach, as it were, with so great a retinue. Much harm is done by a single case of indulgence or greed; the familiar friend, if he be luxurious, weakens and softens us imperceptibly; the neighbor, if he be rich, rouses our covetousness; the companion, if he be slanderous, rubs off some of his rust upon us, even though we be spotless and sincere. What then do you think the effect will be on character, when the world at large assaults it! You must either imitate or loathe the world.

But both courses are to be avoided; you should not copy the bad simply because they are many, nor should you hate the many because they are unlike you. Withdraw into yourself, as far as you can. Associate with those who will make a better man of you. Welcome those whom you yourself can improve. The process is mutual; for men learn while they teach. There is no reason why pride in advertising your abilities should lure you into publicity, so that you should desire to recite or harangue before the general public. Of course I should be willing for you to do so if you had a stock-in-trade that suited such a mob; as it is, there is not a man of them who can understand you. One or two individuals will perhaps come in your way, but even these will have to be molded and trained by you so that they will understand you. You may say: "For what purpose did I learn all these things?" But you need not fear that you have wasted your efforts; it was for yourself that you learned them.

In order, however, that I may not today have learned exclusively for myself, I shall share with you three excellent sayings, of the same general purport, which have come to my attention. This letter

> **Associate with those who will make a better man of you. Welcome those whom you yourself can improve. The process is mutual; for men learn while they teach**

will give you one of them as payment of my debt; the other two you may accept as a contribution in advance. Democritus says: "One man means as much to me as a multitude, and a multitude only as much as one man." The following also was nobly spoken by someone or other, for it is doubtful who the author was; they asked him what was the object of all this study applied to an art that would reach but very few. He replied: "I am content with few, content with one, content with none at all." The third saying—and a noteworthy one, too—is by Epicurus, written to one of the partners of his studies: "I write this not for the many, but for you; each of us is enough of an audience for the other." Lay these words to heart, Lucilius, that you may scorn the pleasure which comes from the applause of the majority. Many men praise you; but have you any reason for being pleased with yourself, if you are a person whom the many can understand? Your good qualities should face inward. Farewell.

XII. ON OLD AGE

WHEREVER I TURN, I SEE EVIDENCES OF MY ADVANCING YEARS. I visited lately my country place, and protested against the money which was spent on the tumble-down building. My bailiff maintained that the flaws were not due to his own carelessness; "he was doing everything possible, but the house was old." And this was the house which grew under my own hands! What has the future in store for me, if stones of my own age are already crumbling? I was angry, and I embraced the first opportunity to vent my spleen in the bailiff's presence. "It is clear," I cried, "that these plane-trees are neglected; they have no leaves. Their branches are so gnarled and shriveled; the boles are so rough and unkempt! This would not happen, if someone loosened the earth at their feet, and watered them." The bailiff swore by my protecting deity that "he was doing everything possible, and never relaxed his efforts, but those trees were old." Between you and me, I had planted those trees myself; I had seen them in their first leaf. Then I turned to the door and asked: "Who is that broken-down dotard? You have done well to place him at the entrance; for he is outward bound. Where did you get him? What pleasure did it give you to take up for burial some other man's dead?" But the slave said: "Don't you know me, sir? I am Felicio; you used to bring me little images. My father was Philositus the steward, and I am your pet slave." "The man is clean crazy," I remarked. "Has my pet slave become a little boy again? But it is quite possible; his teeth are just dropping out."

I owe it to my country-place that my old age became apparent wherever I turned. Let us cherish and love old age; for it is full of pleasure if one knows how to use it. Fruits are most welcome when almost over; youth is most charming at its close; the last drink delights the toper, the glass which souses him and puts the finishing touch on his drunkenness. Each pleasure reserves to the end the greatest delights which it contains. Life is most delightful when it is on the downward slope, but has not yet reached the abrupt decline. And I myself believe that the period which stands, so to speak, on the edge of the roof, possesses pleasures of its own. Or else the very fact of our not wanting pleasures has taken the place of the pleasures themselves. How comforting it is to have tired out one's appetites, and to have done with them! "But," you say, "it is a nuisance to be looking death in the face!" Death, however, should be looked in the face by young and old alike. We are not summoned according to our rating on the censor's list. Moreover, no one is so old that it would be improper for him to hope for another day of existence. And one day, mind you, is a stage on life's journey.

Our span of life is divided into parts; it consists of large circles enclosing smaller. One circle embraces and bounds the rest; it reaches from birth to the last day of existence. The next circle limits the period of our young manhood. The third confines all of childhood in its circumference. Again, there is, in a class by itself, the year; it contains within itself all the divisions of time by the multiplication of which we get the total of life. The month is bounded by a narrower ring. The smallest circle of all is the day; but even a day has its beginning and its ending, its sunrise and its sunset. Hence Heraclitus, whose obscure style gave him his surname, remarked: "One day is equal to every day." Different persons have interpreted the saying in different ways. Some hold that days are equal in number of hours, and this is true; for if by "day" we mean twenty-four hours' time, all days must be equal, inasmuch as the night acquires what the day loses. But others maintain that one day is equal to all days through resemblance, because the very longest space of time possesses no element which cannot be found in a single day—namely, light and darkness—and even to eternity day makes these alternations more numerous, not different when it is shorter and different again when it is longer. Hence, every day ought to be regulated as if it closed the series, as if it rounded out and completed our existence.

Pacuvius, who by long occupancy made Syria his own, used to hold a regular burial sacrifice in his own honor, with wine and the usual funeral feasting, and then would have himself carried from the dining room to his chamber, while eunuchs applauded and sang in Greek to a musical accompaniment: "He has lived his life, he has lived his life!" Thus Pacuvius had himself carried out to burial every day. Let us, however, do from a good motive what he used to do from a debased motive; let us go to our sleep with joy and gladness; let us say:

I have lived; the course which Fortune set for me Is finished.

And if God is pleased to add another day, we should welcome it with glad hearts. That man is happiest, and is secure in his own possession of himself, who can await the morrow without apprehension. When a man has said: "I have lived!", every morning he arises he receives a bonus.

But now I ought to close my letter. "What?" you say; "shall it come to me without any little offering?" Be not afraid; it brings something,—nay, more than something, a great deal. For what is more noble than the following saying of which I make this letter the bearer: "It is wrong to live under constraint; but no man is constrained to live under constraint." Of course not. On all sides lie many short and simple paths to freedom; and let us thank God that no man can be kept in life. We may spurn the very constraints that hold us. "Epicurus," you reply, "uttered these words; what are you doing with another's property?" Any truth, I maintain, is my own property. And I shall continue to heap quotations from Epicurus upon you, so that all persons who swear by the words of another, and put a value upon the speaker and not upon the thing spoken, may understand that the best ideas are common property. Farewell.

XVI. ON PHILOSOPHY,
THE GUIDE OF LIFE

———

I T IS CLEAR TO YOU, I AM SURE, LUCILIUS, THAT NO MAN CAN LIVE A happy life, or even a supportable life, without the study of wisdom; you know also that a happy life is reached when our wisdom is brought to completion, but that life is at least endurable even when our wisdom is only begun. This idea, however, clear though it is, must be strengthened and implanted more deeply by daily reflection; it is more important for you to keep the resolutions you have already made than to go on and make noble ones. You must persevere, must develop new strength by continuous study, until that which is only a good inclination becomes a good settled purpose. Hence you no longer need to come to me with much talk and protestations; I know that you have made great progress. I understand the feelings which prompt your words; they are not feigned or specious words. Nevertheless I shall tell you what I think—that at present I have hopes for you, but not yet perfect trust. And I wish that you would adopt the same attitude toward yourself; there is no reason why you should put confidence in yourself too quickly and readily. Examine yourself; scrutinize and observe yourself in diverse ways; but mark, before all else, whether it is in philosophy or merely in life itself that you have made progress. Philosophy is no trick to catch the public; it is not devised for show. It is a matter, not of words, but of facts. It is not pursued in order that the day may yield some amusement before it is spent, or that our leisure may be relieved of a tedium that irks us. It molds and constructs the soul; it orders our life, guides our conduct, shows us what we should do and what we should leave undone; it sits at the helm and directs our course as we waver amid uncertainties. Without it, no one can live fearlessly or in peace of mind. Countless things that happen every hour call for advice; and such advice is to be sought in philosophy.

Perhaps someone will say: "How can philosophy help me, if Fate exists? Of what avail is philosophy, if God rules the universe? Of what avail is it, if Chance governs everything? For not only is it impossible to change things that are determined, but it is also impossible to plan beforehand against what is undetermined; either God has forestalled my plans, and decided what I am to do, or else Fortune gives no free play to my plans." Whether the truth, Lucilius, lies in one or in all of these views, we must be philosophers; whether Fate binds us down by an inexorable law, or whether God as arbiter of the universe has arranged everything, or whether Chance drives and tosses human affairs without method, philosophy ought to be our defense. She will encourage us to obey God cheerfully, but Fortune defiantly; she will teach us to follow God and endure Chance. But it is not my purpose now to be led into a discussion as to what is within our own control—if foreknowledge is supreme, or if a chain of fated events drags us along in its clutches, or if the sudden and the unexpected play the tyrant over us; I return now to my warning and my exhortation, that you should not allow the impulse of your spirit to weaken and grow cold. Hold fast to it and establish it firmly, in order that what is now impulse may become a habit of the mind.

If I know you well, you have already been trying to find out, from the very beginning of my letter, what little contribution it brings to you. Sift the letter, and you will find it. You need not wonder at any genius of mine; for as yet I am lavish only with other men's property. But why did I say "other men"? Whatever is well said by anyone is mine. This also is a saying of Epicurus: "If you live according to nature, you will never be poor; if you live according to opinion, you will never be rich." Nature's wants are slight; the demands of opinion are boundless. Suppose that the property of many millionaires is heaped up in your possession. Assume that Fortune carries you far beyond the limits of a private income, decks you with gold, clothes you in purple, and brings you to such a degree of luxury and wealth that you can bury the earth under your marble floors; that you may not only possess, but tread upon, riches. Add statues, paintings, and whatever any art has devised for the luxury; you will only learn from such things to crave still greater.

Natural desires are limited; but those which spring from false opinion can have no stopping point. The false has no limits. When you are traveling on a road, there must be an end; but when astray, your wanderings are limitless. Recall your steps, therefore, from idle things, and when you would know whether that which you seek is based upon a natural or upon a misleading desire, consider whether it can stop at any definite point. If you find, after having traveled far, that there is a more distant goal always in view, you may be sure that this condition is contrary to nature. Farewell.

The false has no limits

XVIII. ON FESTIVALS
AND FASTING

———

I T IS THE MONTH OF DECEMBER, AND YET THE CITY IS AT THIS VERY
moment in a sweat. License is given to the general merrymaking. Everything resounds with mighty preparations—as if the Saturnalia differed at
all from the usual business day! So true it is that the difference is nil, that I
regard as correct the remark of the man who said: "Once December was a
month; now it is a year."

If I had you with me, I should be glad to consult you and find out
what you think should be done—whether we ought to make no change in
our daily routine, or whether, in order not to be out of sympathy with the
ways of the public, we should dine in gayer fashion and doff the toga. As
it is now, we Romans have changed our dress for the sake of pleasure and
holiday-making, though in former times that was only customary when
the State was disturbed and had fallen on evil days. I am sure that, if I
know you aright, playing the part of an umpire you would have wished
that we should be neither like the liberty-capped throng in all ways, nor in
all ways unlike them; unless, perhaps, this is just the season when we ought
to lay down the law to the soul, and bid it be alone in refraining from pleasures just when the whole mob has let itself go in pleasures; for this is the
surest proof which a man can get of his own constancy, if he neither seeks
the things which are seductive and allure him to luxury, nor is led into

them. It shows much more courage to remain dry and sober when the mob is drunk and vomiting; but it shows greater self-control to refuse to withdraw oneself and to do what the crowd does, but in a different way—thus neither making oneself conspicuous nor becoming one of the crowd. For one may keep holiday without extravagance.

I am so firmly determined, however, to test the constancy of your mind that, drawing from the teachings of great men, I shall give you also a lesson: Set aside a certain number of days, during which you shall be content with the scantiest and cheapest fare, with coarse and rough dress, saying to yourself the while: "Is this the condition that I feared?" It is precisely in times of immunity from care that the soul should toughen itself beforehand for occasions of greater stress, and it is while Fortune is kind that it should fortify itself against her violence. In days of peace the soldier performs maneuvers, throws up earthworks with no enemy in sight, and wearies himself by gratuitous toil, in order that he may be equal to unavoidable toil. If you would not have a man flinch when the crisis comes, train him before it comes. Such is the course which those men have followed who, in their imitation of poverty, have every month come almost to want, that they might never recoil from what they had so often rehearsed.

You need not suppose that I mean meals like Timon's, or "paupers' huts," or any other device which luxurious millionaires use to beguile the tedium of their lives. Let the pallet be a real one, and the coarse cloak; let the bread be hard and grimy. Endure all this for three or four days at a time, sometimes for more, so that it may be a test of yourself instead of a mere hobby. Then, I assure you, my dear Lucilius, you will leap for joy when filled with a pennyworth of food, and you will understand that a man's peace of mind does not depend upon Fortune; for, even when angry she grants enough for our needs.

There is no reason, however, why you should think that you are doing anything great; for you will merely be doing what many thousands of slaves and many thousands of poor men are doing every day. But you may credit yourself with this item—that you will not be doing it under compulsion, and that it will be as easy for you to endure it permanently as to make the experiment from time to time. Let us practice our strokes on the "dummy"; let us become intimate with poverty, so that Fortune may not catch us off our guard. We shall be rich with all the more comfort, if we once learn how far poverty is from being a burden.

Even Epicurus, the teacher of pleasure, used to observe stated intervals, during which he satisfied his hunger in miserly fashion; he wished to see whether he thereby fell short of full and complete happiness, and, if so, by what amount he fell short, and whether this amount was worth purchasing at the price of great effort. At any rate, he makes such a statement in the well-known letter written to Polyaenus in the archonship of Charinus. Indeed, he boasts that he himself lived on less than a penny, but that Metrodorus, whose progress was not yet so great, needed a whole penny. Do you think that there can be fullness on such fare? Yes, and there is pleasure also—not that shifty and fleeting Pleasure which needs a fillip now and then, but a pleasure that is steadfast and sure. For though water, barley-meal, and crusts of barley-bread, are not a cheerful diet, yet it is the highest kind of Pleasure to be able to derive pleasure from this sort of food, and to have reduced one's needs to that modicum which no unfairness of Fortune can snatch away. Even prison fare is more generous; and those who have been set apart for capital punishment are not so meanly fed by the man who is to execute them. Therefore, what a noble soul must one have, to descend of one's own free will to a diet which even those who have been sentenced to death have not to fear! This is indeed forestalling the spear thrusts of Fortune.

So begin, my dear Lucilius, to follow the custom of these men, and set apart certain days on which you shall withdraw from your business and make yourself at home with the scantiest fare. Establish business relations with poverty.

Dare, O my friend, to scorn the sight of wealth,
And mold yourself to kinship with your God.

For he alone is in kinship with God who has scorned wealth. Of course I do not forbid you to possess it, but I would have you reach the point at which you possess it dauntlessly; this can be accomplished only by persuading yourself that you can live happily without it as well as with it, and by regarding riches always as likely to elude you.

But now I must begin to fold up my letter. "Settle your debts first," you cry. Here is a draft on Epicurus; he will pay down the sum: "Ungoverned anger begets madness." You cannot help knowing the truth of these words, since you have had not only slaves, but also enemies. But indeed this emotion blazes out against all sorts of persons; it springs from love as much as from hate, and shows itself not less in serious matters than in jest and sport. And it makes no difference how important the provocation may be, but into what kind of soul it penetrates. Similarly with fire; it does not matter how great is the flame, but what it falls upon. For solid timbers have repelled a very great fire; conversely, dry and easily inflammable stuff nourishes the slightest spark into a conflagration. So it is with anger, my dear Lucilius; the outcome of a mighty anger is madness, and hence anger should be avoided, not merely that we may escape excess, but that we may have a healthy mind. Farewell.

XIX. ON WORLDLINESS
AND RETIREMENT

———

I LEAP FOR JOY WHENEVER I RECEIVE LETTERS FROM YOU. FOR THEY fill me with hope; they are now not mere assurances concerning you, but guarantees. And I beg and pray you to proceed in this course; for what better request could I make of a friend than one which is to be made for his own sake? If possible, withdraw yourself from all the business of which you speak; and if you cannot do this, tear yourself away. We have dissipated enough of our time already—let us in old age begin to pack up our baggage. Surely there is nothing in this that men can begrudge us. We have spent our lives on the high seas; let us die in harbor. Not that I would advise you to try to win fame by your retirement; one's retirement should neither be paraded nor concealed. Not concealed, I say, for I shall not go so far in urging you as to expect you to condemn all men as mad and then seek out for yourself a hiding place and oblivion; rather make this your business, that your retirement be not conspicuous, though it should be obvious. In the second place, while those whose choice is unhampered from the start will deliberate on that other question, whether they wish to pass their lives in obscurity, in your case there is not a free choice. Your ability and energy have thrust you into the work of the world; so have the charm of your writings and the friendships you have made with famous and notable men. Renown has already taken you by storm. You may sink

yourself into the depths of obscurity and utterly hide yourself; yet your earlier acts will reveal you. You cannot keep lurking in the dark; much of the
old gleam will follow you wherever you fly.

Peace you can claim for yourself without being disliked by anyone,
without any sense of loss, and without any pangs of spirit. For what will
you leave behind you that you can imagine yourself reluctant to leave?
Your clients? But none of these men courts you for yourself; they merely
court something from you. People used to hunt friends, but now they hunt
money; if a lonely old man changes his will, the morning-caller transfers
himself to another door. Great things cannot be bought for small sums;
so reckon up whether it is preferable to leave your own true self, or merely
some of your belongings. Would that you had had the privilege of growing
old amid the limited circumstances of your origin, and that Fortune had
not raised you to such heights! You were removed far from the sight of
wholesome living by your swift rise to prosperity, by your province, by your
position as procurator, and by all that such things promise; you will next
acquire more important duties and after them still more. And what will be
the result? Why wait until there is nothing left for you to crave? That time
will never come. We hold that there is a succession of causes, from which
fate is woven; similarly, you may be sure, there is a succession in our desires;
for one begins where its predecessor ends. You have been thrust into an
existence which will never of itself put an end to your wretchedness and
your slavery. Withdraw your chafed neck from the yoke; it is better that it
should be cut off once for all, than galled for ever. If you retreat to privacy,
everything will be on a smaller scale, but you will be satisfied abundantly;
in your present condition, however, there is no satisfaction in the plenty
which is heaped upon you on all sides. Would you rather be poor and sated,
or rich and hungry? Prosperity is not only greedy, but it also lies exposed
to the greed of others. And as long as nothing satisfies you, you yourself
cannot satisfy others.

"But," you say, "how can I take my leave?" Any way you please. Reflect
how many hazards you have ventured for the sake of money, and how

much toil you have undertaken for a title! You must dare something to
gain leisure, also—or else grow old amid the worries of procuratorships
abroad and subsequently of civil duties at home, living in turmoil and in
ever fresh floods of responsibilities, which no
man has ever succeeded in avoiding by unob-
trusiveness or by seclusion of life. For what
bearing on the case has your personal desire
for a secluded life? Your position in the world
desires the opposite! What if, even now, you
allow that position to grow greater? But all
that is added to your successes will be added to
your fears. At this point I should like to quote a saying of Maecenas, who
spoke the truth when he stood on the very summit: "There's thunder even
on the loftiest peaks." If you ask me in what book these words are found,
they occur in the volume entitled *Prometheus*. He simply meant to say that
these lofty peaks have their tops surrounded with thunderstorms. But is
any power worth so high a price that a man like you would ever, in order to
obtain it, adopt a style so debauched as that? Maecenas was indeed a man
of parts, who would have left a great pattern for Roman oratory to follow,
had his good Fortune not made him effeminate—nay, had it not emascu-
lated him! An end like his awaits you also, unless you forthwith shorten
sail and—as Maecenas was not willing to do until it was too late—hug the
shore!

**You must dare
something to
gain leisure**

This saying of Maecenas's might have squared my account with you;
but I feel sure, knowing you, that you will get out an injunction against me,
and that you will be unwilling to accept payment of my debt in such crude
and debased currency. However that may be, I shall draw on the account
of Epicurus. He says: "You must reflect carefully beforehand with whom
you are to eat and drink, rather than what you are to eat and drink. For a
dinner of meats without the company of a friend is like the life of a lion or a
wolf." This privilege will not be yours unless you withdraw from the world;
otherwise, you will have as guests only those whom your slave-secretary
sorts out from the throng of callers. It is, however, a mistake to select your

friend in the reception hall or to test him at the dinner-table. The most serious misfortune for a busy man who is overwhelmed by his possessions is, that he believes men to be his friends when he himself is not a friend to them, and that he deems his favors to be effective in winning friends, although, in the case of certain men, the more they owe, the more they hate. A trifling debt makes a man your debtor; a large one makes him an enemy. "What," you say, "do not kindnesses establish friendships?" They do, if one has had the privilege of choosing those who are to receive them, and if they are placed judiciously, instead of being scattered broadcast.

Therefore, while you are beginning to call your mind your own, mean-time apply this maxim of the wise: consider that it is more important who receives a thing, than what it is he receives. Farewell.

XX. ON PRACTICING WHAT YOU PREACH

———

IF YOU ARE IN GOOD HEALTH AND IF YOU THINK YOURSELF WORTHY of becoming at last your own master, I am glad. For the credit will be mine, if I can drag you from the floods in which you are being buffeted without hope of emerging. This, however, my dear Lucilius, I ask and beg of you, on your part, that you let wisdom sink into your soul, and test your progress, not by mere speech or writings, but by stoutness of heart and decrease of desire. Prove your words by your deeds.

Far different is the purpose of those who are speech-making and trying to win the approbation of a throng of hearers, far different that of those who allure the ears of young men and idlers by many-sided or fluent argumentation; philosophy teaches us to act, not to speak; it exacts of every man that he should live according to his own standards, that his life should not be out of harmony with his words, and that, further, his inner life should be of one hue and not out of harmony with all his activities. This, I say, is the highest duty and the highest proof of wisdom—that deed and word should be in accord, that a man should be equal to himself under all conditions, and always the same.

"But," you reply, "who can maintain this standard?" Very few, to be sure; but there are some. It is indeed a hard undertaking, and I do not say that the philosopher can always keep the same pace. But he can always travel the same path. Observe yourself, then, and see whether your dress and your house are inconsistent, whether you treat yourself lavishly and your family meanly, whether you eat frugal dinners and yet build luxurious houses. You should lay hold, once and for all, upon a single norm to live by, and should regulate your whole life according to this norm. Some men restrict themselves at home, but strut with swelling port before the public; such discordance is a fault, and it indicates a wavering mind which cannot yet keep its balance. And I can tell you, further, whence arise this unsteadiness and disagreement of action and purpose; it is because no man resolves upon what he wishes, and, even if he has done so, he does not persist in it, but jumps the track; not only does he change, but he returns and slips back to the conduct which he has abandoned and abjured. Therefore, to omit the ancient definitions of wisdom and to include the whole manner of human life, I can be satisfied with the following: "What is wisdom? Always desiring the same things, and always refusing the same things." You may be excused from adding the little proviso—that what you wish, should be right; since no man can always be satisfied with the same thing, unless it is right.

> "What is wisdom? Always desiring the same things, and always refusing the same things."

For this reason men do not know what they wish, except at the actual moment of wishing; no man ever decided once and for all to desire or to refuse. Judgment varies from day to day, and changes to the opposite, making many a man pass his life in a kind of game. Press on, therefore, as you have begun; perhaps you will be led to perfection, or to a point which you alone understand is still short of perfection.

"But what," you say, "will become of my crowded household without a household income?" If you stop supporting that crowd, it will support itself; or perhaps you will learn by the bounty of poverty what you cannot learn by your own bounty. Poverty will keep for you your true and tried friends; you will be rid of the men who were not seeking you for yourself, but for something which you have. Is it not true, however, that you should love poverty, if only for this single reason—that it will show you those by whom you are loved? O when will that time come, when no one shall tell lies to compliment you! Accordingly, let your thoughts, your efforts, your desires, help to make you content with your own self and with the goods that spring from yourself; and commit all your other prayers to God's keeping! What happiness could come closer home to you? Bring yourself down to humble conditions, from which you cannot be ejected and in order that you may do so with greater alacrity, the contribution contained in this letter shall refer to that subject; I shall bestow it upon you immediately.

XXIII. ON THE TRUE JOY WHICH COMES FROM PHILOSOPHY

———

DO YOU SUPPOSE THAT I SHALL WRITE YOU HOW KINDLY THE winter season has dealt with us—a short season and a mild one—or what a nasty spring we are having—cold weather out of season—and all the other trivialities which people write when they are at a loss for topics of conversation? No; I shall communicate something which may help both you and myself. And what shall this "something" be, if not an exhortation to soundness of mind? Do you ask what is the foundation of a sound mind? It is, not to find joy in useless things. I said that it was the foundation; it is really the pinnacle. We have reached the heights if we know what it is that we find joy in and if we have not placed our happiness in the control of externals. The man who is goaded ahead by hope of anything, though it be within reach, though it be easy of access, and though his ambitions have never played him false, is troubled and unsure of himself. Above all, my dear Lucilius, make this your business: learn how to feel joy.

> **Above all, my dear Lucilius, make this your business: learn how to feel joy**

165

Do you think that I am now robbing you of many pleasures when I try to do away with the gifts of chance, when I counsel the avoidance of hope, the sweetest thing that gladdens our hearts? Quite the contrary; I do not wish you ever to be deprived of gladness. I would have it born in your house; and it is born there, if only it be inside of you. Other objects of cheer do not fill a man's bosom; they merely smooth his brow and are inconstant—unless perhaps you believe that he who laughs has joy. The very soul must be happy and confident, lifted above every circumstance.

Real joy, believe me, is a stern matter. Can one, do you think, despise death with a care-free countenance, or with a "blithe and gay" expression, as our young dandies are accustomed to say? Or can one thus open his door to poverty, or hold the curb on his pleasures, or contemplate the endurance of pain? He who ponders these things in his heart is indeed full of joy; but it is not a cheerful joy. It is just this joy, however, of which I would have you become the owner; for it will never fail you when once you have found its source. The yield of poor mines is on the surface; those are really rich whose veins lurk deep, and they will make more bountiful returns to him who delves unceasingly. So too those baubles which delight the common crowd afford but a thin pleasure, laid on as a coating, and even joy that is only plated lacks a real basis. But the joy of which I speak, that to which I am endeavoring to lead you, is something solid, disclosing itself the more fully as you penetrate into it. Therefore I pray you, my dearest Lucilius, do the one thing that can render you really happy: cast aside and trample under foot all the things that glitter outwardly and are held out to you by another or as obtainable from another; look toward the true good, and rejoice only in that which comes from your own store. And what do I mean by "from your own store"? I mean from your very self, that which is the best part of you. The frail body, also, even though we can accomplish nothing without it, is to be regarded as necessary rather than as important; it involves us in vain pleasures, short-lived, and soon to be regretted, which, unless they are reined in by extreme self-control, will be transformed into the opposite. This is what I mean: pleasure, unless it has been kept within bounds, tends to rush headlong into the abyss of sorrow.

But it is hard to keep within bounds in that which you believe to be good. The real good may be coveted with safety. Do you ask me what this real good is, and whence it derives? I will tell you: it comes from a good conscience, from honorable purposes, from right actions, from contempt of the gifts of chance, from an even and calm way of living which treads but one path. For men who leap from one purpose to another, or do not even leap but are carried over by a sort of hazard—how can such wavering and unstable persons possess any good that is fixed and lasting? There are only a few who control themselves and their affairs by a guiding purpose; the rest do not proceed; they are merely swept along, like objects afloat in a river. And of these objects, some are held back by sluggish waters and are transported gently; others are torn along by a more violent current; some, which are nearest the bank, are left there as the current slackens; and others are carried out to sea by the onrush of the stream. Therefore, we should decide what we wish, and abide by the decision.

Now is the time for me to pay my debt. I can give you a saying of your friend Epicurus and thus clear this letter of its obligation. "It is bothersome always to be beginning life." Or another, which will perhaps express the meaning better: "They live ill who are always beginning to live." You are right in asking why; the saying certainly stands in need of a commentary. It is because the life of such persons is always incomplete. But a man cannot stand prepared for the approach of death if he has just begun to live. We must make it our aim already to have lived long enough. No one deems that he has done so, if he is just on the point of planning his life. You need not think that there are few of this kind; practically everyone is of such a stamp. Some men, indeed, only begin to live when it is time for them to leave off living. And if this seems surprising to you, I shall add that which will surprise you still more: Some men have left off living before they have begun. Farewell.

XXIV. ON DESPISING DEATH

YOU WRITE ME THAT YOU ARE ANXIOUS ABOUT THE RESULT OF A lawsuit, with which an angry opponent is threatening you; and you expect me to advise you to picture to yourself a happier issue, and to rest in the allurements of hope. Why, indeed, is it necessary to summon trouble—which must be endured soon enough when it has once arrived, or to anticipate trouble and ruin the present through fear of the future? It is indeed foolish to be unhappy now because you may be unhappy at some future time. But I shall conduct you to peace of mind by another route: if you would put off all worry, assume that what you fear may happen will certainly happen in any event; whatever the trouble may be, measure it in your own mind, and estimate the amount of your fear. You will thus understand that what you fear is either insignificant or short-lived. And you need not spend a long time in gathering illustrations which will strengthen you; every epoch has produced them. Let your thoughts travel into any era of Roman or foreign history, and there will throng before you notable examples of high achievement or of high endeavor.

If you lose this case, can anything more severe happen to you than being sent into exile or led to prison? Is there a worse fate that any man may fear than being burned or being killed? Name such penalties one by one, and mention the men who have scorned them; one does not need to hunt for them—it is simply a matter of selection. Sentence of conviction was borne by Rutilius as if the injustice of the decision were the only thing which annoyed him. Exile was endured by Metellus with courage, by Rutilius even with gladness; for the former consented to come back only because his country called him; the latter refused to return when Sulla summoned him—and nobody in those days said "No" to Sulla! Socrates in prison discoursed, and declined to flee when certain persons gave him the opportunity; he remained there, in order to free mankind from the fear of two most grievous things, death and imprisonment. Mucius put his hand into the fire. It is painful to be burned; but how much more painful to inflict such suffering upon oneself! Here was a man of no learning, not primed to face death and pain by any words of wisdom, and equipped only with the courage of a soldier, who punished himself for his fruitless daring; he stood and watched his own right hand falling away piecemeal on the enemy's brazier, nor did he withdraw the dissolving limb, with its uncovered bones, until his foe removed the fire. He might have accomplished something more successful in that camp, but never anything more brave. See how much keener a brave man is to lay hold of danger than a cruel man is to inflict it: Porsenna was more ready to pardon Mucius for wishing to slay him than Mucius to pardon himself for failing to slay Porsenna!

"Oh," say you, "those stories have been droned to death in all the schools; pretty soon, when you reach the topic "On Despising Death," you will be telling me about Cato." But why should I not tell you about Cato, how he read Plato's book on that last glorious night, with a sword laid at his pillow? He had provided these two requisites for his last moments—the first, that he might have the will to die, and the second, that he might have the means. So he put his affairs in order—as well as one could put in order that which was ruined and near its end—and thought that he ought to see to it that no one should have the power to slay or the good Fortune to save Cato. Drawing the sword—which he had kept unstained from all bloodshed against the final day, he cried: "Fortune, you have accomplished nothing by resisting all my endeavors. I have fought, till now, for my country's freedom, and not for my own; I did not strive so doggedly to be free, but only to live among the free. Now, since the affairs of mankind are beyond hope, let Cato be withdrawn to safety." So saying, he inflicted a mortal wound upon his body. After the physicians had bound it up, Cato had less blood and less strength, but no less courage; angered now not only at Caesar but also at himself, he rallied his unarmed hands against his wound, and expelled, rather than dismissed, that noble soul which had been so defiant of all worldly power.

I am not now heaping up these illustrations for the purpose of exercising my wit, but for the purpose of encouraging you to face that which is thought to be most terrible. And I shall encourage you all the more easily by showing that not only resolute men have despised that moment when the soul breathes its last, but that certain persons, who were craven in other respects, have equaled in this regard the courage of the bravest. Take, for example, Scipio, the father-in-law of Gnaeus Pompeius: he was driven back upon the African coast by a head-wind and saw his ship in the power of the enemy. He therefore pierced his body with a sword; and when they asked where the commander was, he replied: "All is well with the commander." These words brought him up to the level of his ancestors and suffered not the glory which fate gave to the Scipios in Africa to lose its continuity. It was a great deed to conquer Carthage, but a greater deed to conquer death. "All is well with the commander!" Ought a general to die otherwise, especially one of Cato's generals? I shall not refer you to history, or collect examples of those men who throughout the ages have despised death; for they are very many. Consider these times of ours, whose enervation and over-refinement call forth our complaints; they nevertheless will include men of every rank, of every lot in life, and of every age, who have cut short their misfortunes by death.

Believe me, Lucilius; death is so little to be feared that through its good offices nothing is to be feared. Therefore, when your enemy threatens, listen unconcernedly. Although your conscience makes you confident, yet, since many things have weight which are outside your case, both hope for that which is utterly just, and prepare yourself against that which is utterly unjust. Remember, however, before all else, to strip things of all that disturbs and confuses, and to see what each is at bottom; you will then comprehend that they contain nothing fearful except the actual fear. That you see happening to boys happens also to ourselves, who are only slightly bigger boys: when those whom they love, with whom they daily associate, with whom they play, appear with masks on, the boys are frightened out of their wits. We should strip the mask, not only from men, but from things, and restore to each object its own aspect.

"Why dost your hold up before my eyes swords, fires, and a throng of executioners raging about thee? Take away all that vain show, behind which your lurkest and scarest fools! Ah! your art naught but Death, whom only yesterday a manservant of mine and a maidservant did despise! Why dost your again unfold and spread before me, with all that great display, the whip and the rack? Why are those engines of torture made ready, one for each several member of the body, and all the other innumerable machines for tearing a man apart piecemeal? Away with all such stuff, which makes us numb with terror! And your, silence the groans, the cries, and the bitter shrieks ground out of the victim as he is torn on the rack! Forsooth thou are naught but Pain, scorned by yonder gout-ridden wretch, endured by yonder dyspeptic in the midst of his dainties, borne bravely by the girl in travail. Slight your art, if I can bear thee; short your art if I cannot bear thee!"

Death is so little to be feared that through its good offices nothing is to be feared

Ponder these words which you have often heard and often uttered. Moreover, prove by the result whether that which you have heard and uttered is true. For there is a very disgraceful charge often brought against our school—that we deal with the words, and not with the deeds, of philosophy.

What, have you only at this moment learned that death is hanging over your head, at this moment exile, at this moment grief? You were born to these perils. Let us think of everything that can happen as something which will happen. I know that you have really done what I advise you to do; I now warn you not to drown your soul in these petty anxieties of yours; if you do, the soul will be dulled and will have too little vigor left when the time comes for it to arise. Remove the mind from this case of yours to the case of men in general. Say to yourself that our petty bodies are mortal and frail; pain can reach them from other sources than from wrong or the might of the stronger. Our pleasures themselves become torments; banquets bring indigestion, carousals paralysis of the muscles and palsy, sensual habits affect the feet, the hands, and every joint of the body.

I may become a poor man; I shall then be one among many. I may be exiled; I shall then regard myself as born in the place to which I shall be sent. They may put me in chains. What then? Am I free from bonds now? Behold this clogging burden of a body, to which nature has fettered me! "I shall die," you say; you mean to say "I shall cease to run the risk of sickness; I shall cease to run the risk of imprisonment; I shall cease to run the risk of death." I am not so foolish as to go through at this juncture the arguments which Epicurus harps upon, and say that the terrors of the world below are idle—that Ixion does not whirl round on his wheel, that Sisyphus does not shoulder his stone uphill, that a man's entrails cannot be restored and devoured every day; no one is so childish as to fear Cerberus, or the shadows, or the spectral garb of those who are held together by naught but their unfleshed bones. Death either annihilates us or strips us bare. If we are then released, there remains the better part, after the burden has been withdrawn; if we are annihilated, nothing remains; good and bad are alike removed.

Allow me at this point to quote a verse of yours, first suggesting that, when you wrote it, you meant it for yourself no less than for others. It is ignoble to say one thing and mean another; and how much more ignoble to write one thing and mean another! I remember one day you were handling the well-known commonplace—that we do not suddenly fall on death, but advance toward it by slight degrees; we die every day. For every day a little of our life is taken from us; even when we are growing, our life is on the wane. We lose our childhood, then our boyhood, and then our youth. Counting even yesterday, all past time is lost time; the very day which we are now spending is shared between ourselves and death. It is not the last drop that empties the water-clock, but all that which previously has flowed out; similarly, the final hour when we cease to exist does not of itself bring death; it merely of itself completes the death process. We reach death at that moment, but we have been a long time on the way. In describing this situation, you said in your customary style (for you are always impressive, but never more pungent than when you are putting the truth in appropriate words):

> Not single is the death which comes; the death
> Which takes us off is but the last of all.

I prefer that you should read your own words rather than my letter; for then it will be clear to you that this death, of which we are afraid, is the last but not the only death. I see what you are looking for; you are asking what I have packed into my letter, what inspiriting saying from some master-mind, what useful precept. So I shall send you something dealing with this very subject which has been under discussion. Epicurus upbraids those who crave, as much as those who shrink from, death: "It is absurd," he says, "to run toward death

We reach death at that moment, but we have been a long time on the way

because you are tired of life, when it is your manner of life that has made you run toward death." And in another passage: "What is so absurd as to seek death, when it is through fear of death that you have robbed your life of peace?" And you may add a third statement, of the same stamp: "Men are so thoughtless, nay, so mad, that some, through fear of death, force themselves to die."

Whichever of these ideas you ponder, you will strengthen your mind for the endurance alike of death and of life. For we need to be warned and strengthened in both directions—not to love or to hate life overmuch; even when reason advises us to make an end of it, the impulse is not to be adopted without reflection or at headlong speed. The grave and wise man should not beat a hasty retreat from life; he should make a becoming exit. And above all, he should avoid the weakness which has taken possession of so many—the lust for death. For just as there is an unreflecting tendency of the mind toward other things, so, my dear Lucilius, there is an unreflecting tendency toward death; this often seizes upon the noblest and most spirited men, as well as upon the craven and the abject. The former despise life; the latter find it irksome.

Others also are moved by a satiety of doing and seeing the same things, and not so much by a hatred of life as because they are cloyed with it. We slip into this condition, while philosophy itself pushes us on, and we say; "How long must I endure the same things? Shall I continue to wake and sleep, be hungry and be cloyed, shiver and perspire? There is an end to nothing; all things are connected in a sort of circle; they flee and they are pursued. Night is close at the heels of day, day at the heels of night; summer ends in autumn, winter rushes after autumn, and winter softens into spring; all nature in this way passes, only to return. I do nothing new; I see nothing new; sooner or later one sickens of this, also." There are many who think that living is not painful, but superfluous. Farewell.

XXVI. ON OLD AGE
AND DEATH

———

I WAS JUST LATELY TELLING YOU THAT I WAS WITHIN SIGHT OF OLD age. I am now afraid that I have left old age behind me. For some other word would now apply to my years, or at any rate to my body; since old age means a time of life that is weary rather than crushed. You may rate me in the worn-out class—of those who are nearing the end.

Nevertheless, I offer thanks to myself, with you as witness; for I feel that age has done no damage to my mind, though I feel its effects on my constitution. Only my vices, and the outward aids to these vices, have reached senility; my mind is strong and rejoices that it has but slight connexion with the body. It has laid aside the greater part of its load. It is alert; it takes issue with me on the subject of old age; it declares that old age is its time of bloom. Let me take it at its word, and let it make the most of the advantages it possesses. The mind bids me do some thinking and consider how much of this peace of spirit and moderation of character I owe to wisdom and how much to my time of life; it bids me distinguish carefully what I cannot do and what I do not want to do... For why should one complain or regard it as a disadvantage, if powers which ought to come to an end have failed? "But," you say, "it is the greatest possible disadvantage to be worn out and to die off, or rather, if I may speak literally, to melt away! For we are not suddenly smitten and laid low; we are worn away, and every day reduces our powers to a certain extent."

But is there any better end to it all than to glide off to one's proper haven, when nature slips the cable? Not that there is anything painful in a shock and a sudden departure from existence; it is merely because this other way of departure is easy—a gradual withdrawal. I, at any rate, as if the test were at hand and the day were come which is to pronounce its decision concerning all the years of my life, watch over myself and commune thus with myself: "The showing which we have made up to the present time, in word or deed, counts for nothing. All this is but a trifling and deceitful pledge of our spirit, and is wrapped in much charlatanism. I shall leave it to Death to determine what progress I have made. Therefore with no faint heart I am making ready for the day when, putting aside all stage artifice and actor's rouge, I am to pass judgment upon myself—whether I am merely declaiming brave sentiments, or whether I really feel them; whether all the bold threats I have uttered against Fortune are a pretense and a farce. Put aside the opinion of the world; it is always wavering and always takes both sides. Put aside the studies which you have pursued throughout your life; Death will deliver the final judgment in your case. This is what I mean: your debates and learned talks, your maxims gathered from the teachings of the wise, your cultured conversation—all these afford no proof of the real strength of your soul. Even the most timid man can deliver a bold speech. What you have done in the past will be manifest only at the time when you draw your last breath. I accept the terms; I do not shrink from the decision." This is what I say to myself, but I would have you think that I have said it to you also. You are younger; but what does that matter? There is no fixed count of our years. You do not know where death awaits you; so be ready for it everywhere.

You do not know where death awaits you; so be ready for it everywhere

I was just intending to stop, and my hand was making ready for the closing sentence; but the rites are still to be performed and the traveling money for the letter disbursed. And just assume that I am not telling where I intend to borrow the necessary sum; you know upon whose coffers I depend. Wait for me but a moment, and I will pay you from my own account; meanwhile, Epicurus will oblige me with these words: "Think on death," or rather, if you prefer the phrase, on "migration to heaven." The meaning is clear—that it is a wonderful thing to learn thoroughly how to die. You may deem it superfluous to learn a text that can be used only once; but that is just the reason why we ought to think on a thing. When we can never prove whether we really know a thing, we must always be learning it. "Think on death." In saying this, he bids us think on freedom. He who has learned to die has unlearned slavery; he is above any external power, or, at any rate, he is beyond it. What terrors have prisons and bonds and bars for him? His way out is clear. There is only one chain which binds us to life, and that is the love of life. The chain may not be cast off, but it may be rubbed away, so that, when necessity shall demand, nothing may retard or hinder us from being ready to do at once that which at some time we are bound to do. Farewell.

XXVIII. ON TRAVEL
AS A CURE FOR
DISCONTENT

———

D O YOU SUPPOSE THAT YOU ALONE HAVE HAD THIS EXPERIENCE? Are you surprised, as if it were a novelty, that after such long travel and so many changes of scene you have not been able to shake off the gloom and heaviness of your mind? You need a change of soul rather than a change of climate. Though you may cross vast spaces of sea, and though, as our Vergil remarks, "Lands and cities are left astern," your faults will follow you wherever you travel. Socrates made the same remark to one who complained; he said: "Why do you wonder that globe-trotting does not help you, seeing that you always take yourself with you? The reason which set you wandering is ever at your heels." What pleasure is there in seeing new lands? Or in surveying cities and spots of interest? All your bustle is useless. Do you ask why such flight does not help you? It is because you flee along with yourself. You must lay aside the burdens of the mind; until you do this, no place will satisfy you. Reflect that your present behavior is like that of the prophetess whom Vergil describes: she is excited and goaded into fury, and contains within herself much inspiration that is not her own:

The priestess raves, if haply she may shake
The great god from her heart.

You wander hither and yon, to rid yourself of the burden that rests upon you, though it becomes more troublesome by reason of your very restlessness, just as in a ship the cargo when stationary makes no trouble, but when it shifts to this side or that, it causes the vessel to heel more quickly in the direction where it has settled. Anything you do tells against you, and you hurt yourself by your very unrest; for you are shaking up a sick man.

That trouble once removed, all change of scene will become pleasant; though you may be driven to the uttermost ends of the earth, in whatever corner of a savage land you may find yourself, that place, however forbidding, will be to you a hospitable abode. The person you are matters more than the place to which you go; for that reason we should not make the mind a bondsman to any one place. Live in this belief: "I am not born for any one corner of the universe; this whole world is my country." If you saw this fact clearly, you would not be surprised at getting no benefit from the fresh scenes to which you roam each time through weariness of the old scenes. For the first would have pleased you in each case, had you believed it wholly yours. As it is, however, you are not journeying; you are drifting and being driven, only exchanging one place for another, although that which you seek—to live well—is found everywhere. Can there be any spot so full of confusion as the Forum? Yet you can live quietly even there, if necessary. Of course, if one were allowed to make one's own arrangements, I should flee far from the very sight and neighborhood of the Forum. For just as pestilential places assail even the strongest constitution, so there are some places which are also unwholesome for a healthy mind which is not yet quite sound, though recovering from its ailment. I disagree with those who strike out into the midst of the billows and, welcoming a stormy existence, wrestle daily in hardihood of soul with life's problems. The wise man will endure

The person you are matters more than the place to which you go

all that, but will not choose it; he will prefer to be at peace rather than at war. It helps little to have cast out your own faults if you must quarrel with those of others. Says one: "There were thirty tyrants surrounding Socrates, and yet they could not break his spirit"; but what does it matter how many masters a man has? "Slavery" has no plural; and he who has scorned it is free—no matter amid how large a mob of over-lords he stands.

It is time to stop, but not before I have paid duty. "The knowledge of sin is the beginning of salvation." This saying of Epicurus seems to me to be a noble one. For he who does not know that he has sinned does not desire correction; you must discover yourself in the wrong before you can reform yourself. Some boast of their faults. Do you think that the man has any thought of mending his ways who counts over his vices as if they were virtues? Therefore, as far as possible, prove yourself guilty, hunt up charges against yourself; play the part, first of accuser, then of judge, last of intercessor. At times be harsh with yourself. Farewell.

XXXI. ON SIREN SONGS

—

Now I recognize my Lucilius! He is beginning to reveal the character of which he gave promise. Follow up the impulse which prompted you to make for all that is best, treading under your feet that which is approved by the crowd. I would not have you greater or better than you planned; for in your case the mere foundations have covered a large extent of ground; only finish all that you have laid out, and take in hand the plans which you have had in mind. In short, you will be a wise man, if you stop up your ears; nor is it enough to close them with wax; you need a denser stopple than that which they say Ulysses used for his comrades. The song which he feared was alluring, but came not from every side; the song, however, which you have to fear, echoes round you not from a single headland, but from every quarter of the world. Sail, therefore, not past one region which you mistrust because of its treacherous delights, but past every city. Be deaf to those who love you most of all; they pray for bad things with good intentions. And, if you would be happy, entreat the gods that none of their fond desires for you may be brought to pass. What they wish to have heaped upon you are not really good things; there is only one good, the cause and the support of a happy life—trust in oneself. But this cannot be attained, unless one has learned to despise toil and to reckon it among the things which are neither good nor bad. For it is not possible that a single thing should be bad at one time and good at another, at times light and to be endured, and at times a cause of dread. Work is not a good.

Then what is a good? I say, the scorning of work. That is why I should rebuke men who toil to no purpose. But when, on the other hand, a man is struggling toward honorable things, in proportion as he applies himself more and more, and allows himself less and less to be beaten or to halt, I shall recommend his conduct and shout my encouragement, saying: "By so much you are better! Rise, draw a fresh breath, and surmount that hill, if possible, at a single spurt!"

Work is the sustenance of noble minds. There is, then, no reason why, in accordance with that old vow of your parents, you should pick and choose what Fortune you wish should fall to your lot, or what you should pray for; besides, it is base for a man who has already travelled the whole round of highest honors to be still importuning the gods. What need is there of vows? Make yourself happy through your own efforts; you can do this, if once you comprehend that whatever is blended with virtue is good, and that whatever is joined to vice is bad. Just as nothing gleams if it has no light blended with it, and nothing is black unless it contains darkness or draws to itself something of dimness, and as nothing is hot without the aid of fire, and nothing cold without air; so it is the association of virtue and vice that makes things honorable or base.

What then is good? The knowledge of things. What is evil? The lack of knowledge of things

What then is good? The knowledge of things. What is evil? The lack of knowledge of things. Your wise man, who is also a craftsman, will reject or choose in each case as it suits the occasion; but he does not fear that which he rejects, nor does he admire that which he chooses, if only he has a stout and unconquerable soul. I forbid you to be cast down or depressed. It is not enough if you do not shrink from work; ask for it. "But," you say, "is not trifling and superfluous work, and work that has been inspired by ignoble causes, a bad sort of work?" No; no more than that which is expended upon noble endeavors, since the very quality that endures toil and rouses itself to hard and uphill effort, is of the spirit, which says: "Why do you grow slack? It is not the part of a man to fear sweat." And besides this, in order that virtue may be perfect, there should be an even temperament and a scheme of life that is consistent with itself throughout; and this result cannot be attained without knowledge of things, and without the art which enables us to understand things human and things divine. That is the greatest good. If you seize this good, you begin to be the associate of the gods, and not their suppliant.

"But how," you ask, "does one attain that goal?" You do not need to cross the Pennine or Graian hills, or traverse the Candavian waste, or face the Syrtes, or Scylla, or Charybdis, although you have traveled through all these places for the bribe of a petty governorship; the journey for which nature has equipped you is safe and pleasant. She has given you such gifts that you may, if you do not prove false to them, rise level with God. Your money, however, will not place you on a level with God; for God has no property. Your bordered robe will not do this; for God is not clad in raiment; nor will your reputation, nor a display of self, nor a knowledge of your name wide-spread throughout the world; for no one has knowledge of God; many even hold him in low esteem, and do not suffer for so doing. The throng of slaves which carries your litter along the city streets and in foreign places will not help you; for this God of whom I speak, though the highest and most powerful of beings, carries all things on his own shoulders. Neither can beauty or strength make you blessed, for none of these qualities can withstand old age.

What we have to seek for, then, is that which does not each day pass more and more under the control of some power which cannot be withstood. And what is this? It is the soul—but the soul that is upright, good, and great. What else could you call such a soul than a god dwelling as a guest in a human body? A soul like this may descend into a Roman knight just as well as into a freedman's son or a slave. For what is a Roman knight, or a freedman's son, or a slave? They are mere titles, born of ambition or of wrong. One may leap to heaven from the very slums. Only rise

And mold yourself to kinship with your God.

This molding will not be done in gold or silver; an image that is to be in the likeness of God cannot be fashioned of such materials; remember that the gods, when they were kind unto men, were molded in clay. Farewell.

XXXVI. ON THE VALUE OF RETIREMENT

———

ENCOURAGE YOUR FRIEND TO DESPISE STOUT-HEARTEDLY THOSE who upbraid him because he has sought the shade of retirement and has abdicated his career of honors, and, though he might have attained more, has preferred tranquility to them all. Let him prove daily to these detractors how wisely he has looked out for his own interests. Those whom men envy will continue to march past him; some will be pushed out of the ranks, and others will fall. Prosperity is a turbulent thing; it torments itself. It stirs the brain in more ways than one, goading men on to various aims—some to power, and others to high living. Some it puffs up; others it slackens and wholly enervates.

"But," the retort comes, "so-and-so carries his prosperity well." Yes; just as he carries his liquor. So you need not let this class of men persuade you that one who is besieged by the crowd is happy; they run to him as crowds rush for a pool of water, rendering it muddy while they drain it. But you say: "Men call our friend a trifler and a sluggard." There are men, you know, whose speech is awry, who use the contrary terms. They called him happy; what of it? Was he happy? Even the fact that to certain persons he seems a man of a very rough and gloomy cast of mind, does not trouble me. Aristo used to say that he preferred a youth of stern disposition to one who was a jolly fellow and agreeable to the crowd. "For," he added, "wine which, when new, seemed harsh and sour, becomes good wine; but that which

185

tasted well at the vintage cannot stand age." So let them call him stern and a foe to his own advancement, it is just this sternness that will go well when it is aged, provided only that he continues to cherish virtue and to absorb thoroughly the studies which make for culture—not those with which it is sufficient for a man to sprinkle himself, but those in which the mind should be steeped. Now is the time to learn. "What? Is there any time when a man should not learn?" By no means; but just as it is creditable for every age to study, so it is not creditable for every age to be instructed. An old man learning his A B C is a disgraceful and absurd object; the young man must store up, the old man must use. You will therefore be doing a thing most helpful to yourself if you make this friend of yours as good a man as possible; those kindnesses, they tell us, are to be both sought for and bestowed, which benefit the giver no less than the receiver; and they are unquestionably the best kind.

Finally, he has no longer any freedom in the matter; he has pledged his word. And it is less disgraceful to compound with a creditor than to compound with a promising future. To pay his debt of money, the business man must have a prosperous voyage, the farmer must have fruitful fields and kindly weather; but the debt which your friend owes can be completely paid by mere goodwill. Fortune has no jurisdiction over character. Let him so regulate his character that in perfect peace he may bring to perfection that spirit within him which feels neither loss nor gain, but remains in the same attitude, no matter how things fall out. A spirit like this, if it is heaped with worldly goods, rises superior to its wealth; if, on the other hand, chance has stripped him of a part of his wealth, or even all, it is not impaired.

Fortune has no jurisdiction over character

If your friend had been born in Parthia, he would have begun, when a child, to bend the bow; if in Germany, he would forthwith have been brandishing his slender spear; if he had been born in the days of our forefathers, he would have learned to ride a horse and smite his enemy hand to hand. These are the occupations which the system of each race recommends to the individual—yes, prescribes for him. To what, then, shall this friend of yours devote his attention? I say, let him learn that which is helpful against all weapons, against every kind of foe—contempt of death; because no one doubts that death has in it something that inspires terror, so that it shocks even our souls, which nature has so molded that they love their own existence; for otherwise there would be no need to prepare ourselves, and to whet our courage, to face that toward which we should move with a sort of voluntary instinct, precisely as all men tend to preserve their existence. No man learns a thing in order that, if necessity arises, he may lie down with composure upon a bed of roses; but he steels his courage to this end, that he may not surrender his plighted faith to torture, and that, if need be, he may some day stay out his watch in the trenches, even though wounded, without even leaning on his spear; because sleep is likely to creep over men who support themselves by any prop whatsoever.

In death there is nothing harmful; for there must exist something to which it is harmful. And yet, if you are possessed by so great a craving for a longer life, reflect that none of the objects which vanish from our gaze and are re-absorbed into the world of things, from which they have come forth and are soon to come forth again, is annihilated; they merely end their course and do not perish. And death, which we fear and shrink from, merely interrupts life, but does not steal it away; the time will return when we shall be restored to the light of day; and many men would object to this, were they not brought back in forgetfulness of the past.

But I mean to show you later, with more care, that everything which seems to perish merely changes. Since you are destined to return, you ought to depart with a tranquil mind. Mark how the round of the universe repeats its course; you will see that no star in our firmament is extinguished, but that they all set and rise in alternation. Summer has gone, but another year will bring it again; winter lies low, but will be restored by its own proper months; night has overwhelmed the sun, but day will soon rout the night again. The wandering stars retrace their former courses; a part of the sky is rising unceasingly, and a part is sinking. One word more, and then I shall stop; infants, and boys, and those who have gone mad, have no fear of death, and it is most shameful if reason cannot afford us that peace of mind to which they have been brought by their folly. Farewell.

XXXVIII. ON QUIET CONVERSATION

———

YOU ARE RIGHT WHEN YOU URGE THAT WE INCREASE OUR MUTUAL traffic in letters. But the greatest benefit is to be derived from conversation, because it creeps by degrees into the soul. Lectures prepared beforehand and spouted in the presence of a throng have in them more noise but less intimacy. Philosophy is good advice; and no one can give advice at the top of his lungs. Of course we must sometimes also make use of these harangues, if I may so call them, when a doubting member needs to be spurred on; but when the aim is to make a man learn and not merely to make him wish to learn, we must have recourse to the low-toned words of conversation. They enter more easily, and stick in the memory; for we do not need many words, but, rather, effective words.

Words should be scattered like seed; no matter how small the seed may be, if it has once found favorable ground, it unfolds its strength and from an insignificant thing spreads to its greatest growth. Reason grows in the same way; it is not large to the outward view, but increases as it does its work. Few words are spoken; but if the mind has

Philosophy is good advice; and no one can give advice at the top of his lungs

189

truly caught them, they come into their strength and spring up. Yes, precepts and seeds have the same quality; they produce much, and yet they are slight things. Only, as I said, let a favorable mind receive and assimilate them. Then of itself the mind also will produce bounteously in its turn, giving back more than it has received. Farewell.

XLII. ON VALUES

HAS THAT FRIEND OF YOURS ALREADY MADE YOU BELIEVE THAT HE is a good man? And yet it is impossible in so short a time for one either to become good or be known as such. Do you know what kind of man I now mean when I speak of "a good man"? I mean one of the second grade, like your friend. For one of the first class perhaps springs into existence, like the phoenix, only once in five hundred years. And it is not surprising, either, that greatness develops only at long intervals; Fortune often brings into being commonplace powers, which are born to please the mob; but she holds up for our approval that which is extraordinary by the very fact that she makes it rare.

This man, however, of whom you spoke, is still far from the state which he professes to have reached. And if he knew what it meant to be "a good man," he would not yet believe himself such; perhaps he would even despair of his ability to become good. "But," you say, "he thinks ill of evil men." Well, so do evil men themselves; and there is no worse penalty for vice than the fact that it is dissatisfied with itself and all its fellows. "But he hates those who make an ungoverned use of great power suddenly acquired." I retort that he will do the same thing as soon as he acquires the same powers. In the case of many men, their vices, being powerless, escape notice; although, as soon as the persons in question have become satisfied with their own strength, the vices will be no less daring than those which prosperity has already disclosed. These men simply lack the means whereby they may unfold their wickedness. Similarly, one can handle even a poison-ous snake while it is stiff with cold; the poison is not lacking; it is merely numbed into inaction. In the case of many men, their cruelty, ambition, and indulgence only lack the favor of Fortune to make them dare crimes that would match the worst. That their wishes are the same you will in a moment discover, in this way: give them the power equal to their wishes.

Do you remember how, when you declared that a certain person was under your influence, I pronounced him fickle and a bird of passage, and said that you held him not by the foot but merely by a wing? Was I mis-taken? You grasped him only by a feather; he left it in your hands and escaped. You know what an exhibition he afterward made of himself before you, how many of the things he attempted were to recoil upon his own head. He did not see that in endangering others he was tottering to his own downfall. He did not reflect how burdensome were the objects which he was bent upon attaining, even if they were not superfluous.

Therefore, with regard to the objects which we pursue, and for which we strive with great effort, we should note this truth; either there is noth-ing desirable in them, or the undesirable is preponderant. Some objects are superfluous; others are not worth the price we pay for them. But we do not see this clearly, and we regard things as free gifts when they really cost us very dear. Our stupidity may be clearly proved by the fact that we hold that "buying" refers only to the objects for which we pay cash, and we regard as free gifts the things for which we spend our very selves. These we should refuse to buy, if we were compelled to give in payment for them our houses or some attractive and profitable estate; but we are eager to attain them at the cost of anxiety, of danger, and of lost honor, personal freedom, and time; so true it is that each man regards noth-ing as cheaper than himself.

Man regards nothing as cheaper than himself

Let us therefore act, in all our plans and conduct, just as we are accustomed to act whenever we approach a huckster who has certain wares for sale; let us see how much we must pay for that which we crave. Very often the things that cost nothing cost us the most heavily; I can show you many objects the quest and acquisition of which have wrested freedom from our hands. We should belong to ourselves, if only these things did not belong to us.

I would therefore have you reflect thus, not only when it is a question of gain, but also when it is a question of loss. "This object is bound to perish." Yes, it was a mere extra; you will live without it just as easily as you have lived before. If you have possessed it for a long time, you lose it after you have had your fill of it; if you have not possessed it long, then you lose it before you have become wedded to it. "You will have less money." Yes, and less trouble. "Less influence." Yes, and less envy. Look about you and note the things that drive us mad, which we lose with a flood of tears; you will perceive that it is not the loss that troubles us with reference to these things, but a notion of loss. No one feels that they have been lost, but his mind tells him that it has been so. He that owns himself has lost nothing. But how few men are blessed with ownership of self! Farewell.

XLIII. ON THE RELATIVITY OF FAME

———

DO YOU ASK HOW THE NEWS REACHED ME, AND WHO INFORMED me, that you were entertaining this idea, of which you had said nothing to a single soul? It was that most knowing of persons—gossip. "What," you say, "am I such a great personage that I can stir up gossip?" Now there is no reason why you should measure yourself according to this part of the world; have regard only to the place where you are dwelling. Any point which rises above adjacent points is great, at the spot where it rises. For greatness is not absolute; comparison increases it or lessens it. A ship which looms large in the river seems tiny when on the ocean. A rudder which is large for one vessel, is small for another.

> For greatness is not absolute; comparison increases it or lessens it. A ship which looms large in the river seems tiny when on the ocean

So you in your province are really of importance, though you scorn yourself. Men are asking what you do, how you dine, and how you sleep, and they find out, too; hence there is all the more reason for your living circumspectly. Do not, however, deem yourself truly happy until you find that you can live before men's eyes, until your walls protect but do not hide you; although we are apt to believe that these walls surround us, not to enable us to live more safely, but that we may sin more secretly. I shall mention a fact by which you may weigh the worth of a man's character: you will scarcely find anyone who can live with his door wide open. It is our conscience, not our pride, that has put doorkeepers at our doors; we live in such a fashion that being suddenly disclosed to view is equivalent to being caught in the act. What profits it, however, to hide ourselves away, and to avoid the eyes and ears of men? A good conscience welcomes the crowd, but a bad conscience, even in solitude, is disturbed and troubled. If your deeds are honorable, let everybody know them; if base, what matters is that no one knows them, as long as you yourself know them? How wretched you are if you despise such a witness! Farewell.

XLIX. ON THE SHORT-NESS OF LIFE

———

A MAN IS INDEED LAZY AND CARELESS, MY DEAR LUCILIUS, IF HE IS reminded of a friend only by seeing some landscape which stirs the memory; and yet there are times when the old familiar haunts stir up a sense of loss that has been stored away in the soul, not bringing back dead memories, but rousing them from their dormant state, just as the sight of a lost friend's favorite slave, or his cloak, or his house, renews the mourner's grief, even though it has been softened by time.

Now, lo and behold, Campania, and especially Naples and your beloved Pompeii, struck me, when I viewed them, with a wonderfully fresh sense of longing for you. You stand in full view before my eyes. I am on the point of parting from you. I see you choking down your tears and resisting without success the emotions that well up at the very moment when you try to check them. I seem to have lost you but a moment ago. For what is not "but a moment ago" when one begins to use the memory? It was but a moment ago that I sat, as a lad, in the school of the philosopher Sotion, but a moment ago that I began to plead in the courts, but a moment ago that I lost the desire to plead, but a moment ago that I lost the ability. Infinitely swift is the flight of time, as those see more clearly who are looking backward. For when we are intent on the present, we do not notice it, so gentle is the passage of time's headlong flight. Do you ask the reason for this? All past time is in the same place; it all presents the same aspect to us, it lies together. Everything slips into the same abyss. Besides, an event which in its entirety is of brief compass cannot contain long intervals. The time which we spend in living is but a point, nay, even less than a point. But this point of time, infinitesimal as it is, nature has mocked by making it seem outwardly of longer duration; she has taken one portion thereof and made it infancy, another childhood, another youth, another the gradual slope, so to speak, from youth to old age, and old age itself is still another. How many steps for how short a climb! It was but a moment ago that I saw you off on your journey; and yet this "moment ago" makes up a goodly share of our existence, which is so brief, we should reflect, that it will soon come to an end altogether. In other years time did not seem to me to go so swiftly; now, it seems fast beyond belief, perhaps, because I feel that the finish line is moving closer to me, or it may be that I have begun to take heed and reckon up my losses.

For this reason I am all the more angry that some men claim the major portion of this time for superfluous things—time which, no matter how carefully it is guarded, cannot suffice even for necessary things. Cicero declared that if the number of his days were doubled, he should not have time to read the lyric poets. And you may rate the dialecticians in the same class; but they are foolish in a more melancholy way. The lyric poets are avowedly frivolous; but the dialecticians believe that they are themselves engaged upon serious business. I do not deny that one must cast a glance at dialectic; but it ought to be a mere glance, a sort of greeting from the threshold, merely that one may not be deceived, or judge these pursuits to contain any hidden matters of great worth.

Why do you torment yourself and lose weight over some problem which it is more clever to have scorned than to solve? When a soldier is undisturbed and traveling at his ease, he can hunt for trifles along his way; but when the enemy is closing in on the rear, and a command is given to quicken the pace, necessity makes him throw away everything which he picked up in moments of peace and leisure. I have no time to investigate disputed inflections of words, or to try my cunning upon them.

Behold the gathering clans, the fast-shut gates,
And weapons whetted ready for the war.

I need a stout heart to hear without flinching this din of battle which
sounds round about. And all would rightly think me mad if, when gray-
beards and women were heaping up rocks for the fortifications, when the
armor-clad youths inside the gates were awaiting, or even demanding, the
order for a sally, when the spears of the foemen were quivering in our gates
and the very ground was rocking with mines and subterranean passages—I
say, they would rightly think me mad if I were to sit idle, putting such
petty posers as this: "What you have not lost, you have. But you have not
lost any horns. Therefore, you have horns," or other tricks constructed after
the model of this piece of sheer silliness. And yet I may well seem in your
eyes no less mad, if I spend my energies on that sort of thing; for even now I
am in a state of siege. And yet, in the former case it would be merely a peril
from the outside that threatened me, and a wall that sundered me from
the foe; as it is now, death-dealing perils are in my very presence. I have no
time for such nonsense; a mighty undertaking is on my hands. What am I
to do? Death is on my trail, and life is fleeting away; teach me something
with which to face these troubles. Bring it to pass that I shall cease trying
to escape from death, and that life may cease to escape from me. Give me
courage to meet hardships; make me calm in the face of the unavoidable.
Relax the straitened limits of the time which is allotted me. Show me that
the good in life does not depend upon life's length, but upon the use we
make of it; also, that it is possible, or rather usual, for a man who has lived
long to have lived too little. Say to me when I lie down to sleep: "You may
not wake again!" And when I have waked: "You may not go to sleep again!"
Say to me when I go forth from my house: "You may not return!" And
when I return: "You may never go forth again!" You are mistaken if you
think that only on an ocean voyage there is a very slight space between life
and death. No, the distance between is just as narrow everywhere. It is not
everywhere that death shows himself so near at hand; yet everywhere he is
as near at hand.

Rid me of these shadowy terrors; then you will more easily deliver to me the instruction for which I have prepared myself. At our birth nature made us teachable, and gave us reason, not perfect, but capable of being perfected. Discuss for me justice, duty, thrift, and that twofold purity, both the purity which abstains from another's person, and that which takes care of one's own self. If you will only refuse to lead me along by-paths, I shall more easily reach the goal at which I am aiming. For, as the tragic poet says:

The language of truth is simple.

We should not, therefore, make that language intricate; since there is nothing less fitting for a soul of great endeavor than such crafty cleverness. Farewell.

LI. ON BAIAE
AND MORALS

———

EVERY MAN DOES THE BEST HE CAN, MY DEAR LUCILIUS! YOU OVER there have Etna, that lofty and most celebrated mountain of Sicily; (although I cannot make out why Messala—or was it Valgius? for I have been reading in both—has called it "unique," inasmuch as many regions belch forth fire, not merely the lofty ones where the phenomenon is more frequent—presumably because fire rises to the greatest possible height— but low-lying places also.) As for myself, I do the best I can; I have had to be satisfied with Baiae; and I left it the day after I reached it; for Baiae is a place to be avoided, because, though it has certain natural advantages, luxury has claimed it for her own exclusive resort. "What then," you say, "should any place be singled out as an object of aversion?" Not at all. But just as, to the wise and upright man, one style of clothing is more suitable than another, without his having an aversion for any particular color, but because he thinks that some colors do not befit one who has adopted the simple life; so there are places also, which the wise man or he who is on the way toward wisdom will avoid as foreign to good morals. Therefore, if he is contemplating withdrawal from the world, he will not select Canopus (although Canopus does not keep any man from living simply), nor Baiae either; for both places have begun to be resorts of vice. At Canopus luxury pampers itself to the utmost degree; at Baiae it is even more lax, as if the place itself demanded a certain amount of license.

We ought to select abodes which are wholesome not only for the body but also for the character. Just as I do not care to live in a place of torture, neither do I care to live in a cafe. To witness persons wandering drunk along the beach, the riotous reveling of sailing parties, the lakes a-din with choral song, and all the other ways in which luxury, when it is, so to speak, released from the restraints of law not merely sins, but blazons its sins abroad—why must I witness all this? We ought to see to it that we flee to the greatest possible distance from provocations to vice. We should toughen our minds, and remove them far from the allurements of pleasure. A single winter relaxed Hannibal's fiber; his pampering in Campania took the vigor out of that hero who had triumphed over Alpine snows. He conquered with his weapons, but was conquered by his vices. We too have a war to wage, a type of warfare in which there is allowed no rest or furlough. To be conquered, in the first place, are pleasures, which, as you see, have carried off even the sternest characters. If a man has once understood how great is the task which he has entered upon, he will see that there must be no dainty or effeminate conduct.

What have I to do with those hot baths or with the sweating-room where they shut in the dry steam which is to drain your strength? Perspiration should flow only after toil.

We ought to select abodes which are wholesome not only for the body but also for the character

Suppose we do what Hannibal did—check the course of events, give up the war, and give over our bodies to be coddled. Everyone would rightly blame us for our untimely sloth, a thing fraught with peril even for the victor, to say nothing of one who is only on the way to victory. And we have even less right to do this than those followers of the Carthaginian flag; for our danger is greater than theirs if we slacken, and our toil is greater than theirs even if we press ahead. Fortune is fighting against me, and I shall not carry out her commands. I refuse to submit to the yoke; nay rather, I shake off the yoke that is upon me—an act which demands even greater courage. The soul is not to be pampered; surrendering to pleasure means also surrendering to pain, surrendering to toil, surrendering to poverty. Both ambition and anger will wish to have the same rights over me as pleasure, and I shall be torn asunder, or rather pulled to pieces, amid all these conflicting passions. I have set freedom before my eyes; and I am striving for that reward. And what is freedom, you ask? It means not being a slave to any circumstance, to any constraint, to any chance; it means compelling Fortune to enter the lists on equal terms. And on the day when I know that I have the upper hand, her power will be naught. When I have death in my own control, shall I take orders from her?

Therefore, a man occupied with such reflections should choose an austere and pure dwelling place. The spirit is weakened by surroundings that are too pleasant, and without a doubt one's place of residence can contribute toward impairing its vigour. Animals whose hoofs are hardened on rough ground can travel any road; but when they are fattened on soft marshy meadows their hoofs are soon worn out. The bravest soldier comes from rock-ribbed regions; but the town-bred and the home-bred are sluggish in action. The hand which turns from the plough to the sword never objects to toil; but your sleek and well-dressed dandy quails at the first cloud of dust. Being trained in a rugged country strengthens the character and fits it for great undertakings. It was more honorable in Scipio to spend his exile at Liternum, than at Baiae; his downfall did not need a setting so effeminate. Those also into whose hands the rising fortunes of Rome first transferred the wealth of the state, Gaius Marius, Gnaeus Pompey, and Caesar, did indeed build villas near Baiae; but they set them on the very tops of the mountains. This seemed more soldier-like, to look down from a lofty height upon lands spread far and wide below. Note the situation, position, and type of building which they chose; you will see that they were not country places—they were camps. Do you suppose that Cato would ever have dwelt in a pleasure-palace, that he might count the lewd women as they sailed past, the many kinds of barges painted in all sorts of colors, the roses which were wafted about the lake, or that he might listen to the nocturnal brawls of serenaders? Would he not have preferred to remain in the shelter of a trench thrown up by his own hands to serve for a single night? Would not anyone who is a man have his slumbers broken by a war-trumpet rather than by a chorus of serenaders?

But I have been haranguing against Baiae long enough; although I never could harangue often enough against vice. Vice, Lucilius, is what I wish you to proceed against, without limit and without end. For it has neither limit nor end. If any vice rend your heart, cast it away from you; and if you cannot be rid of it in any other way, pluck out your heart also. Above all, drive pleasures from your sight. Hate them beyond all other things, for they are like the bandits whom the Egyptians call "lovers," who embrace us only to garrote us. Farewell.

LVI. ON QUIET AND STUDY

BESHREW ME IF I THINK ANYTHING MORE REQUISITE THAN SILENCE for a man who secludes himself in order to study! Imagine what a variety of noises reverberates about my ears! I have lodgings right over a bathing establishment. So picture to yourself the assortment of sounds, which are strong enough to make me hate my very powers of hearing! When your strenuous gentleman, for example, is exercising himself by flourishing leaden weights; when he is working hard, or else pretends to be working hard, I can hear him grunt; and whenever he releases his imprisoned breath, I can hear him panting in wheezy and high-pitched tones. Or perhaps I notice some lazy fellow, content with a cheap rubdown, and hear the crack of the pummeling hand on his shoulder, varying in sound according as the hand is laid on flat or hollow. Then, perhaps, a professional comes along, shouting out the score; that is the finishing touch. Add to this the arresting of an occasional roisterer or pickpocket, the racket of the man who always likes to hear his own voice in the bathroom, or the enthusiast who plunges into the swimming-tank with unconscionable noise and splashing. Besides all those whose voices, if nothing else, are good, imagine the hair-plucker with his penetrating, shrill voice—for purposes of advertisement—continually giving it vent and never holding his tongue except when he is plucking the armpits and making his victim yell instead. Then the cakeseller with his varied cries, the sausageman, the confectioner, and all the vendors of food hawking their wares, each with his own distinctive intonation.

So you say: "What iron nerves or deadened ears, you must have, if your mind can hold out amid so many noises, so various and so discordant, when our friend Chrysippus is brought to his death by the continual good-morrows that greet him!" But I assure you that this racket means no more to me than the sound of waves or falling water; although you will remind me that a certain tribe once moved their city merely because they could not endure the din of a Nile cataract. Words seem to distract me more than noises; for words demand attention, but noises merely fill the ears and beat upon them. Among the sounds that din round me without distracting, I include passing carriages, a machinist in the same block, a saw-sharpener nearby, or some fellow who is demonstrating with little pipes and flutes at the Trickling Fountain, shouting rather than singing.

Furthermore, an intermittent noise upsets me more than a steady one. But by this time I have toughened my nerves against all that sort of thing, so that I can endure even a boatswain marking the time in high-pitched tones for his crew. For I force my mind to concentrate, and keep it from straying to things outside itself; all outdoors may be bedlam, provided that there is no disturbance within, provided that fear is not wrangling with desire in my breast, provided that meanness and lavishness are not at odds, one harassing the other. For of what benefit is a quiet neighborhood, if our emotions are in an uproar?

'Twas night, and all the world was lulled to rest.

This is not true; for no real rest can be found when reason has not done the lulling. Night brings our troubles to the light, rather than banishes them; it merely changes the form of our worries. For even when we seek slumber, our sleepless moments are as harassing as the daytime. Real tranquility is the state reached by an unperverted mind when it is relaxed. Think of the unfortunate man who courts sleep by surrendering his spacious mansion to silence, who, that his ear may be disturbed by no sound, bids the whole retinue of his slaves be quiet and that whoever approaches him shall walk on tiptoe; he tosses from this side to that and seeks a fitful slumber amid his frettings! He complains that he has heard sounds, when he has not heard them at all. The reason, you ask? His soul's in an uproar; it must be soothed, and its rebellious murmuring checked. You need not suppose that the soul is at peace when the body is still. Sometimes quiet means disquiet.

> You need not suppose that the soul is at peace when the body is still. Sometimes quiet means disquiet

We must therefore rouse ourselves to action and busy ourselves with interests that are good, as often as we are in the grasp of an uncontrollable sluggishness. Great generals, when they see that their men are mutinous, check them by some sort of labor or keep them busy with small forays. The much occupied man has no time for wantonness, and it is an obvious commonplace that the evils of leisure can be shaken off by hard work. Although people may often have thought that I sought seclusion because I was disgusted with politics and regretted my hapless and thankless position, yet, in the retreat to which apprehension and weariness have driven me, my ambition sometimes develops afresh. For it is not because my ambition was rooted out that it has abated, but because it was wearied or perhaps even put out of temper by the failure of its plans. And so with luxury, also, which sometimes seems to have departed, and then when we have made a profession of frugality, begins to fret us and, amid our economies, seeks the pleasures which we have merely left but not condemned. Indeed, the more stealthily it comes, the greater is its force. For all unconcealed vices are less serious; a disease also is farther on the road to being cured when it breaks forth from concealment and manifests its power. So with greed, ambition, and the other evils of the mind—you may be sure that they do most harm when they are hidden behind a pretense of soundness.

Men think that we are in retirement, and yet we are not. For if we have sincerely retired, and have sounded the signal for retreat, and have scorned outward attractions, then, as I remarked above, no outward thing will distract us; no music of men or of birds can interrupt good thoughts, when they have once become steadfast and sure. The mind which starts at words or at chance sounds is unstable and has not yet withdrawn into itself; it contains within itself an element of anxiety and rooted fear, and this makes one a prey to care, as our Vergil says:

I, whom of yore no dart could cause to flee,
Nor Greeks, with crowded lines of infantry,
Now shake at every sound, and fear the air,
Both for my child and for the load I bear.

This man in his first state is wise; he blenches neither at the brandished spear, nor at the clashing armor of the serried foe, nor at the din of the stricken city. This man in his second state lacks knowledge fearing for his own concerns, he pales at every sound; any cry is taken for the battle-shout and overthrows him; the slightest disturbance renders him breathless with fear. It is the load that makes him afraid. Select anyone you please from among your favorites of Fortune, trailing their many responsibilities, carrying their many burdens, and you will behold a picture of Vergil's hero, "fearing both for his child and for the load he bears."

You may therefore be sure that you are at peace with yourself, when no noise readies you, when no word shakes you out of yourself, whether it be of flattery or of threat, or merely an empty sound buzzing about you with unmeaning din. "What then?" you say, "is it not sometimes a simpler matter just to avoid the uproar?" I admit this. Accordingly, I shall change from my present quarters. I merely wished to test myself and to give myself practice. Why need I be tormented any longer, when Ulysses found so simple a cure for his comrades even against the songs of the Sirens? Farewell.

LVII. ON THE TRIALS
OF TRAVEL

———

WHEN IT WAS TIME FOR ME TO RETURN TO NAPLES FROM BAIAE, I easily persuaded myself that a storm was raging, that I might avoid another trip by sea; and yet the road was so deep in mud, all the way, that I may be thought none the less to have made a voyage. On that day I had to endure the full fate of an athlete; the anointing with which we began was followed by the sand-sprinkle in the Naples tunnel. No place could be longer than that prison; nothing could be dimmer than those torches, which enabled us, not to see amid the darkness, but to see the darkness. But, even supposing that there was light in the place, the dust, which is an oppressive and disagreeable thing even in the open air, would destroy the light; how much worse the dust is there, where it rolls back upon itself, and, being shut in without ventilation, blows back in the faces of those who set it going! So we endured two inconveniences at the same time, and they were diametrically different: we struggled both with mud and with dust on the same road and on the same day.

The gloom, however, furnished me with some food for thought; I felt a certain mental thrill, and a transformation unaccompanied by fear, due to the novelty and the unpleasantness of an unusual occurrence. Of course I am not speaking to you of myself at this point, because I am far from being a perfect person, or even a man of middling qualities; I refer to one over

208

whom Fortune has lost her control. Even such a man's mind will be smitten with a thrill and he will change color. For there are certain emotions, my dear Lucilius, which no courage can avoid; nature reminds courage how perishable a thing it is. And so he will contract his brow when the prospect is forbidding, will shudder at sudden apparitions, and will become dizzy when he stands at the edge of a high precipice and looks down. This is not fear; it is a natural feeling which reason cannot rout. That is why certain brave men, most willing to shed their own blood, cannot bear to see the blood of others. Some persons collapse and faint at the sight of a freshly inflicted wound; others are affected similarly on handling or viewing an old wound which is festering. And others meet the sword-stroke more readily than they see it dealt.

Accordingly, as I said, I experienced a certain transformation, though it could not be called confusion. Then at the first glimpse of restored daylight my good spirits returned without forethought or command. And I began to muse and think how foolish we are to fear certain objects to a greater or less degree, since all of them end in the same way. For what difference does it make whether a watchtower or a mountain crashes down upon us? No difference at all, you will find. Nevertheless, there will be some men who fear the latter mishap to a greater degree, though both accidents are equally deadly; so true it is that fear looks not to the effect, but to the cause of the effect. Do you suppose that I am now referring to the Stoics, who hold that the soul of a man crushed by a great weight cannot abide, and is scattered forthwith, because it has not had a free opportunity to depart? That is not what I am doing; those who think thus are, in my opinion, wrong. Just as fire cannot be crushed out, since it will escape round the edges of the body which overwhelms it; just as the air cannot be damaged by lashes and blows, or even cut into, but flows back about the object to which it gives place; similarly the soul, which consists of the subtlest particles, cannot be arrested or destroyed inside the body, but, by virtue of its delicate substance, it will rather escape through the very object by which it is being crushed. Just as lightning, no matter how widely it strikes and flashes, makes its return through a narrow opening, so the soul, which is still subtler than fire, has a way of escape through any part of the body. We therefore come to this question—whether the soul can be immortal. But be sure of this: if the soul survives the body after the body is crushed, the soul can in no wise be crushed out, precisely because it does not perish; for the rule of immortality never admits of exceptions, and nothing can harm that which is everlasting. Farewell.

LIX. ON PLEASURE
AND JOY

—

I RECEIVED GREAT PLEASURE FROM YOUR LETTER; KINDLY ALLOW ME to use these words in their everyday meaning, without insisting upon their Stoic import. For we Stoics hold that pleasure is a vice. Very likely it is a vice; but we are accustomed to use the word when we wish to indicate a happy state of mind. I am aware that if we test words by our formula, even pleasure is a thing of ill repute, and joy can be attained only by the wise. For "joy" is an elation of spirit, of a spirit which trusts in the goodness and truth of its own possessions. The common usage, however, is that we derive great "joy" from a friend's position as consul, or from his marriage, or from the birth of his child; but these events, so far from being matters of joy, are more often the beginnings of sorrow to come. No, it is a characteristic of real joy that it never ceases, and never changes into its opposite.

Accordingly, when our Vergil speaks of

The evil joys of the mind,

his words are eloquent, but not strictly appropriate. For no "joy" can be evil. He has given the name "joy" to pleasures, and has thus expressed his meaning. For he has conveyed the idea that men take delight in their own evil. Nevertheless, I was not wrong in saying that I received great "plea-sure" from your letter; for although an ignorant man may derive "joy" if the cause be an honorable one, yet, since his emotion is wayward, and is likely soon to take another direction, I call it "pleasure"; for it is inspired by an opinion concerning a spurious good; it exceeds control and is carried to excess.

But, to return to the subject, let me tell you what delighted me in your letter. You have your words under control. You are not carried away by your language, or borne beyond the limits which you have determined upon. Many writers are tempted by the charm of some alluring phrase to some topic other than that which they had set themselves to discuss. But this has not been so in your case; all your words are compact, and suited to the subject. You say all that you wish, and you mean still more than you say. This is a proof of the importance of your subject matter, showing that your mind, as well as your words, contains nothing superfluous or bombastic.

I do, however, find some metaphors, not, indeed, daring ones, but the kind which have stood the test of use. I find similes also; of course, if anyone forbids us to use them, maintaining that poets alone have that privilege, he has not, apparently, read any of our ancient prose writers, who had not yet learned to affect a style that should win applause. For those writers, whose eloquence was simple and directed only toward proving their case, are full of comparisons; and I think that these are necessary, not for the same reason which makes them necessary for the poets, but in order that they may serve as props to our feebleness, to bring both speaker and listener face to face with the subject under discussion. For example, I am at this very moment reading Sextius; he is a keen man, and a philosopher who, though he writes in Greek, has the Roman standard of ethics. One of his similes appealed especially to me, that of an army marching in hollow square, in a place where the enemy might be expected to appear from any quarter, ready for battle. "This," said he, "is just what the wise man ought to do; he should have all his fighting qualities deployed on every side, so that wherever the attack threatens, there his supports may be ready to hand and may obey the captain's command without confusion." This is what we notice in armies which serve under great leaders; we see how all the troops simultaneously understand their general's orders, since they are so arranged that a signal given by one man passes down the ranks of cavalry and infantry at the same moment. This, he declares, is still more necessary for men like ourselves; for soldiers have often feared an enemy without reason, and the march which they thought most dangerous has in fact been most secure; but folly brings no repose, fear haunts it both in the van and in the rear of the column, and both flanks are in a panic. Folly is pursued, and confronted, by peril. It blenches at everything; it is unprepared; it is frightened even by auxiliary troops. But the wise man is fortified against all inroads; he is alert; he will not retreat before the attack of poverty, or of sorrow, or of disgrace, or of pain. He will walk undaunted both against them and among them.

We human beings are fettered and weakened by many vices; we have wallowed in them for a long time and it is hard for us to be cleansed. We are not merely defiled; we are dyed by them. But, to refrain from passing from one figure to another, I will raise this question, which I often consider in my own heart: why is it that folly holds us with such an insistent grasp? It is, primarily, because we do not combat it strongly enough, because we do not struggle toward salvation with all our might; secondly, because we do not put sufficient trust in the discoveries of the wise, and do not drink in their words with open hearts; we approach this great problem in too trifling a spirit. But how can a man learn, in the struggle against his vices, an amount that is enough, if the time which he gives to learning is only the amount left over from his vices? None of us goes deep below the surface. We skim the top only, and we regard the smattering of time spent in the search for wisdom as enough to spare for a busy man. What hinders us most of all is that we are too readily satisfied with ourselves; if we meet with someone who calls us good men, or sensible men, or holy men, we see ourselves in his description, not content with praise in moderation, we accept everything that shameless flattery heaps upon us, as if it were our due. We agree with those who declare us to be the best and wisest of men, although we know that they are given to much lying. And we are so self-complacent that we desire praise for certain actions when we are especially addicted to the very opposite. Yonder person hears himself called "most gentle" when he is inflicting tortures, or "most generous" when he is engaged in looting, or "most temperate" when he is in the midst of drunkenness and lust. Thus it follows that we are unwilling to be reformed, just because we believe ourselves to be the best of men.

Alexander was roaming as far as India, ravaging tribes that were but little known, even to their neighbors. During the blockade of a certain city, while he was reconnoitering the walls and hunting for the weakest spot in the fortifications, he was wounded by an arrow. Nevertheless, he long continued the siege, intent on finishing what he had begun. The pain of his wound, however, as the surface became dry and as the flow of blood was checked, increased; his leg gradually became numb as he sat his horse; and finally, when he was forced to withdraw, he exclaimed: "All men swear that I am the son of Jupiter, but this wound cries out that I am mortal." Let us also act in the same way. Each man, according to his lot in life, is stultified by flattery. We should say to him who flatters us: "You call me a man of sense, but I understand how many of the things which I crave are useless, and how many of the things which I desire will do me harm. I have not even the knowledge, which satiety teaches to animals, of what should be the measure of my food or my drink. I do not yet know how much I can hold."

I shall now show you how you may know that you are not wise. The wise man is joyful, happy and calm, unshaken, he lives on a plane with the gods. Now go, question yourself; if you are never downcast, if your mind is not harassed by my apprehension, through anticipation of what is to come, if day and night your soul keeps on its even and unswerving course, upright and content with itself, then you have attained to the greatest good that mortals can possess. If, however, you seek pleasures of all kinds in all directions, you must know that you are as far short of wisdom as you are short of joy. Joy is the goal which you desire to reach, but you are wandering from the path, if you expect to reach your goal while you are in the midst of riches and official titles—in other words, if you seek joy in the midst of cares, these objects for which you strive so eagerly, as if they would give you happiness and pleasure, are merely causes of grief.

All men of this stamp, I maintain, are pressing on in pursuit of joy, but they do not know where they may obtain a joy that is both great and enduring. One person seeks it in feasting and self-indulgence; another, in canvassing for honors and in being surrounded by a throng of clients; another, in his mistress; another, in idle display of culture and in literature that has no power to heal; all these men are led astray by delights which are deceptive and short-lived—like drunkenness for example, which pays for a single hour of hilarious madness by a sickness of many days, or like applause and the popularity of enthusiastic approval which are gained, and atoned for, at the cost of great mental disquietude.

Reflect, therefore, on this, that the effect of wisdom is a joy that is unbroken and continuous. The mind of the wise man is like the ultra-lunar firmament; eternal calm pervades that region. You have, then, a reason for wishing to be wise, if the wise man is never deprived

The effect of wisdom is a joy that is unbroken and continuous

of joy. This joy springs only from the knowledge that you possess the virtues. None but the brave, the just, the self-restrained, can rejoice. And when you query: "What do you mean? Do not the foolish and the wicked also rejoice?" I reply, no more than lions who have caught their prey. When men have wearied themselves with wine and lust, when night fails them before their debauch is done, when the pleasures which they have heaped upon a body that is too small to hold them begin to fester, at such times they utter in their wretchedness those lines of Vergil:

Your knowest how, amid false-glittering joys,
We spent that last of nights.

Pleasure-lovers spend every night amid false-glittering joys, and just as if it were their last. But the joy which comes to the gods, and to those who imitate the gods, is not broken off, nor does it cease; but it would surely cease were it borrowed from without. Just because it is not in the power of another to bestow, neither is it subject to another's whims. That which Fortune has not given, she cannot take away. Farewell.

LXI. ON MEETING DEATH CHEERFULLY

———

LET US CEASE TO DESIRE THAT WHICH WE HAVE BEEN DESIRING. I, at least, am doing this: in my old age I have ceased to desire what I desired when a boy. To this single end my days and my nights are passed; this is my task, this the object of my thoughts—to put an end to my chronic ills. I am endeavoring to live every day as if it were a complete life. I do not indeed snatch it up as if it were my last; I do regard it, however, as if it might even be my last. The present letter is written to you with this in mind as if death were about to call me away in the very act of writing. I am ready to depart, and I shall enjoy life just because I am not over-anxious as to the future date of my departure.

Before I became old I tried to live well; now that I am old, I shall try to die well; but dying well means dying gladly. See to it that you never do anything unwillingly. That which is bound to be a necessity if you rebel, is not a necessity if you desire it. This is what I mean: he who takes his orders gladly, escapes the bitterest part of slavery—doing what one does not want to do. The man who does something under orders is not unhappy; he is unhappy who does something against his will. Let us therefore so set our minds in order that we may desire whatever is demanded

Dying well means dying gladly

217

of us by circumstances, and above all that we may reflect upon our end without sadness. We must make ready for death before we make ready for life. Life is well enough furnished, but we are too greedy with regard to its furnishings; something always seems to us lacking, and will always seem lacking. To have lived long enough depends neither upon our years nor upon our days, but upon our minds. I have lived, my dear friend Lucilius, long enough. I have had my fill; I await death. Farewell.

LXIII. ON GRIEF FOR LOST FRIENDS

I AM GRIEVED TO HEAR THAT YOUR FRIEND FLACCUS IS DEAD, BUT I would not have you sorrow more than is fitting. That you should not mourn at all I shall hardly dare to insist; and yet I know that it is the better way. But what man will ever be so blessed with that ideal steadfastness of soul, unless he has already risen far above the reach of Fortune? Even such a man will be stung by an event like this, but it will be only a sting. We, however, may be forgiven for bursting into tears, if only our tears have not flowed to excess, and if we have checked them by our own efforts. Let not the eyes be dry when we have lost a friend, nor let them overflow. We may weep, but we must not wail.

Do you think that the law which I lay down for you is harsh, when the greatest of Greek poets has extended the privilege of weeping to one day only, in the lines where he tells us that even Niobe took thought of food? Do you wish to know the reason for lamentations and excessive weeping? It is because we seek the proofs of our bereavement in our tears, and do not give way to sorrow, but merely parade it. No man goes into mourning for his own sake. Shame on our ill-timed folly! There is an element of self-seeking even in our sorrow.

"What," you say, "am I to forget my friend?" It is surely a short-lived memory that you vouchsafe to him, if it is to endure only as long as your grief; presently that brow of yours will be smoothed out in laughter by some circumstance, however casual. It is to a time no more distant than this that I put off the soothing of every regret, the quieting of even the bitterest grief. As soon as you cease to observe yourself, the picture of sorrow which you have contemplated will fade away; at present you are keeping watch over your own suffering. But even while you keep watch it slips away from you, and the sharper it is, the more speedily it comes to an end.

Let us see to it that the recollection of those whom we have lost becomes a pleasant memory to us. No man reverts with pleasure to any subject which he will not be able to reflect upon without pain. So too it cannot but be that the names of those whom we have loved and lost come back to us with a sort of sting; but there is a pleasure even in this sting. For, as my friend Attalus used to say: "The remembrance of lost friends is pleasant in the same way that certain fruits have an agreeably acid taste, or as in extremely old wines it is their very bitterness that pleases us. Indeed, after a certain lapse of time, every thought that gave pain is quenched, and the pleasure comes to us unalloyed." If we take the word of Attalus for it, "to think of friends who are alive and well is like enjoying a meal of cakes and honey; the recollection of friends who have passed away gives a pleasure that is not without a touch of bitterness. Yet who will deny that even these things, which are bitter and contain an element of sourness, do serve to arouse the stomach?" For my part, I do not agree with him. To me, the thought of my dead friends is sweet and appealing. For I have had them as if I should one day lose them; I have lost them as if I have them still.

Therefore, Lucilius, act as befits your own serenity of mind, and cease to put a wrong interpretation on the gifts of Fortune. Fortune has taken away, but Fortune has given. Let us greedily enjoy our friends, because we do not know how long this privilege will be ours. Let us think how often we shall leave them when we go upon distant journeys, and how often we shall fail to see them when we tarry together in the same place; we shall thus understand that we have lost too much of their time while they were alive. But will you tolerate men who are most careless of their friends, and then mourn them most abjectly, and do not love anyone unless they have lost him? The reason why they lament too unrestrainedly at such times is that they are afraid lest men doubt whether they really have loved; all too late they seek for proofs of their emotions. If we have other friends, we surely deserve ill at their hands and think ill of them, if they are of so little account that they fail to console us for the loss of one. If, on the other hand, we have no other friends, we have injured ourselves more than Fortune has injured us; since Fortune has robbed us of one friend, but we have robbed ourselves of every friend whom we have failed to make. Again, he who has been unable to love more than one, has had none too much love even for that one. If a man who has lost his one and only tunic through robbery chooses to bewail his plight rather than look about him for some way to escape the cold, or for something with which to cover his shoulders, would you not think him an utter fool?

You have buried one whom you loved; look about for someone to love. It is better to replace your friend than to weep for him. What I am about to add is, I know, a very hackneyed remark, but I shall not omit it simply because it is a common phrase: a man ends his grief by the mere passing of time, even if he has not ended it of his own accord. But the most shameful cure for sorrow, in the case of a sensible man, is to grow weary of sorrowing. I should prefer you to abandon grief, rather than have grief abandon you; and you should stop grieving as soon as possible, since, even if you wish to do so, it is impossible to keep it up for a long time. Our forefathers have enacted that, in the case of women, a year should be the limit for mourning; not that they needed to mourn for so long, but that they should mourn no longer. In the case of men, no rules are laid down, because to mourn at all is not regarded as honorable. For all that, what woman can you show me, of all the pathetic females that could scarcely be dragged away from the funeral-pile or torn from the corpse, whose tears have lasted a whole month? Nothing becomes offensive so quickly as grief; when fresh, it finds someone to console it and attracts one or another to itself; but after becoming chronic, it is ridiculed, and rightly. For it is either assumed or foolish.

He who writes these words to you is no other than I, who wept so excessively for my dear friend Annaeus Serenus that, in spite of my wishes,

I must be included among the examples of men who have been overcome by grief. Today, however, I condemn this act of mine, and I understand that the reason why I lamented so greatly was chiefly that I had never imagined it possible for his death to precede mine. The only thought which occurred to my mind was that he was the younger, and much younger, too—as if the Fates kept to the order of our ages!

Therefore let us continually think as much about our own mortality as about that of all those we love. In former days I ought to have said: "My friend Serenus is younger than I; but what does that matter? He would naturally die after me, but he may precede me." It was just because I did not do this that I was unprepared when Fortune dealt me the sudden blow. Now is the time for you to reflect, not only that all things are mortal, but also that their mortality is subject to no fixed law. Whatever can happen at any time can happen today. Let us therefore reflect, my beloved Lucilius, that we shall soon come to the goal which this friend, to our own sorrow, has reached. And perhaps, if only the tale told by wise men is true and there is a bourne to welcome us, then he whom we think we have lost has only been sent on ahead. Farewell.

LXVII. ON ILL-HEALTH
AND ENDURANCE
OF SUFFERING

———

I F I MAY BEGIN WITH A COMMONPLACE REMARK, SPRING IS GRADU-
ally disclosing itself; but though it is rounding into summer, when you
would expect hot weather, it has kept rather cool, and one cannot yet be
sure of it. For it often slides back into winter weather. Do you wish to know
how uncertain it still is? I do not yet trust myself to a bath which is absolutely cold; even at this time I break its chill. You may say that this is no
way to show the endurance either of heat or of cold; very true, dear Lucilius, but at my time of life one is at length contented with the natural chill
of the body. I can scarcely thaw out in the middle of summer. Accordingly,
I spend most of the time bundled up; and I thank old age for keeping me
fastened to my bed. Why should I not thank old age on this account? That
which I ought not to wish to do, I lack the ability to do. Most of my converse is with books. Whenever your letters arrive, I imagine that I am with
you, and I have the feeling that I am about to speak my answer, instead of
writing it. Therefore let us together investigate the nature of this problem
of yours, just as if we were conversing with one another.

You ask me whether every good is desirable. You say: "If it is a good
to be brave under torture, to go to the stake with a stout heart, to endure
illness with resignation, it follows that these things are desirable. But I do

not see that any of them is worth praying for. At any rate I have as yet known of no man who has paid a vow by reason of having been cut to pieces by the rod, or twisted out of shape by the gout, or made taller by the rack." My dear Lucilius, you must distinguish between these cases; you will then comprehend that there is something in them that is to be desired. I should prefer to be free from torture; but if the time comes when it must be endured, I shall desire that I may conduct myself therein with bravery, honor, and courage. Of course I prefer that war should not occur; but if war does occur, I shall desire that I may nobly endure the wounds, the starvation, and all that the exigency of war brings. Nor am I so mad as to crave illness; but if I must suffer illness, I shall desire that I may do nothing which shows lack of restraint, and nothing that is unmanly. The conclusion is, not that hardships are desirable, but that virtue is desirable, which enables us patiently to endure hardships.

> The conclusion is, not that hardships are desirable, but that virtue is desirable, which enables us patiently to endure hardships

Certain of our school think that, of all such qualities, a stout endurance is not desirable—though not to be deprecated either—because we ought to seek by prayer only the good which is unalloyed, peaceful, and beyond the reach of trouble. Personally, I do not agree with them. And why? First, because it is impossible for anything to be good without being also desirable. Because, again, if virtue is desirable, and if nothing that is good lacks virtue, then everything good is desirable. And, lastly, because a brave endurance even under torture is desirable. At this point I ask you: is not bravery desirable? And yet bravery despises and challenges danger. The most beautiful and most admirable part of bravery is that it does not shrink from the stake, advances to meet wounds, and sometimes does not even avoid the spear, but meets it with opposing breast. If bravery is desirable, so is patient endurance of torture; for this is a part of bravery. Only sift these things, as I have suggested; then there will be nothing which can lead you astray. For it is not mere endurance of torture, but brave endurance, that is desirable. I therefore desire that "brave" endurance; and this is virtue.

"But," you say, "whoever desired such a thing for himself?" Some prayers are open and outspoken, when the requests are offered specifically; other prayers are indirectly expressed, when they include many requests under one title. For example, I desire a life of honor. Now a life of honor includes various kinds of conduct; it may include the chest in which Regulus was confined, or the wound of Cato which was torn open by Cato's own hand, or the exile of Rutilius, or the cup of poison which removed Socrates from gaol to heaven. Accordingly, in praying for a life of honor, I have prayed also for those things without which, on some occasions, life cannot be honorable

> O thrice and four times blest were they
> Who underneath the lofty walls of Troy
> Met happy death before their parents' eyes!

What does it matter whether you offer this prayer for some individual, or admit that it was desirable in the past? Decius sacrificed himself for the State; he set spurs to his horse and rushed into the midst of the foe, seeking death. The second Decius, rivalling his father's valor, reproducing the words which had become sacred and already household words, dashed into the thickest of the fight, anxious only that his sacrifice might bring omen of success, and regarding a noble death as a thing to be desired. Do you doubt, then, whether it is best to die glorious and performing some deed of valor? When one endures torture bravely, one is using all the virtues. Endurance may perhaps be the only virtue that is on view and most manifest; but bravery is there too, and endurance and resignation and long-suffering are its branches. There, too, is foresight; for without foresight no plan can be undertaken; it is foresight that advises one to bear as bravely as possible the things one cannot avoid. There also is steadfastness, which cannot be dislodged from its position, which the wrench of no force can cause to abandon its purpose. There is the whole inseparable company of virtues; every honorable act is the work of one single virtue, but it is in accordance with the judgment of the whole council. And that which is approved by all the virtues, even though it seems to be the work of one alone, is desirable.

What? Do you think that those things only are desirable which come to us amid pleasure and ease, and which we bedeck our doors to welcome? There are certain goods whose features are forbidding. There are certain prayers which are offered by a throng, not of men who rejoice, but of men who bow down reverently and worship. Was it not in this fashion, think you, that Regulus prayed that he might reach Carthage? Clothe yourself with a hero's courage, and withdraw for a little space from the opinions of the common man. Form a proper conception of the image of virtue, a thing of exceeding beauty and grandeur; this image is not to be worshipped by us with incense or garlands, but with sweat and blood. Behold Marcus Cato, laying upon that hallowed breast his unspotted hands, and tearing apart the wounds which had not gone deep enough to kill him! Which, pray, shall you say to him: "I hope all will be as you wish," and "I am grieved," or shall it be "Good Fortune in your undertaking!"?

In this connection I think of our friend Demetrius, who calls an easy existence, untroubled by the attacks of Fortune, a "Dead Sea." If you have nothing to stir you up and rouse you to action, nothing which will test your resolution by its threats and hostilities; if you recline in unshaken comfort, it is not tranquility; it is merely a flat calm. The Stoic Attalus was wont to say: "I should prefer that Fortune keep me in her camp rather than in the lap of luxury. If I am tortured, but bear it bravely, all is well; if I die, but die bravely, it is also well." Listen to Epicurus; he will tell you that it is actually pleasant. I myself shall never apply an effeminate word to an act so honorable and austere. If I go to the stake, I shall go unbeaten. Why should I not regard this as desirable—not because the fire burns me, but because it does not overcome me? Nothing is more excellent or more beautiful than virtue; whatever we do in obedience to her orders is both good and desirable. Farewell.

LXVIII. ON WISDOM
AND RETIREMENT

I FALL IN WITH YOUR PLAN; RETIRE AND CONCEAL YOURSELF IN repose. But at the same time conceal your retirement also. In doing this, you may be sure that you will be following the example of the Stoics, if not their precept. But you will be acting according to their precept also; you will thus satisfy both yourself and any Stoic you please. We Stoics do not urge men to take up public life in every case, or at all times, or without any qualification. Besides, when we have assigned to our wise man that field of public life which is worthy of him—in other words, the universe— he is then not apart from public life, even if he withdraws; nay, perhaps he has abandoned only one little corner thereof and has passed over into greater and wider regions; and when he has been set in the heavens, he understands how lowly was the place in which he sat when he mounted the curule chair or the judgment-seat. Lay this to heart, that the wise man is never more active in affairs than when things divine as well as things human have come within his ken.

I now return to the advice which I set out to give you—that you keep your retirement in the background. There is no need to fasten a placard upon yourself with the words: "Philosopher and Quietist." Give your purpose some other name; call it ill-health and bodily weakness, or mere laziness. To boast of our retirement is but idle self-seeking. Certain animals hide themselves from discovery by confusing the marks of their foot-prints in the neighborhood of their lairs. You should do the same. Otherwise, there will always be someone dogging your footsteps. Many men pass by that which is visible, and peer after things hidden and concealed; a locked room invites the thief. Things which lie in the open appear cheap; the house-breaker passes by that which is exposed to view. This is the way of the world, and the way of all ignorant men: they crave to burst in upon hidden things. It is therefore best not to vaunt one's retirement. It is, however, a sort of vaunting to make too much of one's concealment and of one's withdrawal from the sight of men. So-and-so has gone into his retreat at Tarentum; that other man has shut himself up at Naples; this third person for many years has not crossed the threshold of his own house. To advertise one's retirement is to collect a crowd. When you withdraw from the world your business is to talk with yourself, not to have men talk about you. But what shall you talk about? Do just what people are fond of doing when they talk about their neighbors—speak ill of yourself when by yourself; then you will become accustomed both to speak and to hear the truth. Above all, however, ponder that which you come to feel is your greatest weakness. Each man knows best the defects of his own body. And so one relieves his stomach by vomiting, another props it up by frequent eating, another drains and purges his body by periodic fasting. Those whose feet are visited by pain abstain either from wine or from the bath. In general, men who are careless in other respects go out of their way to relieve the disease which frequently afflicts them. So it is with our souls; there are in them certain parts which are, so to speak, on the sick-list, and to these parts the cure must be applied.

What, then, am I myself doing with my leisure? I am trying to cure my own sores. If I were to show you a swollen foot, or an inflamed hand, or some shriveled sinews in a withered leg, you would permit me to lie quiet in one place and to apply lotions to the diseased member. But my trouble is greater than any of these, and I cannot show it to you. The abscess, or ulcer, is deep within my breast. Pray, pray, do not commend me, do not say: "What a great man! He has learned to despise all things; condemning the madnesses of man's life, he has made his escape!" I have condemned nothing except myself. There is no reason why you should desire to come to me for the sake of making progress. You are mistaken if you think that you will get any assistance from this quarter; it is not a physician that dwells here, but a sick man. I would rather have you say, on leaving my presence: "I used to think him a happy man and a learned one, and I had pricked up my ears to hear him; but I have been defrauded. I have seen nothing, heard nothing which I craved and which I came back to hear." If you feel thus, and speak thus, some progress has been made. I prefer you to pardon rather than envy my retirement.

Then you say: "Is it retirement, Seneca, that you are recommending to me? You will soon be falling back upon the maxims of Epicurus!" I do recommend retirement to you, but only that you may use it for greater and more beautiful activities than those which you have resigned; to knock at the haughty doors of the influential, to make alphabetical lists of childless old men, to wield the highest authority in public life—this kind of power exposes you to hatred, is short-lived, and, if you rate it at its true value, is tawdry. One man shall be far ahead of me as regards his influence in public life, another in salary as an army officer and in the position which results from this, another in the throng of his clients; but it is worthwhile to be outdone by all these men, provided that I myself can outdo Fortune. And I am no match for her in the throng; she has the greater backing.

Would that in earlier days you had been minded to follow this purpose! Would that we were not discussing the happy life in plain view of death! But even now let us have no delay. For now we can take the word of experience, which tells us that there are many superfluous and hostile things; for this we should long since have taken the word of reason. Let us do what men are wont to do when they are late in setting forth, and wish to make up for lost time by increasing their speed—let us ply the spur. Our time of life is the best possible for these pursuits; for the period of boiling and foaming is now past. The faults that were uncontrolled in the first fierce heat of youth are now weakened, and but little further effort is needed to extinguish them.

"And when," you ask, "will that profit you which you do not learn until your departure, and how will it profit you?" Precisely in this way, that I shall depart a better man. You need not think, however, that any time of life is more fitted to the attainment of a sound mind than that which has gained the victory over itself by many trials and by long and oft-repeated regret for past mistakes, and, its passions assuaged, has reached a state of health. This is indeed the time to have acquired this good; he who has attained wisdom in his old age, has attained it by his years. Farewell.

LXXI. ON THE SUPREME GOOD

————

You are continually referring special questions to me, forgetting that a vast stretch of sea sunders us. Since, however, the value of advice depends mostly on the time when it is given, it must necessarily result that by the time my opinion on certain matters reaches you, the opposite opinion is the better. For advice conforms to circumstances; and our circumstances are carried along, or rather whirled along. Accordingly, advice should be produced at short notice; and even this is too late; it should "grow while we work," as the saying is. And I propose to show you how you may discover the method.

When a man does not know what harbor he is making for, no wind is the right wind

As often as you wish to know what is to be avoided or what is to be sought, consider its relation to the Supreme Good, to the purpose of your whole life. For whatever we do ought to be in harmony with this; no man can set in order the details unless he has already set before himself the chief purpose of his life. The artist may have his colors all prepared, but he cannot produce a likeness unless

232

he has already made up his mind what he wishes to paint. The reason we make mistakes is because we all consider the parts of life, but never life as a whole. The archer must know what he is seeking to hit; then he must aim and control the weapon by his skill. Our plans miscarry because they have no aim. When a man does not know what harbor he is making for, no wind is the right wind. Chance must necessarily have great influence over our lives, because we live by chance. It is the case with certain men, however, that they do not know that they know certain things. Just as we often go searching for those who stand beside us, so we are apt to forget that the goal of the Supreme Good lies near us.

To infer the nature of this Supreme Good, one does not need many words or any round-about discussion; it should be pointed out with the forefinger, so to speak, and not be dissipated into many parts. For what good is there in breaking it up into tiny bits, when you can say: the Supreme Good is that which is honorable? Besides (and you may be still more surprised at this), that which is honorable is the only good; all other goods are alloyed and debased. If you once convince yourself of this, and if you come to love virtue devotedly (for mere loving is not enough), anything that has been touched by virtue will be fraught with blessing and prosperity for you, no matter how it shall be regarded by others. Torture, if only, as you lie suffering, you are more calm in mind than your very torturer; illness, if only you curse not Fortune and yield not to the disease—in short, all those things which others regard as ills will become manageable and will end in good, if you succeed in rising above them.

Let this once be clear, that there is nothing good except that which is honorable, and all hardships will have a just title to the name of "goods," when once virtue has made them honorable. Many think that we Stoics are holding out expectations greater than our human lot admits of; and they have a right to think so. For they have regard to the body only. But let them turn back to the soul, and they will soon measure man by the standard of God. Rouse yourself, most excellent Lucilius, and leave off all this word-play of the philosophers, who reduce a most glorious subject to a matter of syllables, and lower and wear out the soul by teaching fragments; then you will become like the men who discovered these precepts, instead of those who by their teaching do their best to make philosophy seem difficult rather than great.

Socrates, who recalled the whole of philosophy to rules of conduct, and asserted that the highest wisdom consisted in distinguishing between good and evil, said: "Follow these rules, if my words carry weight with you, in order that you may be happy; and let some men think you even a fool. Allow any man who so desires to insult you and work you wrong; but if only virtue dwells with you, you will suffer nothing. If you wish to be happy, if you would be in good faith a good man let one person or another despise you." No man can accomplish this unless he has come to regard all goods as equal, for the reason that no good exists without that which is honorable, and that which is honorable is in every case equal. You may say: "What then? Is there no difference between Cato's being elected praetor and his failure at the polls? Or whether Cato is conquered or conqueror in the battle-line of Pharsalia? And when Cato could not be defeated, though his party met defeat, was not this goodness of his equal to that which would have been his if he had returned victorious to his native land and arranged a peace?" Of course it was; for it is by the same virtue that evil Fortune is overcome and good Fortune is controlled. Virtue, however, cannot be increased or decreased; its stature is uniform. "But," you will object, "Gnaeus Pompey will lose his army; the patricians, those noblest patterns of the State's creation, and the front-rank men of Pompey's party, a Senate under arms, will be routed in a single engagement; the ruins of that great oligarchy will be scattered all over the world; one division will fall in Egypt, another in Africa, and another in Spain! And the poor State will not be allowed even the privilege of being ruined once for all!" Yes, all this may happen; Juba's familiarity with every position in his own kingdom may be of no avail to him, of no avail the resolute bravery of his people when fighting for their king; even the men of Utica, crushed by their troubles, may waver in their allegiance; and the good Fortune which ever attended men of the name of Scipio may desert Scipio in Africa. But long ago destiny "saw to it that Cato should come to no harm."

"He was conquered in spite of it all!" Well, you may include this among Cato's "failures"; Cato will bear with an equally stout heart anything that thwarts him of his victory, as he bore that which thwarted him of his praetorship. The day whereon he failed of election, he spent in play; the night wherein he intended to die, he spent in reading. He regarded in the same light both the loss of his praetorship and the loss of his life; he had convinced himself that he ought to endure anything which might happen. Why should he not suffer, bravely and calmly, a change in the government? For what is free from the risk of change? Neither earth, nor sky, nor the whole fabric of our universe, though it be controlled by the hand of God. It will not always preserve its present order; it will be thrown from its course in days to come. All things move in accord with their appointed times; they are destined to be born, to grow, and to be destroyed. The stars which you see moving above us, and this seemingly immovable earth to which we cling and on which we are set, will be consumed and will cease to exist. There is nothing that does not have its old age; the intervals are merely unequal at which Nature sends forth all these things toward the same goal. Whatever is will cease to be, and yet it will not perish, but will be resolved into its elements. To our minds, this process means perishing, for we behold only that which is nearest; our sluggish mind, under allegiance to the body, does not penetrate to bournes beyond. Were it not so, the mind would endure with greater courage its own ending and that of its possessions, if only it could hope that life and death, like the whole universe about us, go by turns, that whatever has been put together is broken up again, that whatever has been broken up is put together again, and that the eternal craftsmanship of God, who controls all things is working at this task.

Therefore the wise man will say just what a Marcus Cato would say, after reviewing his past life: "The whole race of man, both that which is and that which is to be, is condemned to die. Of all the cities that at any time have held sway over the world, and of all that have been the splendid ornaments of empires not their own, men shall some day ask where they were, and they shall be swept away by destructions of various kinds; some shall be ruined by wars, others shall be wasted away by inactivity and by the kind of peace which ends in sloth, or by that vice which is fraught with destruction even for mighty dynasties—luxury. All these fertile plains shall be buried out of sight by a sudden overflowing of the sea, or a slipping of the soil, as it settles to lower levels, shall draw them suddenly into a yawning chasm. Why then should I be angry or feel sorrow, if I precede the general destruction by a tiny interval of time?" Let great souls comply with God's wishes, and suffer unhesitatingly whatever fate the law of the universe ordains; for the soul at death is either sent forth into a better life, destined to dwell with deity amid greater radiance and calm, or else, at least, without suffering any harm to itself, it will be mingled with nature again, and will return to the universe.

Therefore Cato's honorable death was no less a good than his honorable life, since virtue admits of no stretching. Socrates used to say that verity and virtue were the same. Just as truth does not grow, so neither does virtue grow; for it has its due proportions and is complete. You need not, therefore, wonder that goods are equal, both those which are to be deliberately chosen, and those which circumstances have imposed. For if you once adopt the view that they are unequal, deeming, for instance, a brave endurance of torture as among the lesser goods, you will be including it among the evils also; you will pronounce Socrates unhappy in his prison, Cato unhappy when he reopens his wounds with more courage than he allowed in inflicting them, and Regulus the most ill-starred of all when he pays the penalty for keeping his word even with his enemies. And yet no man, even the most effeminate person in the world, has ever dared to maintain such an opinion. For though such persons deny that a man like Regulus is happy, yet for all that they also deny that he is wretched. The earlier Academics do indeed admit that a man is happy even amid such tortures, but do not admit that he is completely or fully happy. With this view we cannot in any wise agree; for unless a man is happy, he has not attained the Supreme Good; and the good which is supreme admits of no higher degree, if only virtue exists within this man, and if adversity does not impair his virtue, and if, though the body be injured, the virtue abides unharmed. And it does abide. For I understand virtue to be high-spirited and exalted, so that it is aroused by anything that molests it. This spirit, which young men of noble breeding often assume, when they are so deeply stirred by the beauty of some honorable object that they despise all the gifts of chance, is assuredly infused in us and communicated to us by wisdom. Wisdom will bring the conviction that there is but one good—that which is honorable; that this can neither be shortened nor extended, any more than a carpenter's rule, with which straight lines are tested, can be bent. Any change in the rule means spoiling the straight line. Applying, therefore, this same figure to virtue, we shall say: virtue also is straight, and admits of no bending. What can be made more tense than a thing which is already rigid? Such is virtue, which passes judgment on everything, but nothing passes judgment on virtue. And if this rule, virtue, cannot itself be made more straight, neither can the things created by virtue be in one case straighter and in another less straight. For they must necessarily correspond to virtue; hence they are equal.

"What," you say, "do you call reclining at a banquet and submitting to torture equally good?" Does this seem surprising to you? You may be still more surprised at the following—that reclining at a banquet is an evil, while reclining on the rack is a good, if the former act is done in a shameful, and the latter in an honorable manner. It is not the material that makes these actions good or bad; it is the virtue. All acts in which virtue has disclosed itself are of the same measure and value. At this moment the man who measures the souls of all men by his own is shaking his fist in my face because I hold that there is a parity between the goods involved in the case of one who passes sentence honorably, and of one who suffers sentence honorably; or because I hold that there is a parity between the goods of one who celebrates a triumph, and of one who, unconquered in spirit, is carried before the victor's chariot. For such critics think that whatever they themselves cannot do, is not done; they pass judgment on virtue in the

light of their own weaknesses. Why do you marvel if it helps a man, and
on occasion even pleases him, to be burned, wounded, slain, or bound in
prison? To a luxurious man, a simple life is a penalty; to a lazy man, work
is punishment; the dandy pities the diligent man; to the slothful, studies
are torture. Similarly, we regard those things with respect to which we are
all infirm of disposition, as hard and beyond endurance, forgetting what a
torment it is to many men to abstain from wine or to be routed from their
beds at break of day. These actions are not essentially difficult; it is we ourselves that are soft and flabby. We must pass judgment concerning great
matters with greatness of soul; otherwise, that which is really our fault
will seem to be their fault. So it is that certain objects which are perfectly
straight, when sunk in water appear to the onlooker as bent or broken off.
It matters not only what you see, but with what eyes you see it; our souls
are too dull of vision to perceive the truth. But give me an unspoiled and
sturdy-minded young man; he will pronounce more fortunate one who
sustains on unbending shoulders the whole weight of adversity, who stands
out superior to Fortune. It is not a cause for wonder that one is not tossed
about when the weather is calm; reserve your wonderment for cases where a
man is lifted up when all others sink, and keeps his footing when all others
are prostrate.

What element of evil is there in torture and in the other things which
we call hardships? It seems to me that there is this evil—that the mind
sags, and bends, and collapses. But none of these things can happen to
the sage; he stands erect under any load. Nothing can subdue him; nothing that must be endured annoys him. For he does not complain that he
has been struck by that which can strike any man. He knows his own
strength; he knows that he was born to carry burdens. I do not withdraw
the wise man from the category of man, nor do I deny to him the sense of
pain as though he were a rock that has no feelings at all. I remember that
he is made up of two parts: the one part is irrational—it is this that may
be bitten, burned, or hurt; the other part is rational—it is this which
holds resolutely to opinions, is courageous, and unconquerable. In the

latter is situated man's Supreme Good. Before this is completely attained, the mind wavers in uncertainty; only when it is fully achieved is the mind fixed and steady. And so when one has just begun, or is on one's way to the heights and is cultivating virtue, or even if one is drawing near the perfect good but has not yet put the finishing touch upon it, one will retrograde at times and there will be a certain slackening of mental effort. For such a man has not yet traversed the doubtful ground; he is still standing in slippery places. But the happy man, whose virtue is complete, loves himself most of all when his bravery has been submitted to the severest test, and when he not only, endures but welcomes that which all other men regard with fear if it is the price which he must pay for the performance of a duty which honor imposes, and he greatly prefers to have men say of him: "how much more noble!" rather than "how much more lucky!"

And now I have reached the point to which your patient waiting summons me. You must not think that our human virtue transcends nature; the wise man will tremble, will feel pain, will turn pale. For all these are sensations of the body. Where, then, is the abode of utter distress, of that which is truly an evil? In the other part of us, no doubt, if it is the mind that these trials drag down, force to a confession of its servitude, and cause to regret its existence. The wise man, indeed, overcomes Fortune by his virtue, but many who profess wisdom are sometimes frightened by the most unsubstantial threats. And at this stage it is a mistake on our part to make the same demands upon the wise man and upon the learner. I still exhort myself to do that which I recommend; but my exhortations are not yet followed. And even if this were the case, I should not have these principles so ready for practice, or so well trained, that they would rush to my assistance in every crisis. Just as wool takes up certain colors at once, while there are others which it will not absorb unless it is soaked and steeped in them many times; so other systems of doctrine can be immediately applied by men's minds after once being accepted, but this system of which I speak, unless it has gone deep and has sunk in for a long time, and has not merely colored but thoroughly permeated the soul, does not fulfill any of its promises. The matter can be imparted quickly and in very few words: "Virtue is the only good; at any rate there is no good without virtue; and virtue itself is situated in our nobler part, that is, the rational part." And what will this virtue be? A true and never-swerving judgment. For therefrom will spring all mental impulses, and by its agency every external appearance that stirs our impulses will be clarified. It will be in keeping with this judgment to judge all things that have been colored by virtue as goods, and as equal goods.

Bodily goods are, to be sure, good for the body; but they are not absolutely good. There will indeed be some value in them; but they will possess no genuine merit, for they will differ greatly; some will be less, others greater. And we are constrained to acknowledge that there are great differences among the very followers of wisdom. One man has already made so much progress that he dares to raise his eyes and look Fortune in the face, but not persistently, for his eyes soon drop, dazzled by her overwhelming splendor; another has made so much progress that he is able to match glances with her—that is, unless he has already reached the summit and is full of confidence. That which is short of perfection must necessarily be unsteady, at one time progressing, at another slipping or growing faint; and it will surely slip back unless it keeps struggling ahead; for if a man slackens at all in zeal and faithful application, he must retrograde. No one can resume his progress at the point where he left off. Therefore let us press on and persevere. There remains much more of the road than we have put behind us; but the greater part of progress is the desire to progress.

I fully understand what this task is. It is a thing which I desire, and I desire it with all my heart. I see that you also have been aroused and are hastening with great zeal toward infinite beauty. Let us, then, hasten; only on these terms will life be a boon to us; otherwise, there is delay, and indeed disgraceful delay, while we busy ourselves with revolting things. Let us see to it that all time belongs to us. This, however, cannot be unless first of all our own selves begin to belong to us. And when will it be our privilege to despise both kinds of fortune? When will it be our privilege, after all the passions have been subdued and brought under our own control, to utter the words "I have conquered!"? Do you ask me whom I have conquered? Neither the Persians, nor the far-off Medes, nor any warlike race that lies beyond the Dahae; not these, but greed, ambition, and the fear of death that has conquered the conquerors of the world. Farewell.

LXXV. ON THE DISEASES
OF THE SOUL

——

YOU HAVE BEEN COMPLAINING THAT MY LETTERS TO YOU ARE rather carelessly written. Now who talks carefully unless he also desires to talk affectedly? I prefer that my letters should be just what my conversation would be if you and I were sitting in one another's company or taking walks together, spontaneous and easy; for my letters have nothing strained or artificial about them. If it were possible, I should prefer to show, rather than speak, my feelings. Even if I were arguing a point, I should not stamp my foot, or toss my arms about, or raise my voice; but I should leave that sort of thing to the orator, and should be content to have conveyed my feelings to you without having either embellished them or lowered their dignity. I should like to convince you entirely of this one fact—that I feel whatever I say, that I not only feel it, but am wedded to it. It is one sort of kiss which a man gives his mistress and another which he gives his children; yet in the father's embrace also, holy and restrained as it is, plenty of affection is disclosed.

I prefer, however, that our conversation on matters so important should not be meager and dry; for even philosophy does not renounce the company of cleverness. One should not, however, bestow very much attention upon mere words. Let this be the kernel of my idea: let us say what we feel, and feel what we say; let speech harmonize with life. That man has fulfilled his promise who is the same person both when you see him and when you hear him. We shall not fail to see what sort of man he is and how large a man he is, if only he is one and the same. Our words should aim not to please, but to help. If, however, you can attain eloquence without pains-taking, and if you either are naturally gifted or can gain eloquence at slight cost, make the most of it and apply it to the noblest uses. But let it be of such a kind that it displays facts rather than itself. It and the other arts are wholly concerned with cleverness; but our business here is the soul.

A sick man does not call in a physician who is eloquent; but if it so happens that the physician who can cure him likewise discourses elegantly about the treatment which is to be followed, the patient will take it in good part. For all that, he will not find any reason to congratulate himself on having discovered a physician who is eloquent. For the case is no different from that of a skilled pilot who is also handsome. Why do you tickle my ears? Why do you entertain me? There is other business at hand; I am to be cauterized, operated upon, or put on a diet. That is why you were summoned to treat me!

You are required to cure a disease that is chronic and serious—one which affects the general well-being. You have as serious a business on hand as a physician has during a plague. Are you concerned about words? Rejoice this instant if you can cope with *things*. When shall you learn all that there is to learn? When shall you so plant in your mind that which you have learned, that it cannot escape? When shall you put it all into practice? For it is not sufficient merely to commit these things to memory, like other matters; they must be practically tested. He is not happy who only knows them, but he who does them. You reply: "What? Are there no degrees of happiness below your 'happy' man? Is there a sheer descent immediately below wisdom?" I think not. For though he who makes progress is still numbered with the fools, yet he is separated from them by a long interval. Among the very persons who are making progress there are also great spaces intervening. They fall into three classes, as certain philosophers believe. First come those who have not yet attained wisdom but have already gained a place nearby. Yet even that which is not far away is still outside. These, if you ask me, are men who have already laid aside all passions and vices, who have learned what things are to be embraced; but their assurance is not yet tested. They have not yet put their good into practice, yet from now on they cannot slip back into the faults which they have escaped. They have already arrived at a point from which there is no slipping back, but they are not yet aware of the fact; as I remember writing in another letter, "They are ignorant of their knowledge." It has now been vouchsafed to them to enjoy their good, but not yet to be sure of it. Some define this class, of which I have been speaking—a class of men who are making progress—as having escaped the diseases of the mind, but not yet the passions, and as still standing upon slippery ground; because no one is beyond the dangers of evil except him who has cleared himself of it wholly. But no one has so cleared himself except the man who has adopted wisdom in its stead.

I have often before explained the difference between the diseases of the mind and its passions. And I shall remind you once more: the diseases are hardened and chronic vices, such as greed and ambition; they have enfolded the mind in too close a grip, and have begun to be permanent evils thereof. To give a brief definition: by "disease" we mean a persistent perversion of the judgment, so that things which are mildly desirable are thought to be highly desirable. Or, if you prefer, we may define it thus: to be too zealous in striving for things which are only mildly desirable or not desirable at all, or to value highly things which ought to be valued but slightly or valued not at all. "Passions" are objectionable impulses of the spirit, sudden and vehement; they have come so often, and so little attention has been paid to them, that they have caused a state of disease; just as a catarrh, when there has been but a single attack and the catarrh has not yet become habitual, produces a cough, but causes consumption when it has become regular and chronic. Therefore we may say that those who have made most progress are beyond the reach of the "diseases"; but they still feel the "passions" even when very near perfection.

The second class is composed of those who have laid aside both the greatest ills of the mind and its passions, but yet are not in assured possession of immunity. For they can still slip back into their former state. The third class are beyond the reach of many of the vices and particularly of the great vices, but not beyond the reach of all. They have escaped avarice, for example, but still feel anger; they no longer are troubled by lust, but are still troubled by ambition; they no longer have desire, but they still have fear. And just because they fear, although they are strong enough to withstand certain things, there are certain things to which they yield; they scorn death, but are in terror of pain.

Let us reflect a moment on this topic. It will be well with us if we are admitted to this class. The second stage is gained by great good Fortune with regard to our natural gifts and by great and unceasing application to study. But not even the third type is to be despised. Think of the host of evils which you see about you; behold how there is no crime that is not exemplified, how far wickedness advances every day, and how prevalent are sins in home and commonwealth. You will see, therefore, that we are making a considerable gain, if we are not numbered among the basest.

"But as for me," you say, "I hope that it is in me to rise to a higher rank than that!" I should pray, rather than promise, that we may attain this; we have been forestalled. We hasten toward virtue while hampered by vices. I am ashamed to say it; but we worship that which is honorable only in so far as we have time to spare. But what a rich reward awaits us if only we break off the affairs which forestall us and the evils that cling to us with utter tenacity! Then neither desire nor fear shall rout us. Undisturbed by fears, unspoiled by pleasures, we shall be afraid neither of death nor of the gods; we shall know that death is no evil and that the gods are not powers of evil. That which harms has no greater power than that which receives harm, and things which are utterly good have no power at all to harm. There await us, if ever we escape from these low dregs to that sublime and lofty height, peace of mind and, when all error has been driven out, perfect liberty. You ask what this freedom is? It means not fearing either men or gods; it means not craving wickedness or excess; it means possessing supreme power over oneself. And it is a priceless good to be master of oneself. Farewell.

LXXVI. ON LEARNING WISDOM IN OLD AGE

———

YOU HAVE BEEN THREATENING ME WITH YOUR ENMITY, IF I DO NOT keep you informed about all my daily actions. But see, now, upon what frank terms you and I live: for I shall confide even the following fact to your ears. I have been hearing the lectures of a philosopher; four days have already passed since I have been attending his school and listening to the harangue, which begins at two o'clock. "A fine time of life for that!" you say. Yes, fine indeed! Now what is more foolish than refusing to learn, simply because one has not been learning for a long time? "What do you mean? Must I follow the fashion set by the fops and youngsters?" But I am pretty well off if this is the only thing that discredits my declining years. Men of all ages are admitted to this classroom. You retort: "Do we grow old merely in order to tag after the youngsters?" But if I, an old man, go to the theater, and am carried to the races, and allow no duel in the arena to be fought to a finish without my presence, shall I blush to attend a philosopher's lecture?

You should keep learning as long as you are ignorant—even to the end of your life, if there is anything in the proverb. And the proverb suits the present case as well as any: "As long as you live, keep learning how to live." For all that, there is also something which I can teach in that school. You ask, do you, what I can teach? That even an old man should keep learning. But I am ashamed of mankind, as often as I enter the lecture hall. On my

246

way to the house of Metronax I am compelled to go, as you know, right past the Neapolitan Theatre. The building is jammed; men are deciding, with tremendous zeal, who is entitled to be called a good flute player; even the Greek piper and the herald draw their crowds. But in the other place, where the question discussed is: "What is a good man?" and the lesson which we learn is "How to be a good man," very few are in attendance, and the majority think that even these few are engaged in no good business; they have the name of being empty-headed idler. I hope I may be blessed with that kind of mockery; for one should listen in an unruffled spirit to the railings of the ignorant; when one is marching toward the goal of honor, one should scorn scorn itself.

Proceed, then, Lucilius, and hasten, lest you yourself be compelled to learn in your old age, as is the case with me. Nay, you must hasten all the more, because for a long time you have not approached the subject, which is one that you can scarcely learn thoroughly when you are old. "How much progress shall I make?" you ask. Just as much as you try to make. Why do you wait? Wisdom comes haphazard to no man. Money will come of its own accord; titles will be given to you; influence and authority will perhaps be thrust upon you; but virtue will not fall upon you by chance. Either is knowledge thereof to be won by light effort or small toil; but toiling is worthwhile when one is about to win all goods at a single stroke. For there is but a single good—namely, that which is honorable; in all those other things of which the general opinion approves, you will find no truth or certainty. Why it is, however, that there is but one good, namely, that which is honorable, I shall now tell you, inasmuch as you judge that in my earlier letter I did not carry the discussion far enough, and think that this theory was commended to you rather than proved. I shall also compress the remarks of other authors into narrow compass.

Everything is estimated by the standard of its own good. The vine is valued for its productiveness and the flavor of its wine, the stag for his speed. We ask, with regard to beasts of burden, how sturdy of back they are; for their only use is to bear burdens. If a dog is to find the trail of a wild beast, keenness of scent is of first importance; if to catch his quarry, swiftness of foot; if to attack and harry it, courage. In each thing that quality should be best for which the thing is brought into being and by which it is judged. And what quality is best in man? It is reason; by virtue of reason he surpasses the animals, and is surpassed only by the gods. Perfect reason is therefore the good peculiar to man; all other qualities he shares in some degree with animals and plants. Man is strong; so is the lion. Man is comely; so is the peacock. Man is swift; so is the horse. I do not say that man is surpassed in all these qualities. I am not seeking to find that which is greatest in him, but that which is peculiarly his own. Man has body; so also have trees. Man has the power to act and to move at will; so have beasts and worms. Man has a voice; but how much louder is the voice of the dog, how much shriller that of the eagle, how much deeper that of the bull, how much sweeter and more melodious that of the nightingale! What then is peculiar to man? Reason. When this is right and has reached perfection, man's felicity is complete. Hence, if everything is praiseworthy and has arrived at the end intended by its nature, when it has brought its peculiar good to perfection, and if man's peculiar good is reason; then, if a man has brought his reason to perfection, he is praiseworthy and has readied the end suited to his nature. This perfect reason is called virtue, and is likewise that which is honorable.

Hence that in man is alone a good which alone belongs to man. For we are not now seeking to discover what is a good, but what good is man's. And if there is no other attribute which belongs peculiarly to man except reason, then reason will be his one peculiar good, but a good that is worth all the rest put together. If any man is bad, he will, I suppose, be regarded with disapproval; if good, I suppose he will be regarded with approval. Therefore, that attribute of man whereby he is approved or disapproved is his chief and only good. You do not doubt whether this is a good; you merely doubt whether it is the sole good. If a man possess all other things, such as health, riches, pedigree, a crowded reception hall, but is confessedly bad, you will disapprove of him. Likewise, if a man possess none of the things which I have mentioned, and lacks money, or an escort of clients, or rank and a line of grandfathers and great-grandfathers, but is confessedly good, you will approve of him. Hence, this is man's one peculiar good, and the possessor of it is to be praised even if he lacks other things; but he who does not possess it, though he possess everything else in abundance is condemned and rejected. The same thing holds good regarding men as regarding things. A ship is said to be good not when it is decorated with costly colors, nor when its prow is covered with silver or gold or its figurehead embossed in ivory, nor when it is laden with the imperial revenues or with the wealth of kings, but when it is steady and staunch and taut, with seams that keep out the water, stout enough to endure the buffeting of the waves obedient to its helm, swift and caring naught for the winds. You will speak of a sword as good, not when its sword-belt is of gold, or its scabbard studded with gems, but when its edge is fine for cutting and its point will pierce any armor. Take the carpenter's rule: we do not ask how beautiful it is, but how straight it is. Each thing is praised in regard to that attribute which is taken as its standard, in regard to that which is its peculiar quality.

Therefore in the case of man also, it is not pertinent to the question to know how many acres he ploughs, how much money he has out at interest, how many callers attend his receptions, how costly is the couch on which he lies, how transparent are the cups from which he drinks, but how good he is. He is good, however, if his reason is well-ordered and right and adapted to that which his nature has willed. It is this that is called virtue; this is what we mean by "honorable"; it is man's unique good. For since reason alone brings man to perfection, reason alone, when perfected, makes man happy. This, moreover, is man's only good, the only means by which he is made happy. We do indeed say that those things also are goods which are furthered and brought together by virtue—that is, all the works of virtue; but virtue itself

For since reason alone brings man to perfection, reason alone, when perfected, makes man happy

is for this reason the only good, because there is no good without virtue. If every good is in the soul, then whatever strengthens, uplifts, and enlarges the soul, is a good; virtue, however, does make the soul stronger, loftier, and larger. For all other things, which arouse our desires, depress the soul and weaken it, and when we think that they are uplifting the soul, they are merely puffing it up and cheating it with much emptiness. Therefore, that alone is good which will make the soul better.

All the actions of life, taken as a whole, are controlled by the consideration of what is honorable or base; it is with reference to these two things that our reason is governed in doing or not doing a particular thing. I shall explain what I mean: A good man will do what he thinks it will be honorable for him to do, even if it involves toil; he will do it even if it involves harm to him; he will do it even if it involves peril; again, he will not do that which will be base, even if it brings him money, or pleasure, or power. Nothing will deter him from that which is honorable, and nothing will tempt him into baseness. Therefore, if he is determined invariably to follow that which is honorable, invariably to avoid baseness, and in every act of his life to have regard for these two things, deeming nothing else good except that which is honorable, and nothing else bad except that which is base; if virtue alone is unperverted in him and by itself keeps its even course, then virtue is that man's only good, and nothing can thenceforth happen to it which may make it anything else than good. It has escaped all risk of change; folly may creep upward toward wisdom, but wisdom never slips back into folly.

You may perhaps remember my saying that the things which have been generally desired and feared have been trampled down by many a man in moments of sudden passion. There have been found men who would place their hands in the flames, men whose smiles could not be stopped by the torturer, men who would shed not a tear at the funeral of their children, men who would meet death unflinchingly. It is love, for example, anger, lust, which have challenged dangers. If a momentary stubbornness can accomplish all this when roused by some goad that pricks the spirit, how much more can be accomplished by virtue, which does not act impulsively or suddenly, but uniformly and with a strength that is lasting! It follows that the things which are often scorned by the men who are moved with a sudden passion, and are always scorned by the wise, are neither goods nor evils. Virtue itself is therefore the only good; she marches proudly between the two extremes of fortune, with great scorn for both.

If, however, you accept the view that there is anything good besides that which is honorable, all the virtues will suffer. For it will never be possible for any virtue to be won and held, if there is anything outside itself which virtue must take into consideration. If there is any such thing, then it is at variance with reason, from which the virtues spring, and with truth also, which cannot exist without reason. Any opinion, however, which is at variance with truth, is wrong. A good man, you will admit, must have the highest sense of duty toward the gods. Hence he will endure with an unruffled spirit whatever happens to him; for he will know that it has happened as a result of the divine law, by which the whole creation moves. This being so, there will be for him one good, and only one, namely, that which is honorable; for one of its dictates is that we shall obey the gods and not blaze forth in anger at sudden misfortunes or deplore our lot, but rather patiently accept fate and obey its commands. If anything except the honorable is good, we shall be hounded by greed for life, and by greed for the things which provide life with its furnishings—an intolerable state, subject to no limits, unstable. The only good, therefore, is that which is honorable, that which is subject to bounds.

I have declared that man's life would be more blest than that of the gods, if those things which the gods do not enjoy are goods—such as money and offices of dignity. There is this further consideration: if only it is true that our souls, when released from the body, still abide, a happier condition is in store for them than is theirs while they dwell in the body. And yet, if those things are goods which we make use of for our bodies' sake, our souls will be worse off when set free; and that is contrary to our belief, to say that the soul is happier when it is cabined and confined than when it is free and has betaken itself to the universe. I also said that if those things which dumb animals possess equally with man are goods, then dumb animals also will lead a happy life; which is of course impossible. One must endure all things in defense of that which is honorable; but this would not be necessary if there existed any other good besides that which is honorable.

Although this question was discussed by me pretty extensively in a previous letter, I have discussed it summarily and briefly run through the argument. But an opinion of this kind will never seem true to you unless you exalt your mind and ask yourself whether, at the call of duty, you would be willing to die for your country, and buy the safety of all your fellow citizens at the price of your own; whether you would offer your neck not only with patience, but also with gladness. If you would do this, there is no other good in your eyes. For you are giving up everything in order to acquire this good. Consider how great is the power of that which is honorable: you will die for your country, even at a moment's notice, when you know that you ought to do so. Sometimes, as a result of noble conduct, one wins great joy even in a very short and fleeting space of time; and though none of the fruits of a deed that has been done will accrue to the doer after he is dead and removed from the sphere of human affairs, yet the mere contemplation of a deed that is to be done is a delight, and the brave and upright man, picturing to himself the guerdons of his death—guerdons such as the freedom of his country and the deliverance of all those for whom he is paying out his life—partakes of the greatest pleasure and enjoys the fruit of his own peril. But that man also who is deprived of this joy, the joy which is afforded by the contemplation of some last noble effort, will leap to his death without a moment's hesitation, content to act rightly and dutifully. Moreover, you may confront him with many discouragements; you may say: "Your deed will speedily be forgotten," or "Your fellow citizens will offer you scant thanks." He will answer: "All these matters lie outside my task. My thoughts are on the deed itself. I know that this is honorable. Therefore, whithersoever I am led and summoned by honor, I will go."

This, therefore, is the only good, and not only is every soul that has reached perfection aware of it, but also every soul that is by nature noble and of right instincts; all other goods are trivial and mutable. For this reason we are harassed if we possess them. Even though, by the kindness of Fortune, they have been heaped together, they weigh heavily upon their owners, always pressing them down and sometimes crushing them. None of those whom you behold clad in purple is happy, any more than one of these actors upon whom the play bestows a scepter and a cloak while on the stage; they strut their hour before a crowded house, with swelling port and buskined foot; but when once they make their exit the foot-gear is removed and they return to their proper stature. None of those who have been raised to a loftier height by riches and honors is really great. Why then does he seem great to you? It is because you are measuring the pedestal along with the man. A dwarf is not tall, though he stand upon a mountaintop; a colossal statue will still be tall, though you place it in a well. This is the error under which we labor; this is the reason why we are imposed upon: we value no man at what he is, but add to the man himself the trappings in which he is clothed. But when you wish to inquire into a man's true worth, and to know what manner of man he is, look at him when he is naked; make him lay aside his inherited estate, his titles, and the other deceptions of fortune; let him even strip off his body. Consider his soul, its quality and its stature, and thus learn whether its greatness is borrowed, or its own.

If a man can behold with unflinching eyes the flash of a sword, if he knows that it makes no difference to him whether his soul takes flight through his mouth or through a wound in his throat, you may call him happy; you may also call him happy if, when he is threatened with bodily torture, whether it be the result of accident or of the might of the stronger, he can without concern hear talk of chains, or of exile, or of all the idle fears that stir men's minds, and can say:

"O maiden, no new sudden form of toil
Springs up before my eyes; within my soul
I have forestalled and surveyed everything.
Today it is you who threaten me with these terrors;

but I have always threatened myself with them,
and have prepared myself as a man to meet man's destiny."

If an evil has been pondered beforehand, the blow is gentle when it comes. To the fool, however, and to him who trusts in Fortune, each event as it arrives "comes in a new and sudden form," and a large part of evil, to the inexperienced, consists in its novelty. This is proved by the fact that men endure with greater courage, when they have once become accustomed to them, the things which they had at first regarded as hardships. Hence, the wise man accustoms himself to coming trouble, lightening by long reflection the evils which others lighten by long endurance. We sometimes hear the inexperienced say: "I knew that this was in store for me." But the wise man knows that all things are in store for him. Whatever happens, he says: "I knew it." Farewell.

LXXXI. ON BENEFITS

——

YOU COMPLAIN THAT YOU HAVE MET WITH AN UNGRATEFUL PER-son. If this is your first experience of that sort, you should offer thanks either to your good luck or to your caution. In this case, however, caution can effect nothing but to make you ungenerous. For if you wish to avoid such a danger, you will not confer benefits; and so, that benefits may not be lost with another man, they will be lost to yourself.

It is better, however, to get no return than to confer no benefits. Even after a poor crop one should sow again; for often losses due to continued barrenness of an unproductive soil have been made good by one year's fertility. In order to discover one grateful person, it is worthwhile to make trial of many ungrateful ones. No man has so unerring a hand when he confers benefits that he is not frequently deceived; it is well for the traveler to wander, that he may again cleave to the path. After a shipwreck, sailors try the sea again. The banker is not frightened away from the forum by the swindler. If one were compelled to drop everything that caused trouble, life would soon grow dull amid sluggish idleness; but in your case this very condition may prompt you to become more charitable. For when the outcome of any undertaking is unsure, you must try again and again, in order to succeed ultimately. I have, however, discussed the matter with sufficient fullness in the volumes which I have written, entitled "On Benefits."

What I think should rather be investigated is this—a question which I feel has not been made sufficiently clear: "Whether he who has helped

255

us has squared the account and has freed us from our debt, if he has done us harm later." You may add this question also, if you like: "when the harm done later has been more than the help rendered previously." If you are seeking for the formal and just decision of a strict judge, you will find that he checks off one act by the other, and declares: "Though the injuries outweigh the benefits, yet we should credit to the benefits anything that stands over even after the injury." The harm done was indeed greater, but the helpful act was done first. Hence the time also should be taken into account. Other cases are so clear that I need not remind you that you should also look into such points as: How gladly was the help offered, and how reluctantly was the harm done—since benefits, as well as injuries, depend on the spirit. "I did not wish to confer the benefit; but I was won over by my respect for the man, or by the importunity of his request, or by hope." Our feeling about every obligation depends in each case upon the spirit in which the benefit is conferred; we weigh not the bulk of the gift, but the quality of the good-will which prompted it. So now let us do away with guess-work; the former deed was a benefit, and the latter, which transcended the earlier benefit, is an injury. The good man so arranges the two sides of his ledger that he voluntarily cheats himself by adding to the benefit and subtracting from the injury.

The more indulgent magistrate, however (and I should rather be such a one), will order us to forget the injury and remember the accommodation. "But surely," you say, "it is the part of justice to render to each that which is his due—thanks in return for a benefit, and retribution, or at any rate ill-will, in return for an injury!" This, I say, will be true when it is one man who has inflicted the injury, and a different man who has conferred the benefit; for if it is the same man, the force of the injury is nullified by the benefit conferred. Indeed, a man who ought to be pardoned, even though there were no good deeds credited to him in the past, should receive something more than mere leniency if he commits a wrong when he has a benefit to his credit. I do not set an equal value on benefits and injuries. I reckon a benefit at a higher rate than an injury. Not all grateful persons know what it involves to be in debt for a benefit; even a thoughtless, crude fellow, one of the common herd, may know, especially soon after he has received the gift; but he does not know how deeply he stands in debt therefore. Only the wise man knows exactly what value should be put upon everything; for the fool whom I just mentioned, no matter how good his intentions may be, either pays less than he owes, or pays it at the wrong time or the wrong place. That for which he should make return he wastes and loses. There is a marvelously accurate phraseology applied to certain subjects, a long-established terminology which indicates certain acts by means of symbols that are most efficient and that serve to outline men's duties. We are, as you know, wont to speak thus: "A. has made a return for the favor bestowed by B." Making a return means handing over of your own accord that which you owe. We do not say, "He has paid back the favor"; for "pay back" is used of a man upon whom a demand for payment is made, of those who pay against their will. Of those who pay under any circumstances whatsoever, and of those who pay through a third party. We do not say, "He has "restored" the benefit," or "settled" it; we have never been satisfied with a word which applies properly to a debt of money. Making a return means offering something to him from whom you have received something. The phrase implies a voluntary return; he who has made such a return has served the writ upon himself.

The wise man will inquire in his own mind into all the circumstances: how much he has received, from whom, when, where, how. And so we declare that none but the wise man knows how to make return for a favor; moreover, none but the wise man knows how to confer a benefit—that man, I mean, who enjoys the giving more than the recipient enjoys the receiving. Now some person will reckon this remark as one of the generally surprising statements such as we Stoics are wont to make and such as the Greeks call "paradoxes," and will say: "Do you maintain, then, that only the wise man knows how to return a favor? Do you maintain that no one else knows how to make restoration to a creditor for a debt? Or, on buying a commodity, to pay full value to the seller?" In order not to bring any odium upon myself, let me tell you that Epicurus says the same thing. At any rate, Metrodorus remarks that only the wise man knows how to return a favor. Again, the objector mentioned above wonders at our saying: "The wise man alone knows how to love, the wise man alone is a real friend." And yet it is a part of love and of friendship to return favors; nay, further, it is an ordinary act, and happens more frequently than real friendship. Again, this same objector wonders at our saying, "There is no loyalty except in the wise man," just as if he himself does not say the same thing! Or do you think that there is any loyalty in him who does not know how to return a favor? These men, accordingly, should cease to discredit us, just as if we were uttering an impossible boast; they should understand that the essence of honor resides in the wise man, while among the crowd we find only the ghost and the semblance of honor. None but the wise man knows how to return a favor. Even a fool can return it in proportion to his knowledge and his power; his fault would be a lack of knowledge rather than a lack of will or desire. To will does not come by teaching.

The wise man will compare all things with one another; for the very same object becomes greater or smaller, according to the time, the place, and the cause. Often the riches that are spent in profusion upon a palace cannot accomplish as much as a thousand *denarii* given at the right time. Now it makes a great deal of difference whether you give outright, or come to a man's assistance, whether your generosity saves him, or sets him up in life. Often the gift is small, but the consequences great. And what a distinction do you imagine there is between taking something which one lacks—something which was offered—and receiving a benefit in order to confer one in return?

But we should not slip back into the subject which we have already sufficiently investigated. In this balancing of benefits and injuries, the good man will, to be sure, judge with the highest degree of fairness, but he will incline toward the side of the benefit; he will turn more readily in this direction. Moreover, in affairs of this kind the person concerned is wont to count for a great deal. Men say: "You conferred a benefit upon me in that matter of the slave, but you did me an injury in the case of my father" or, "You saved my son, but robbed me of a father." Similarly, he will follow up all other matters in which comparisons can be made, and if the difference be very slight, he will pretend not to notice it. Even though the difference be great, yet if the concession can be made without impairment of duty and loyalty, our good man will overlook it, that is, provided the injury exclusively affects the good man himself. To sum up, the matter stands thus: the good man will be easy-going in striking a balance; he will allow too much to be set against his credit. He will be unwilling to pay a benefit by balancing the injury against it. The side toward which he will lean, the tendency which he will exhibit, is the desire to be under obligations for the favor, and the desire to make return therefore. For anyone who receives a benefit more gladly than he repays it is mistaken. By as much as he who pays is more lighthearted than he who borrows, by so much ought he to be more joyful who unburdens himself of the greatest debt—a benefit received—than he who incurs the greatest obligations. For ungrateful men make mistakes in this respect also: they have to pay their creditors both capital and interest, but they think that benefits are currency which they can use without interest. So the debts grow through postponement, and the later the action is postponed the more remains to be paid. A man is an ingrate if he repays a favor without interest. Therefore, interest also should be allowed for, when you compare your receipts and your expenses. We should try by all means to be as grateful as possible.

For gratitude is a good thing for ourselves, in a sense in which justice, that is commonly supposed to concern other persons, is not; gratitude returns in large measure unto itself. There is not a man who, when he has benefited his neighbor, has not benefited himself—I do not mean for the reason that he whom you have aided will desire to aid you, or that he whom you have defended will desire to protect you, or that an example of good conduct returns in a circle to benefit the doer, just as examples of bad conduct recoil upon their authors, and as men find no pity if they suffer wrongs which they themselves have demonstrated the possibility of committing; but that the reward for all the virtues lies in the virtues themselves. For they are not practiced with a view to recompense; the wages of a good deed is to have done it. I am grateful, not in order that my neighbor, provoked by the earlier act of kindness, may be more ready to benefit me, but simply in order that I may perform a most pleasant and beautiful act; I feel grateful, not because it profits me, but because it pleases me. And, to prove the truth of this to you, I declare that even if I may not be grateful without seeming ungrateful, even if I am able to retain a benefit only by an act which resembles an injury; even so, I shall strive in the utmost calmness of spirit toward the purpose which honor demands, in the very midst of disgrace. No one, I think, rates virtue higher or is more consecrated to virtue than he who has lost his reputation for being a good man in order to keep from losing the approval of his conscience. Thus, as I have said, your being grateful is more conducive to your own good than to your neighbor's good. For while your neighbor has had a common, everyday experience—namely, receiving back the gift which he had bestowed—you have had a great experience which is the outcome of an utterly happy condition of soul—to have felt gratitude. For if wickedness makes men unhappy and virtue makes men blessed, and if it is a virtue to be grateful, then the return which you have made is only the customary thing, but the thing to which you have attained is priceless—the consciousness of gratitude, which comes only to the soul that is divine and blessed. The opposite feeling to this, however, is immediately attended by the greatest unhappiness; no man, if he be ungrateful, will be unhappy in the future. I allow him no day of grace; he is unhappy forthwith.

Let us therefore avoid being ungrateful, not for the sake of others but for our own sakes. When we do wrong, only the least and lightest portion of it flows back upon our neighbor; the worst and, if I may use the term, the densest portion of it stays at home and troubles the owner. My master Attalus used to say: "Evil herself drinks the largest portion of her own poison." The poison which serpents carry for the destruction of others, and secrete without harm to themselves, is not like this poison; for this sort is ruinous to the possessor. The ungrateful man tortures and torments himself; he hates the gifts which he has accepted, because he must make a return for them, and he tries to belittle their value, but he really enlarges and exaggerates the injuries which he has received. And what is more wretched than a man who forgets his benefits and clings to his injuries?

Wisdom, on the other hand, lends grace to every benefit, and of her own free will commends it to her own favor, and delights her soul by continued recollection thereof. Evil men have but one pleasure in benefits, and a very short-lived pleasure at that; it lasts only while they are receiving them. But the wise man derives therefrom an abiding and eternal joy. For he takes delight not so much in receiving the gift as in having received it; and this joy never perishes; it abides with him always. He despises the wrongs done him; he forgets them, not accidentally, but voluntarily. He does not put a wrong construction upon everything, or seek for someone whom he may hold responsible for each happening; he rather ascribes even the sins of men to chance. He will not misinterpret a word or a look; he makes light of all mishaps by interpreting them in a generous way. He does not remember an injury rather than a service. As far as possible, he lets his memory rest upon the earlier and the better deed, never changing his attitude toward those who have deserved well of him, except in climes where the bad deeds far outdistance the good, and the space between them is obvious even to one who closes his eyes to it; even then only to this extent, that he strives, after receiving the preponderant injury, to resume the attitude which he held before he received the benefit. For when the injury merely equals the benefit, a certain amount of kindly feeling is left over. Just as a defendant is acquitted when the votes are equal, and just as the spirit of kindliness always tries to bend every doubtful case toward the better interpretation, so the mind of the wise man, when another's merits merely equal his bad deeds, will, to be sure, cease to feel an obligation, but does not cease to desire to feel it, and acts precisely like the man who pays his debts even after they have been legally cancelled.

But no man can be grateful unless he has learned to scorn the things which drive the common herd to distraction; if you wish to make return for a favor, you must be willing to go into exile—or to pour forth your blood, or to undergo poverty, or—and this will frequently happen—even to let your very innocence be stained and exposed to shameful slanders. It is no slight price that a man must pay for being grateful. We hold nothing dearer than a benefit, so long as we are seeking one; we hold nothing cheaper after we have received it. Do you ask what it is that makes us forget benefits received? It is our extreme greed for receiving others. We consider not what we have obtained, but what we are to seek. We are deflected from the right course by riches, titles, power, and everything which is valuable in our opinion but worthless when rated at its real value. We do not know how to weigh matters; we should take counsel regarding them, not with their reputation but with their nature; those things possess no grandeur wherewith to enthrall our minds, except the fact that we have become accustomed to marvel at them. For they are not praised because they ought to be desired, but they are desired because they have been praised; and when the error of individuals has once created error on the part of the public, then the public error goes on creating error on the part of individuals.

But just as we take on faith such estimates of values, so let us take on the faith of the people this truth that nothing is more honorable than a grateful heart. This phrase will be echoed by all cities, and by all races, even those from savage countries. Upon this point—good and bad will agree. Some praise pleasure, some prefer toil; some say that pain is the greatest of evils, some say it is no evil at all; some will include riches in the Supreme Good, others will say that their discovery meant harm to the human race, and that none is richer than he to whom Fortune has found nothing to give. Amid all this diversity of opinion all men will yet with one voice, as the saying is, vote "aye" to the proposition that thanks should be returned to those who have deserved well of us. On this question the common herd, rebellious as they are, will all agree, but at present we keep paying back injuries instead of benefits, and the primary reason why a man is ungrateful is that he has found it impossible to be grateful enough. Our madness has gone to such lengths that it is a very dangerous thing to confer great benefits upon a person; for just because he thinks it shameful not to repay, so he would have none left alive whom he should repay. "Keep for yourself what you have received; I do not ask it back—I do not demand it. Let it be safe to have conferred a favor." There is no worse hatred than that which springs from shame at the desecration of a benefit. Farewell.

LXXXII. ON THE NATU-RAL FEAR OF DEATH

I HAVE ALREADY CEASED TO BE ANXIOUS ABOUT YOU. "WHOM THEN of the gods," you ask, "have you found as your voucher?" A god, let me tell you, who deceives no one—a soul in love with that which is upright and good. The better part of yourself is on safe ground. Fortune can inflict injury upon you; what is more pertinent is that I have no fears lest you do injury to yourself. Proceed as you have begun, and settle yourself in this way of living, not luxuriously, but calmly. I prefer to be in trouble rather than in luxury; and you had better interpret the term "in trouble" as popular usage is wont to interpret it: living a "hard," "rough," "toilsome" life. We are wont to hear the lives of certain men praised as follows, when they are objects of unpopularity: "So-and-So lives luxuriously"; but by this they mean: "He is softened by luxury." For the soul is made womanish by degrees, and is weakened until it matches the ease and laziness in which it lies. Lo, is it not better for one who is really a man even to become hardened? Next, these same dandies fear that which they have made their own lives resemble. Much difference is there between lying idle and lying buried! "But," you say, "is it not better even to lie idle than to whirl round in these eddies of business distraction?" Both extremes are to be deprecated—both tension and sluggishness. I hold that he who lies on a perfumed couch is no less dead than he who is dragged along by the executioner's hook.

Leisure without study is death; it is a tomb for the living man. What then is the advantage of retirement? As if the real causes of our anxieties did not follow us across the seas! What hiding place is there, where the fear of death does not enter? What peaceful haunts are there, so fortified and so far withdrawn that pain does not fill them with fear? Wherever you hide yourself, human ills will make an uproar all around. There are many external things which compass us about, to deceive us or to weigh upon us; there are many things within which, even amid solitude, fret and ferment.

Therefore, gird yourself about with philosophy, an impregnable wall. Though it be assaulted by many engines, Fortune can find no passage into it. The soul stands on unassailable ground, if it has abandoned external things; it is independent in its own fortress; and every weapon that is hurled falls short of the mark. Fortune has not the long reach with which we credit her; she can seize none except him that clings to her. Let us then recoil from her as far as we are able. This will be possible for us only through knowledge of self and of the world of Nature. The soul should know whither it is going and whence it came, what is good for it and what is evil, what it seeks and what it avoids, and what is that Reason which distinguishes between the desirable and the undesirable, and thereby tames the madness of our desires and calms the violence of our fears.

Some men flatter themselves that they have checked these evils by themselves even without the aid of philosophy; but when some accident catches them off their guard, a tardy confession of error is wrung from them. Their boastful words perish from their lips when the torturer commands them to stretch forth their hands, and when death draws nearer! You might say to such a man: "It was easy for you to challenge evils that were not near-by; but here comes pain, which you declared you could endure; here comes death, against which you uttered many a courageous boast! The whip cracks, the sword flashes:

Ah now, Aeneas, your must needs be stout
And strong of heart!"

This strength of heart, however, will come from constant study, provided that you practice, not with the tongue but with the soul, and provided that you prepare yourself to meet death. To enable yourself to meet death, you may expect no encouragement or cheer from those who try to make you believe, by means of their hair-splitting logic, that death is no evil. For I take pleasure, excellent Lucilius, in poking fun at the absurdities of the Greeks, of which, to my continual surprise, I have not yet succeeded in ridding myself. Our master Zeno uses a syllogism like this: "No evil is glorious; but death is glorious; therefore death is no evil." A cure, Zeno! I have been freed from fear; henceforth I shall not hesitate to bare my neck on the scaffold. Will you not utter sterner words instead of rousing a dying man to laughter? Indeed, Lucilius, I could not easily tell you whether he who thought that he was quenching the fear of death by setting up this syllogism was the more foolish, or he who attempted to refute it, just as if it had anything to do with the matter! For the refuter himself proposed a counter-syllogism, based upon the proposition that we regard death as "indifferent,"—one of the things which the Greeks call ἀδιάφορα. "Nothing," he says, "that is indifferent can be glorious; death is glorious; therefore death is not indifferent." You comprehend the tricky fallacy which is contained in this syllogism. Mere death is, in fact, not glorious; but a brave death is glorious. And when you say, "Nothing that is indifferent is glorious," I grant you this much, and declare that nothing is glorious except as it deals with indifferent things. I classify as "indifferent," that is, neither good nor evil—sickness, pain, poverty, exile, death. None of these things is intrinsically glorious; but nothing can be glorious apart from them. For it is not poverty that we praise, it is the man whom poverty cannot humble or bend. Nor is it exile that we praise, it is the man who withdraws into exile in the spirit in which he would have sent another into exile. It is not pain that we praise, it is the man whom pain has not coerced. One praises not death, but the man whose soul death takes away before it can confound it. All these things are in themselves neither honorable nor glorious; but any one of them that virtue has visited and touched is made honorable and glorious by virtue; they merely lie in between, and the decisive question is only whether wickedness or virtue has laid hold upon them. For instance, the death which in Cato's case is glorious, is in the case of Brutus forthwith base and disgraceful. For this Brutus, condemned to death, was trying to obtain postponement; he withdrew a moment in order to ease himself; when summoned to die and ordered to bare his throat, he exclaimed: "I will bare my throat, if only I may live!" What madness it is to run away, when it is impossible to turn back! "I will bare my throat, if only I may live!" He came very near saying also: "even under Antony!" This fellow deserved indeed to be consigned to *life*!

But, as I was going on to remark, you see that death in itself is neither an evil nor a good; Cato experienced death most honorably, Brutus most basely. Everything, if you add virtue, assumes a glory which it did not possess before. We speak of a sunny room, even though the same room is pitch dark at night. It is the day which fills it with light, and the night which steals the light away; thus it is with the things which we call indifferent and "middle," like riches, strength, beauty, titles, kingship, and their opposites—death, exile, ill-health, pain, and all such evils, the fear of which upsets us to a greater or less extent; it is the wickedness or the virtue that bestows the name of good or evil. An object is not by its own essence either hot or cold; it is heated when thrown into a furnace, and chilled when dropped into water. Death is honorable when related to that which is honorable; by this I mean virtue and a soul that despises the worst hardships.

Furthermore, there are vast distinctions among these qualities which we call "middle." For example, death is not so indifferent as the question whether your hair should be worn evenly or unevenly. Death belongs among those things which are not indeed evils, but still have in them a semblance of evil; for there are implanted in us love of self, a desire for existence and self-preservation, and also an abhorrence of dissolution, because death seems to rob us of many goods and to withdraw us from the abundance to which we have become accustomed. And there is another element which estranges us from death: we are already familiar with the present, but are ignorant of the future into which we shall transfer ourselves, and we shrink from the unknown. Moreover, it is natural to fear the world of shades, whither death is supposed to lead. Therefore, although death is something indifferent, it is nevertheless not a thing which we can easily ignore. The soul must be hardened by long practice, so that it may learn to endure the sight and the approach of death.

Death ought to be despised more than it is wont to be despised. For we believe too many of the stories about death. Many thinkers have striven hard to increase its ill repute; they have portrayed the prison in the world below and the land overwhelmed by everlasting night, where

Within his blood-stained cave Hell's warder huge
Doth sprawl his ugly length on half-crunched bones,
And terrifies the disembodied ghosts
With never-ceasing bark.

Even if you can win your point and prove that these are mere stories and that nothing is left for the dead to fear, another fear steals upon you. For the fear of going to the underworld is equaled by the fear of going nowhere.

In the face of these notions, which longstanding opinion has dinned in our ears, how can brave endurance of death be anything else than glorious, and fit to rank among the greatest accomplishments of the human mind? For the mind will never rise to virtue if it believes that death is an evil; but it will so rise if it holds that death is a matter of indifference. It is not in the order of nature that a man shall proceed with a great heart to a destiny which he believes to be evil; he will go sluggishly and with reluctance. But nothing glorious can result from unwillingness and cowardice; virtue does nothing under compulsion. Besides, no deed that a man does is honorable unless he has devoted himself thereto and attended to it with all his heart, rebelling against it with no portion of his being. When, however, a man goes to face an evil, either through fear of worse evils or in the hope of goods whose attainment is of sufficient moment to him that he can swallow the one evil which he must endure—in that case the judgment of the agent is drawn in two directions. On the one side is the motive which bids him carry out his purpose; on the other, the motive which restrains him and makes him flee from something which has aroused his apprehension or leads to danger. Hence he is torn in different directions; and if this happens, the glory of his act is gone. For virtue accomplishes its plans only when the spirit is in harmony with itself. There is no element of fear in any of its actions.

> Yield not to evils, but, still braver, go
> Where'er your Fortune shall allow.

You cannot "still braver go," if you are persuaded that those things are the real evils. Root out this idea from your soul; otherwise your apprehensions will remain undecided and will thus check the impulse to action. You will be pushed into that toward which you ought to advance like a soldier.

Those of our school, it is true, would have men think that Zeno's syllogism is correct, but that the second I mentioned, which is set up against his, is deceptive and wrong. But I for my part decline to reduce such questions to a matter of dialectical rules or to the subtleties of an utterly worn-out system. Away, I say, with all that sort of thing, which makes a man feel, when a question is propounded to him, that he is hemmed in, and forces him to admit a premise, and then makes him say one thing in his answer when his real opinion is another. When truth is at stake, we must act more frankly; and when fear is to be combated, we must act more bravely. Such questions, which the dialecticians involve in subtleties, I prefer to solve and weigh rationally, with the purpose of winning conviction and not of forcing the judgment.

When a general is about to lead into action an army prepared to meet death for their wives and children, how will he exhort them to battle? I remind you of the Fabii, who took upon a single clan a war which concerned the whole state. I point out to you the Lacedaemonians in position at the very pass of Thermopylae! They have no hope of victory, no hope of returning. The place where they stand is to be their tomb. In what language do you encourage them to bar the way with their bodies and take upon themselves the ruin of their whole tribe, and to retreat from life rather than from their post? Shall you say: "That which is evil is not glorious; but death is glorious; therefore death is not an evil"? What a powerful discourse! After such words, who would hesitate to throw himself upon the serried spears of the foemen, and die in his tracks? But take Leonidas: how bravely did he address his men! He said: "Fellow-soldiers, let us to our breakfast, knowing that we shall sup in Hades!" The food of these men did not grow lumpy in their mouths, or stick in their throats, or slip from their fingers; eagerly did they accept the invitation to breakfast, and to supper also! Think, too, of the famous Roman general; his soldiers had been dispatched to seize a position, and when they were about to make their way through a huge army of the enemy, he addressed them with the words: "You must go now, fellow-soldiers, to yonder place, whence there is no 'must' about your returning!"

You see, then, how straightforward and peremptory virtue is; but what man on earth can your deceptive logic make more courageous or more upright? Rather does it break the spirit, which should never be less straitened or forced to deal with petty and thorny problems than when some great work is being planned. It is not the Three Hundred,—it is all mankind that should be relieved of the fear of death. But how can you prove to all those men that death is no evil? How can you overcome the notions of all our past life—notions with which we are tinged from our very infancy? What succour can you discover for man's helplessness? What can you say that will make men rush, burning with zeal, into the midst of danger? By what persuasive speech can you turn aside this universal feeling of fear, by what strength of wit can you turn aside the conviction of the human race which steadfastly opposes you? Do you propose to construct catchwords for me, or to string together petty syllogisms? It takes great weapons to strike down great monsters. You recall the fierce serpent in Africa, more frightful to the Roman legions than the war itself, and assailed in vain by arrows and slings; it could not be wounded even by "Pythius," since its huge size, and the toughness which matched its bulk, made spears, or any weapon hurled by the hand of man, glance off. It was finally destroyed by rocks equal in size to millstones. Are you, then, hurling petty weapons like yours even against death? Can you stop a lion's charge by an awl? Your arguments are indeed sharp; but there is nothing sharper than a stalk of grain. And certain arguments are rendered useless and unavailing by their very subtlety. Farewell.

LXXXIII. ON DRUNKENNESS

———

YOU BID ME GIVE YOU AN ACCOUNT OF EACH SEPARATE DAY, AND OF the whole day too; so you must have a good opinion of me if you think that in these days of mine there is nothing to hide. At any rate, it is thus that we should live—as if we lived in plain sight of all men; and it is thus that we should think—as if there were someone who could look into our inmost souls; and there is one who can so look. For what avails it that something is hidden from man? Nothing is shut off from the sight of God. He is witness of our souls, and he comes into the very midst of our thoughts—comes into them, I say, as one who may at any time depart. I shall therefore do as you bid, and shall gladly inform you by letter what I am doing, and in what sequence. I shall keep watching myself continually, and—a most useful habit—shall review each day. For this is what makes us wicked: that no one of us looks back over his own life. Our thoughts are devoted only to what we are about to do. And yet our plans for the future always depend on the past.

Today has been unbroken; no one has filched the slightest part of it from me. The whole time has been divided between rest and reading. A brief space has been given over to bodily exercise, and on this ground I can thank old age—my exercise costs very little effort; as soon as I stir, I am tired. And weariness is the aim and end of exercise, no matter how strong one is. Do you ask who are my pacemakers? One is enough for me—the slave Pharius, a pleasant fellow, as you know; but I shall exchange him for another. At my time of life I need one who is of still more tender years. Pharius, at any rate, says that he and I are at the same period of life; for we are both losing our teeth. Yet even now I can scarcely follow his pace as he runs, and within a very short time I shall not be able to follow him at all; so you see what profit we get from daily exercise. Very soon does a wide interval open between two persons who travel different ways. My slave is climbing up at the very moment when I am coming down, and you surely know how much quicker the latter is. Nay, I was wrong; for now my life is not coming down; it is falling outright. Do you ask, for all that, how our race resulted today? We raced to a tie—something which rarely happens in a running contest. After tiring myself out in this way (for I cannot call it exercise), I took a cold bath; this, at my house, means just short of hot. I, the former cold-water enthusiast, who used to celebrate the new year by taking a plunge into the canal, who, just as naturally as I would set out to do some reading or writing, or to compose a speech, used to inaugurate the first of the year with a plunge into the Virgo aqueduct, have changed my allegiance, first to the Tiber, and then to my favorite tank, which is warmed only by the sun, at times when I am most robust and when there is not a flaw in my bodily processes. I have very little energy left for bathing. After the bath, some stale bread and breakfast without a table; no need to wash the hands after such a meal. Then comes a very short nap. You know my habit; I avail myself of a scanty bit of sleep—unharnessing, as it were. For I am satisfied if I can just stop staying awake. Sometimes I know that I have slept; at other times, I have a mere suspicion.

Lo, now the din of the Races sounds about me! My ears are smitten with sudden and general cheering. But this does not upset my thoughts or even break their continuity. I can endure an uproar with complete resignation. The medley of voices blended in one note sounds to me like the dashing of waves, or like the wind that lashes the treetops, or like any other sound which conveys no meaning.

What is it, then, you ask, to which I have been giving my attention? I will tell you, a thought sticks in my mind, left over from yesterday— namely, what men of the greatest sagacity have meant when they have offered the most trifling and intricate proofs for problems of the greatest importance—proofs which may be true, but none the less resemble falla- cies. Zeno, that greatest of men, the revered founder of our brave and holy school of philosophy, wishes to discourage us from drunkenness. Listen, then, to his arguments proving that the good man will not get drunk: "No one entrusts a secret to a drunken man; but one will entrust a secret to a good man; therefore, the good man will not get drunk." Mark how ridicu- lous Zeno is made when we set up a similar syllogism in contrast with his. There are many, but one will be enough: "No one entrusts a secret to a man when he is asleep; but one entrusts a secret to a good man; therefore, the good man does not go to sleep." Posidonius pleads the cause of our master Zeno in the only possible way; but it cannot, I hold, be pleaded even in this way. For Posidonius maintains that the word "drunken" is used in two ways—in the one case of a man who is loaded with wine and has no con- trol over himself; in the other, of a man who is accustomed to get drunk, and is a slave to the habit. Zeno, he says, meant the latter—the man who is accustomed to get drunk, not the man who is drunk; and no one would entrust to this person any secret, for it might be blabbed out when the man was in his cups. This is a fallacy. For the first syllogism refers to him who is actually drunk and not to him who is about to get drunk. You will surely admit that there is a great difference between a man who is drunk and a drunkard. He who is actually drunk may be in this state for the first time and may not have the habit, while the drunkard is often free from drunkenness. I therefore interpret the word in its usual meaning, especially since the syllogism is set up by a man who makes a business of the careful use of words, and who weighs his language. Moreover, if this is what Zeno meant, and what he wished it to mean to us, he was trying to avail himself of an equivocal word in order to work in a fallacy; and no man ought to do this when truth is the object of inquiry.

But let us admit, indeed, that he meant what Posidonius says; even so, the conclusion is false, that secrets are not entrusted to an habitual drunkard. Think how many soldiers who are not always sober have been entrusted by a general or a captain or a centurion with messages which might not be divulged! With regard to the notorious plot to murder Gaius Caesar—I mean the Caesar who conquered Pompey and got control of the state—Tillius Cimber was trusted with it no less than Gaius Cassius. Now Cassius throughout his life drank water; while Tillius Cimber was a sot as well as a brawler. Cimber himself alluded to this fact, saying: "*I* carry a master? I cannot carry my liquor!" So let each one call to mind those who, to his knowledge, can be ill trusted with wine, but well trusted with the spoken word; and yet one case occurs to my mind, which I shall relate, lest it fall into oblivion. For life should be provided with conspicuous illustrations. Let us not always be harking back to the dim past.

Lucius Piso, the director of Public Safety at Rome, was drunk from the very time of his appointment. He used to spend the greater part of the night at banquets, and would sleep until noon. That was the way he spent his morning hours. Nevertheless, he applied himself most diligently to his official duties, which included the guardianship of the city. Even the sainted Augustus trusted him with secret orders when he placed him in command of Thrace. Piso conquered that country. Tiberius, too, trusted him when he took his holiday in Campania, leaving behind him in the city many a critical matter that aroused both suspicion and hatred. I fancy that it was because Piso's drunkenness turned out well for the Emperor that he appointed to the office of city prefect Cossus, a man of authority and balance, but so soaked and steeped in drink that once, at a meeting of the Senate, whither he had come after banqueting, he was overcome by a slumber from which he could not be roused, and had to be carried home. It was to this man that Tiberius sent many orders, written in his own hand—orders which he believed he ought not to trust even to the officials of his household. Cossus never let a single secret slip out, whether personal or public.

So let us abolish all such harangues as this: "No man in the bonds of drunkenness has power over his soul. As the very vats are burst by new wine, and as the dregs at the bottom are raised to the surface by the strength of the fermentation; so, when the wine effervesces, whatever lies hidden below is brought up and made visible. As a man overcome by liquor cannot keep down his food when he has overindulged in wine, so he cannot keep back a secret either. He pours forth impartially both his own secrets and those of other persons." This, of course, is what commonly happens, but so does this—that we take counsel on serious subjects with those whom we know to be in the habit of drinking freely. Therefore this proposition, which is laid down in the guise of a defense of Zeno's syllogism, is false—that secrets are not entrusted to the habitual drunkard.

How much better it is to arraign drunkenness frankly and to expose its vices! For even the middling good man avoids them, not to mention the perfect sage, who is satisfied with slaking his thirst; the sage, even if now and then he is led on by good cheer which, for a friend's sake, is carried somewhat too far, yet always stops short of drunkenness. We shall investigate later the question whether the mind of the sage is upset by too much wine and commits follies like those of the toper; but meanwhile, if you wish to prove that a good man ought not to get drunk, why work it out by logic? Show how base it is to pour down more liquor than one can carry, and not to know the capacity of one's own stomach; show how often the drunkard does things which make him blush when he is sober; state that drunkenness is nothing but a condition of insanity purposely assumed. Prolong the drunkard's condition to several days; will you have any doubt about his madness? Even as it is, the madness is no less; it merely lasts a shorter time. Think of Alexander of Macedon, who stabbed Clitus, his dearest and most loyal friend, at a banquet; after Alexander understood what he had done, he wished to die, and assuredly he ought to have died.

Drunkenness kindles and discloses every kind of vice, and removes the sense of shame that veils our evil undertakings. For more men abstain from forbidden actions because they are ashamed of sinning than because their inclinations are good. When the strength of wine has become too great and has gained control over the mind, every lurking evil comes forth from its hiding place. Drunkenness does not create vice, it merely brings it into view; at such times the lustful man does not wait even for the privacy of a bedroom, but without postponement gives free play to the demands of his passions; at such times the unchaste man proclaims and publishes his malady; at such times your cross-grained fellow does not restrain his tongue or his hand. The haughty man increases his arrogance, the ruthless man his cruelty, the slanderer his spitefulness. Every vice is given free play and comes to the front. Besides, we forget who we are, we utter words that are halting and poorly enunciated, the glance is unsteady, the step falters,

Drunkenness does not create vice, it merely brings it into view

the head is dizzy, the very ceiling moves about as if a cyclone were whirling the whole house, and the stomach suffers torture when the wine generates gas and causes our very bowels to swell. However, at the time, these troubles can be endured, so long as the man retains his natural strength; but what can he do when sleep impairs his powers, and when that which was drunkenness becomes indigestion?

Think of the calamities caused by drunkenness in a nation! This evil has betrayed to their enemies the most spirited and warlike races; this evil has made breaches in walls defended by the stubborn warfare of many years; this evil has forced under alien sway peoples who were utterly unyielding and defiant of the yoke; this evil has conquered by the wine-cup those who in the field were invincible. Alexander, whom I have just mentioned, passed through his many marches, his many battles, his many winter campaigns (through which he worked his way by overcoming disadvantages of time or place), the many rivers which flowed from unknown sources, and the many seas, all in safety; it was intemperance in drinking that laid him low, and the famous death-dealing bowl of Hercules.

What glory is there in carrying much liquor? When you have won the prize, and the other banqueters, sprawling asleep or vomiting, have declined your challenge to still other toasts; when you are the last survivor of the revels; when you have vanquished everyone by your magnificent show of prowess and there is no man who has proved himself of so great capacity as you, you are vanquished by the cask. Mark Antony was a great man, a man of distinguished ability; but what ruined him and drove him into foreign habits and un-Roman vices, if it was not drunkenness and—no less potent than wine—love of Cleopatra? This it was that made him an enemy of the state; this it was that rendered him no match for his enemies; this it was that made him cruel, when as he sat at table the heads of the leaders of the state were brought in; when amid the most elaborate feasts and royal luxury he would identify the faces and hands of men whom he had proscribed; when, though heavy with wine, he yet thirsted for blood. It was intolerable that he was getting drunk while he did such things; how much more intolerable that he did these things while actually drunk! Cruelty usually follows wine-bibbing; for a man's soundness of mind is corrupted and made savage. Just as a lingering illness makes men querulous and irritable and drives them wild at the least crossing of their desires, so continued bouts of drunkenness bestialize the soul. For when people are often beside themselves, the habit of madness lasts on, and the vices which liquor generated retain their power even when the liquor is gone.

Therefore you should state why the wise man ought not to get drunk. Explain by facts, and not by mere words, the hideousness of the thing, and its haunting evils. Do that which is easiest of all—namely, demonstrate that what men call pleasures are punishments as soon as they have exceeded due bounds. For if you try to prove that the wise man can souse himself with much wine and yet keep his course straight, even though he be in his cups, you may go on to infer by syllogisms that he will not die if he swallows poison, that he will not sleep if he takes a sleeping-potion, that he will not vomit and reject the matter which clogs his stomach when you give him hellebore. But, when a man's feet totter and his tongue is unsteady, what reason have you for believing that he is half sober and half drunk? Farewell.

LXXXV. ON SOME VAIN SYLLOGISMS

I HAD BEEN INCLINED TO SPARE YOU, AND HAD OMITTED ANY KNOTTY problems that still remained undiscussed; I was satisfied to give you a sort of taste of the views held by the men of our school, who desire to prove that virtue is of itself sufficiently capable of rounding out the happy life. But now you bid me include the entire bulk either of our own syllogisms or of those which have been devised by other schools for the purpose of belittling us. If I shall be willing to do this, the result will be a book, instead of a letter. And I declare again and again that I take no pleasure in such proofs. I am ashamed to enter the arena and undertake battle on behalf of gods and men armed only with an awl.

"He that possesses prudence is also self-restrained; he that possesses self-restraint is also unwavering; he that is unwavering is unperturbed; he that is unperturbed is free from sadness; he that is free from sadness is happy. Therefore, the prudent man is happy, and prudence is sufficient to constitute the happy life."

Certain of the Peripatetics reply to this syllogism by interpreting "unperturbed," "unwavering," and "free from sadness" in such a way as to make "unperturbed" mean one who is rarely perturbed and only to a moderate degree, and not one who is never perturbed. Likewise, they say that a person is called "free from sadness" who is not subject to sadness, one who falls into this objectionable state not often nor in too great a degree. It is not, they say, the way of human nature that a man's spirit should be exempt from sadness, or that the wise man is not overcome by grief but is merely touched by it, and other arguments of this sort, all in accordance with the teachings of their school. They do not abolish the passions in this way; they only moderate them. But how petty is the superiority which we attribute to the wise man, if he is merely braver than the most craven, happier than the most dejected, more self-controlled than the most unbridled, and greater than the lowliest! Would Ladas boast his swiftness in running by comparing himself with the halt and the weak?

> For she could skim the topmost blades of corn
> And touch them not, nor bruise the tender ears;
> Or travel over seas, well-poised above
> The swollen floods, nor dip her flying feet
> In ocean's waters.

This is speed estimated by its own standard, not the kind which wins praise by comparison with that which is slowest. Would you call a man well who has a light case of fever? No, for good health does not mean moderate illness. They say, "The wise man is called unperturbed in the sense in which pomegranates are called mellow—not that there is no hardness at all in their seeds, but that the hardness is less than it was before." That view is wrong; for I am not referring to the gradual weeding out of evils in a good man, but to the complete absence of evils; there should be in him no evils at all, not even any small ones. For if there are any, they will grow, and as they grow will hamper him. Just as a large and complete cataract wholly blinds the eyes, so a medium-sized cataract dulls their vision.

If by your definition the wise man has any passions whatever, his reason will be no match for them and will be carried swiftly along, as it were, on a rushing stream—particularly if you assign to him, not one passion with which he must wrestle, but all the passions. And a throng of such, even though they be moderate, can affect him more than the violence of one powerful passion. He has a craving for money, although in a moderate degree. He has ambition, but it is not yet fully aroused. He has a hot temper, but it can be appeased. He has inconstancy, but not the kind that is very capricious or easily set in motion. He has lust, but not the violent kind. We could deal better with a person who possessed one full-fledged vice, than with one who possessed all the vices, but none of them in extreme form. Again, it makes no difference how great the passion is; no matter what its size may be, it knows no obedience, and does not welcome advice. Just as no animal, whether wild or tamed and gentle, obeys reason, since nature made it deaf to advice; so the passions do not follow or listen, however slight they are. Tigers and lions never put off their wildness; they some-times moderate it, and then, when you are least prepared, their softened fierceness is roused to madness. Vices are never genuinely tamed. Again, if reason prevails, the passions will not even get a start; but if they get under way against the will of reason, they will maintain themselves against the will of reason. For it is easier to stop them in the beginning than to control them when they gather force. This half-way ground is accordingly mislead-ing and useless; it is to be regarded just as the declaration that we ought to be "moderately" insane, or "moderately" ill. Virtue alone possesses moder-ation; the evils that afflict the mind do not admit of moderation. You can more easily remove than control them. Can one doubt that the vices of the human mind, when they have become chronic and callous ("diseases" we call them), are beyond control, as, for example, greed, cruelty, and wan-tonness? Therefore the passions also are beyond control; for it is from the passions that we pass over to the vices. Again, if you grant any privileges to sadness, fear, desire, and all the other wrong impulses, they will cease to lie within our jurisdiction. And why? Simply because the means of arousing them lie outside our own power. They will accordingly increase in propor-tion as the causes by which they are stirred up are greater or less. Fear will grow to greater proportions, if that which causes the terror is seen to be of greater magnitude or in closer proximity; and desire will grow keener in proportion as the hope of a greater gain has summoned it to action. If the existence of the passions is not in our own control, neither is the extent of their power; for if you once permit them to get a start, they will increase along with their causes, and they will be of whatever extent they shall grow to be. Moreover, no matter how small these vices are, they grow greater. That which is harmful never keeps within bounds. No matter how trifling diseases are at the beginning, they creep on apace; and sometimes the slightest augmentation of disease lays low the enfeebled body!

But what folly it is, when the beginnings of certain things are situated outside our control, to believe that their endings are within our control! How have I the power to bring something to a close, when I have not had the power to check it at the beginning? For it is easier to keep a thing out than to keep it under after you have let it in. Some men have made a distinction as follows, saying: "If a man has self-control and wisdom, he is indeed at peace as regards the attitude and habit of his mind, but not as regards the outcome. For, as far as his habit of mind is concerned, he is not perturbed, or saddened, or afraid; but there are many extraneous causes which strike him and bring perturbation upon him." What they mean to say is this: "So-and-so is indeed not a man of an angry disposition, but still he sometimes gives way to anger," and "He is not, indeed, inclined to fear, but still he sometimes experiences fear"; in other words, he is free from the fault, but is not free from the passion of fear. If, however, fear is once given an entrance, it will by frequent use pass over into a vice; and anger, once admitted into the mind, will alter the earlier habit of a mind that was formerly free from anger. Besides, if the wise man, instead of despising all causes that come from without, ever fears anything, when the time arrives for him to go bravely to meet the spear, or the flames, on behalf of his country, his laws, and his liberty, he will go forth reluctantly and with flagging spirit. Such inconsistency of mind, however, does not suit the character of a wise man.

Then, again, we should see to it that two principles which ought to be tested separately should not be confused. For the conclusion is reached independently that that alone is good which is honorable, and again independently the conclusion that virtue is sufficient for the happy life. If that alone is good which is honorable, everyone agrees that virtue is sufficient for the purpose of living happily; but, on the contrary, if virtue alone makes men happy, it will not be conceded that that alone is good which is honorable. Xenocrates and Speusippus hold that a man can become happy even by virtue alone, not, however, that that which is honorable is the only good. Epicurus also decides that one who possesses virtue is happy, but that virtue of itself is not sufficient for the happy life, because the pleasure that results from virtue, and not virtue itself, makes one happy. This is a futile distinction. For the same philosopher declares that virtue never exists without pleasure; and therefore, if virtue is always connected with pleasure and always inseparable therefrom, virtue is of itself sufficient. For virtue keeps pleasure in its company, and does not exist without it, even when alone. But it is absurd to say that a man will be happy by virtue alone, and yet not absolutely happy. I cannot discover how that may be, since the happy life contains in itself a good that is perfect and cannot be excelled. If a man has this good, life is completely happy.

Now if the life of the gods contains nothing greater or better, and the happy life is divine, then there is no further height to which a man can be raised. Also, if the happy life is in want of nothing, then every happy life is perfect; it is happy and at the same time most happy. Have you any doubt that the happy life is the Supreme Good? Accordingly, if it possesses the Supreme Good, it is supremely happy. Just as the Supreme Good does not admit of increase (for what will be superior to that which is supreme?), exactly so the happy life cannot be increased either; for it is not without the Supreme Good. If then you bring in one man who is "happier" than another, you will also bring in one who is "much happier"; you will then be making countless distinctions in the Supreme Good; although I understand the Supreme Good to be that good which admits of no degree above itself. If one person is less happy than another, it follows that he eagerly desires the life of that other and happier man in preference to his own. But the happy man prefers no other man's life to his own. Either of these two things is incredible: that there should be anything left for a happy man to wish for in preference to what is, or that he should not prefer the thing which is better than what he already has. For certainly, the more prudent he is, the more he will strive after the best, and he will desire to attain it by every possible means. But how can one be happy who is still able, or rather who is still bound, to crave something else? I will tell you what is the source of this error: men do not understand that the happy life is a unit; for it is its essence, and not its extent, that establishes such a life on the noblest plane. Hence there is complete equality between the life that is long and the life that is short, between that which is spread out and that which is confined, between that whose influence is felt in many places and in many directions, and that which is restricted to one interest. Those who reckon life by number, or by measure, or by parts, rob it of its distinctive quality. Now, in the happy life, what is the distinctive quality? It is its fulness. Satiety, I think, is the limit to our eating or drinking. A eats more and B eats less; what difference does it make? Each is now sated. Or A drinks more and B drinks less; what difference does it make? Each is no longer thirsty. Again, A lives for many years and B for fewer; no matter, if only A's many years have brought as much happiness as B's few years. He whom you maintain to be "less happy" is not happy; the word admits of no diminution.

"He who is brave is fearless; he who is fearless is free from sadness; he who is free from sadness is happy." It is our own school which has framed this syllogism; they attempt to refute it by this answer, namely, that we Stoics are assuming as admitted a premise which is false and distinctly controverted—that the brave man is fearless. "What!" they say, "will the brave man have no fear of evils that threaten him? That would be the condition of a madman, a lunatic, rather than of a brave man. The brave man will, it is true, feel fear in only a very slight degree; but he is not absolutely free from fear." Now those who assert this are doubling back to their old argument, in that they regard vices of less degree as equivalent to virtues. For indeed the man who does feel fear, though he feels it rather seldom and to a slight degree, is not free from wickedness, but is merely troubled by it in a milder form. "Not so," is the reply, "for I hold that a man is mad if he does not fear evils which hang over his head." What you say is perfectly true, if the things which threaten are really evils; but if he knows that they are not evils and believes that the only evil is baseness, he will be bound to face dangers without anxiety and to despise things which other men cannot help fearing. Or, if it is the characteristic of a fool and a madman not to fear evils, then the wiser a man is the more he will fear such things! "It is the doctrine of you Stoics, then," they reply, "that a brave man will expose himself to dangers." By no means; he will merely not fear them, though he will avoid them. It is proper for him to be careful, but not to be fearful. "What then? Is he not to fear death, imprisonment, burning, and all the other missiles of Fortune?" Not at all; for he knows that they are not evils, but only seem to be. He reckons all these things as the bugbears of man's existence. Paint him a picture of slavery, lashes, chains, want, mutilation by disease or by torture—or anything else you may care to mention; he will count all such things as terrors caused by the derangement of the mind. These things are only to be feared by those who are fearful. Or do you regard as an evil that to which some day we may be compelled to resort of our own free will?

What then, you ask, is an evil? It is the yielding to those things which are called evils; it is the surrendering of one's liberty into their control, when really we ought to suffer all things in order to preserve this liberty. Liberty is lost unless we despise those things which put the yoke upon our necks. If men knew what bravery was, they would have no doubts as to what a brave man's conduct should be. For bravery is not thoughtless rashness, or love of danger, or the courting of fear-inspiring objects; it is the knowledge which enables us to distinguish between that which is evil and that which is not. Bravery takes the greatest care of itself, and likewise endures with the greatest patience all things which have a false appearance of being evil. "What then?" is the query; "if the sword is brandished over your brave man's neck, if he is pierced in this place and in that continually, if he sees his entrails in his lap, if he is tortured again after being kept waiting in order that he may thus feel the torture more keenly, and if the blood flows afresh out of bowels where it has but lately ceased to flow, has he no fear? Shall you say that he has felt no pain either?" Yes, he has felt pain; for no human virtue can rid itself of feelings. But he has no fear; unconquered he looks down from a lofty height upon his sufferings. Do you ask me what spirit animates him in these circumstances? It is the spirit of one who is comforting a sick friend.

"That which is evil does harm; that which does harm makes a man worse. But pain and poverty do not make a man worse; therefore they are not evils." "Your proposition," says the objector, "is wrong; for what harms one does not necessarily make one worse. The storm and the squall work harm to the pilot, but they do not make a worse pilot of him for all that." Certain of the Stoic school reply to this argument as follows: "The pilot becomes a worse pilot because of storms or squalls, inasmuch as he cannot carry out his purpose and hold to his course; as far as his art is concerned, he becomes no worse a pilot, but in his work he does become worse." To this the Peripatetics retort: "Therefore, poverty will make even the wise man worse, and so will pain, and so will anything else of that sort. For although those things will not rob him of his virtue, yet they will hinder the work of virtue." This would be a correct statement, were it not for the fact that the pilot and the wise man are two different kinds of person. The wise man's purpose in conducting his life is not to accomplish at all hazards what he tries, but to do all things rightly; the pilot's purpose, however, is to bring his ship into port at all hazards. The arts are handmaids; they must accomplish what they promise to do. But wisdom is mistress and ruler. The arts render a slave's service to life; wisdom issues the commands.

For myself, I maintain that a different answer should be given: that the pilot's art is never made worse by the storm, nor the application of his art either. The pilot has promised you, not a prosperous voyage, but a serviceable performance of his task—that is, an expert knowledge of steering a ship. And the more he is hampered by the stress of Fortune, so much the more does his knowledge become apparent. He who has been able to say, "Neptune, you shall never sink this ship except on an even keel," has fulfilled the requirements of his art; the storm does not interfere with the pilot's work, but only with his success. "What then," you say, "is not a pilot harmed by any circumstance which does not permit him to make port, frustrates all his efforts, and either carries him out to sea, or holds the ship in irons, or strips her masts?" No, it does not harm him as a pilot, but only as a voyager; otherwise, he is no pilot. It is indeed so far from hindering the pilot's art that it even exhibits the art; for anyone, in the words of the proverb, is a pilot on a calm sea. These mishaps obstruct the voyage but not the steersman *qua* steersman. A pilot has a double rôle: one he shares with all his fellow-passengers, for he also is a passenger; the other is peculiar to him, for he is the pilot. The storm harms him as a passenger, but not as a pilot. Again, the pilot's art is another's good—it concerns his passengers just as a physician's art concerns his patients. But the wise man's good is a common good—it belongs both to those in whose company he lives, and to himself also. Hence our pilot may perhaps be harmed, since his services, which have been promised to others, are hindered by the storm; but the wise man is not harmed by poverty, or by pain, or by any other of life's storms. For all his functions are not checked, but only those which pertain to others; he himself is always in action, and is greatest in performance at the very time when Fortune has blocked his way. For then he is actually engaged in the business of wisdom; and this wisdom I have declared already to be, both the good of others, and also his own. Besides, he is not prevented from helping others, even at the time when constraining circumstances press him down. Because of his poverty he is prevented from showing how the State should be handled; but he teaches, none the less, how poverty should be handled. His work goes on throughout his whole life.

Thus no fortune, no external circumstance, can shut off the wise man from action. For the very thing which engages his attention prevents him from attending to other things. He is ready for either outcome: if it brings goods, he controls them; if evils, he conquers them. So thoroughly, I mean, has he schooled himself that he makes manifest his virtue in prosperity as well as in adversity, and keeps his eyes on virtue itself, not on the objects with which virtue deals. Hence neither poverty, nor pain, nor anything else that deflects the inexperienced and drives them headlong, restrains him from his course. Do you suppose that he is weighed down by evils? He makes use of them. It was not of ivory only that Phidias knew how to make statues; he also made statues of bronze. If you had given him marble, or a still meaner material, he would have made of it the best statue that the material would permit. So the wise man will develop virtue, if he may, in the midst of wealth, or, if not, in poverty; if possible, in his own country—if not, in exile; if possible, as a commander—if not, as a common soldier; if possible, in sound health—if not, enfeebled. Whatever Fortune he finds, he will accomplish from that something noteworthy.

Animal-tamers are unerring; they take the most savage animals, which may well terrify those who encounter them, and subdue them to the will of man; not content with having driven out their ferocity, they even tame them so that they dwell in the same abode. The trainer puts his hand into the lion's mouth; the tiger is kissed by his keeper. The tiny Aethiopian orders the elephant to sink down on its knees, or to walk the rope. Similarly, the wise man is a skilled hand at taming evils. Pain, want, disgrace, imprisonment, exile—these are universally to be feared; but when they encounter the wise man, they are tamed. Farewell.

XCII. ON THE HAPPY LIFE

———

Y‌OU AND I WILL AGREE, I THINK, THAT OUTWARD THINGS ARE sought for the satisfaction of the body, that the body is cherished out of regard for the soul, and that in the soul there are certain parts which minister to us, enabling us to move and to sustain life, bestowed upon us just for the sake of the primary part of us. In this primary part there is something irrational, and something rational. The former obeys the latter, while the latter is the only thing that is not referred back to another, but rather refers all things to itself. For the divine reason also is set in supreme command over all things, and is itself subject to none; and even this reason which we possess is the same, because it is derived from the divine reason. Now if we are agreed on this point, it is natural that we shall be agreed on the following also—namely, that the happy life depends upon this and this alone: our attainment of perfect reason. For it is naught but this that keeps the soul from being bowed down, that stands its ground against Fortune; whatever the condition of their affairs may be, it keeps men untroubled. And that alone is a good which is never subject to impairment. That man, I declare, is happy whom nothing makes less strong than he is; he keeps to the heights, leaning upon none but himself; for one who sustains himself by any prop may fall. If the case is otherwise, then things which do not pertain to us will begin to have great influence over us. But who desires Fortune to have the upper hand, or what sensible man prides himself upon that which is not his own?

What is the happy life? It is peace of mind, and lasting tranquility. This will be yours if you possess greatness of soul; it will be yours if you possess the steadfastness that resolutely clings to a good judgment just reached. How does a man reach this condition? By gaining a complete view of truth, by maintaining, in all that he does, order, measure, fitness, and a will that is inoffensive and kindly, that is intent upon reason and never departs therefrom, that commands at the same time love and admiration. In short, to give you the principle in brief compass, the wise man's soul ought to be such as would be proper for a god. What more can one desire who possesses all honorable things? For if dishonorable things can contribute to the best estate, then there will be the possibility of a happy life under conditions which do not include an honorable life. And what is more base or foolish than to connect the good of a rational soul with things irrational? Yet there are certain philosophers who hold that the Supreme Good admits of increase because it is hardly complete when the gifts of Fortune are adverse. Even Antipater, one of the great leaders of this school, admits that he ascribes some influence to externals, though only a very slight influence. You see, however, what absurdity lies in not being content with the daylight unless it is increased by a tiny fire. What importance can a spark have in the midst of this clear sunlight? If you are not contented with only that which is honorable, it must follow that you desire in addition either the kind of quiet which the Greeks call "undisturbedness," or else pleasure. But the former may be attained in any case. For the mind is free from disturbance when it is fully free to contemplate the universe, and nothing distracts it from the contemplation of nature. The second, pleasure, is simply the good of cattle. We are but adding the irrational to the rational, the dishonorable to the honorable. A pleasant physical sensation affects this life of ours; why, therefore, do you hesitate to say that all is well with a man just because all is well with his appetite? And do you rate, I will not say among heroes, but among men, the person whose Supreme Good is a matter of flavors and colors and sounds? Nay, let him withdraw from the ranks of this, the noblest class of living beings, second only to the gods; let him herd with the dumb brutes—an animal whose delight is in fodder!

The irrational part of the soul is twofold: the one part is spirited, ambitious, uncontrolled; its seat is in the passions; the other is lowly, sluggish, and devoted to pleasure. Philosophers have neglected the former, which, though unbridled, is yet better, and is certainly more courageous and more worthy of a man, and have regarded the latter, which is nerveless and ignoble, as indispensable to the happy life. They have ordered reason to serve this latter; they have made the Supreme Good of the noblest living being an abject and mean affair, and a monstrous hybrid, too, composed of various members which harmonize but ill. For as our Vergil, describing Scylla, says

Above, a human face and maiden's breast,
A beauteous breast—below, a monster huge
Of bulk and shapeless, with a dolphin's tail
Joined to a wolf-like belly.

And yet to this Scylla are tacked on the forms of wild animals, dreadful and swift; but from what monstrous shapes have these wiseacres compounded wisdom! Man's primary art is virtue itself; there is joined to this the useless and fleeting flesh, fitted only for the reception of food, as Posidonius remarks. This divine virtue ends in foulness, and to the higher parts, which are worshipful and heavenly, there is fastened a sluggish and flabby animal. As for the second desideratum—quiet—although it would indeed not of itself be of any benefit to the soul, yet it would relieve the soul of hindrances; pleasure, on the contrary, actually destroys the soul and softens all its vigor. What elements so inharmonious as these can be found united? To that which is most vigorous is joined that which is most sluggish, to that which is austere that which is far from serious, to that which is most holy that which is unrestrained even to the point of impurity. "What, then," comes the retort, "if good health, rest, and freedom from pain are not likely to hinder virtue, shall you not seek all these?" Of course I shall seek them, but not because they are goods—I shall

seek them because they are according to nature and because they will
be acquired through the exercise of good judgment on my part. What,
then, will be good in them? This alone—that it is a good thing to choose
them. For when I don suitable attire, or walk as I should, or dine as I
ought to dine, it is not my dinner, or my walk, or my dress that are goods,
but the deliberate choice which I show in regard to them, as I observe,
in each thing I do, a mean that conforms with reason. Let me also add
that the choice of neat clothing is a fitting object of a man's efforts; for
man is by nature a neat and well-groomed animal. Hence the choice of
neat attire, and not neat attire in itself, is a good; since the good is not
in the thing selected, but in the quality of the selection. Our actions are
honorable, but not the actual things which we do. And you may assume
that what I have said about dress applies also to the body. For nature has
surrounded our soul with the body as with a sort of garment; the body is
its cloak. But who has ever reckoned the value of clothes by the wardrobe
which contained them? The scabbard does not make the sword good or
bad. Therefore, with regard to the body I shall return the same answer to
you—that, if I have the choice, I shall choose health and strength, but
that the good involved will be my judgment regarding these things, and
not the things themselves.

Another retort is: "Granted that the wise man is happy; nevertheless,
he does not attain the Supreme Good which we have defined, unless the
means also which nature provides for its attainment are at his call. So,
while one who possesses virtue cannot be unhappy, yet one cannot be perfectly happy if one lacks such natural gifts as health, or soundness of limb."
But in saying this, you grant the alternative which seems the more difficult
to believe—that the man who is in the midst of unremitting and extreme
pain is not wretched, nay, is even happy; and you deny that which is much
less serious—that he is completely happy. And yet, if virtue can keep a man
from being wretched, it will be an easier task for it to render him completely
happy. For the difference between happiness and complete happiness is less
than that between wretchedness and happiness. Can it be possible that a
thing which is so powerful as to snatch a man from disaster, and place him

among the happy, cannot also accomplish what remains, and render him supremely happy? Does its strength fail at the very top of the climb? There are in life things which are advantageous and disadvantageous—both beyond our control. If a good man, in spite of being weighed down by all kinds of disadvantages, is not wretched, how is he not supremely happy, no matter if he does lack certain advantages? For as he is not weighted down to wretchedness by his burden of disadvantages, so he is not withdrawn from supreme happiness through lack of any advantages; nay, he is just as supremely happy without the advantages as he is free from wretchedness though under the load of his disadvantages. Otherwise, if his good can be impaired, it can be snatched from him altogether.

A short space above, I remarked that a tiny fire does not add to the sun's light. For by reason of the sun's brightness any light that shines apart from the sunlight is blotted out. "But," one may say, "there are certain objects that stand in the way even of the sunlight." The sun, however, is unimpaired even in the midst of obstacles, and, though an object may intervene and cut off our view thereof, the sun sticks to his work and goes on his course. Whenever he shines forth from amid the clouds, he is no smaller, nor less punctual either, than when he is free from clouds; since it makes a great deal of difference whether there is merely something in the way of his light or something which interferes with his shining. Similarly, obstacles take nothing away from virtue; it is no smaller, but merely shines with less brilliancy. In our eyes, it may perhaps be less visible and less luminous than before; but as regards itself it is the same and, like the sun when he is eclipsed, is still, though in secret, putting forth its strength. Disasters, therefore, and losses, and wrongs, have only the same power over virtue that a cloud has over the sun.

We meet with one person who maintains that a wise man who has met with bodily misfortune is neither wretched nor happy. But he also is in error, for he is putting the results of chance upon a parity with the virtues, and is attributing only the same influence to things that are honorable as to things that are devoid of honor. But what is more detestable and more unworthy than to put contemptible things in the same class with things worthy of reverence! For reverence is due to justice, duty, loyalty, bravery, and prudence; on the contrary, those attributes are worthless with which the most worthless men are often blessed in fuller measure—such as a sturdy leg, strong shoulders, good teeth, and healthy and solid muscles. Again, if the wise man whose body is a trial to him shall be regarded as neither wretched nor happy, but shall be left in a sort of half-way position, his life also will be neither desirable nor undesirable. But what is so foolish as to say that the wise man's life is not desirable? And what is so far beyond the bounds of credence as the opinion that any life is neither desirable nor undesirable? Again, if bodily ills do not make a man wretched, they consequently allow him to be happy. For things which have no power to change his condition for the worse, have not the power, either, to disturb that condition when it is at its best.

"But," someone will say, "we know what is cold and what is hot; a lukewarm temperature lies between. Similarly, A is happy, and B is wretched, and C is neither happy nor wretched." I wish to examine this figure, which is brought into play against us. If I add to your lukewarm water a larger quantity of cold water, the result will be cold water. But if I pour in a larger quantity of hot water, the water will finally become hot. In the case, however, of your man who is neither wretched nor happy, no matter how much I add to his troubles, he will not be unhappy, according to your argument; hence your figure offers no analogy. Again, suppose that I set before you a man who is neither miserable nor happy. I add blindness to his misfortunes; he is not rendered unhappy. I cripple him; he is not rendered unhappy. I add afflictions which are unceasing and severe; he is not rendered unhappy. Therefore, one whose life is not changed to misery by all these ills is not dragged by them, either, from his life of happiness. Then if, as you say, the wise man cannot fall from happiness to wretchedness, he cannot fall into non-happiness. For how, if one has begun to slip, can one stop at any particular place? That which prevents him from rolling to the bottom, keeps him at the summit. Why, you urge, may not a happy life possibly be destroyed? It cannot even be disjointed; and for that reason virtue is of itself sufficient for the happy life.

"But," it is said, "is not the wise man happier if he has lived longer and has been distracted by no pain, than one who has always been compelled to grapple with evil fortune?" Answer me now—is he any better or more honorable? If he is not, then he is not happier either. In order to live more happily, he must live more rightly; if he cannot do that, then he cannot live more happily either. Virtue cannot be strained tighter, and therefore neither can the happy life, which depends on virtue. For virtue is so great a good that it is not affected by such insignificant assaults upon it as shortness of life, pain, and the various bodily vexations. For pleasure does not deserve that virtue should even glance at it. Now what is the chief thing in virtue? It is the quality of not needing a single day beyond the present, and of not reckoning up the days that are ours; in the slightest possible moment of time virtue completes an eternity of good. These goods seem to us incredible and transcending man's nature; for we measure its grandeur by the standard of our own weakness, and we call our vices by the name of virtue. Furthermore, does it not seem just as incredible that any man in the midst of extreme suffering should say, "I am happy"? And yet this utterance was heard in the very factory of pleasure, when Epicurus said: "Today and one other day have been the happiest of all!" although in the one case he was tortured by strangury, and in the other by the incurable pain of an ulcerated stomach. Why, then, should those goods which virtue bestows be incredible in the sight of us, who cultivate virtue, when they are found even in those who acknowledge pleasure as their mistress? These also, ignoble and base-minded as they are, declare that even in the midst of excessive pain and misfortune the wise man will be neither wretched nor happy. And yet this also is incredible—nay, still more incredible, than the other case. For I do not understand how, if virtue falls from her heights, she can help being hurled all the way to the bottom. She either must preserve one in happiness, or, if driven from this position, she will not prevent us from becoming unhappy. If virtue only stands her ground, she cannot be driven from the field; she must either conquer or be conquered.

But some say: "Only to the immortal gods is given virtue and the happy life; we can attain but the shadow, as it were, and semblance of such goods as theirs. We approach them, but we never reach them." Reason, however, is a common attribute of both gods and men; in the gods it is already perfected, in us it is capable of being perfected. But it is our vices that bring us to despair; for the second class of rational being, man, is of an inferior order—a guardian, as it were, who is too unstable to hold fast to what is best, his judgment still wavering and uncertain. He may require the faculties of sight and hearing, good health, a bodily exterior that is not loathsome, and, besides, greater length of days conjoined with an unimpaired constitution. Though by means of reason he can lead a life which will not bring regrets, yet there resides in this imperfect creature, man, a certain power that makes for badness, because he possesses a mind which is easily moved to perversity. Suppose, however, the badness which is in full view, and has previously been stirred to activity, to be removed; the man is still not a good man, but he is being molded to goodness. One, however, in whom there is lacking any quality that makes for goodness, is bad.

But:

> He in whose body virtue dwells, and spirit
> E'er present

is equal to the gods; mindful of his origin, he strives to return thither. No man does wrong in attempting to regain the heights from which he once came down. And why should you not believe that something of divinity exists in one who is a part of God? All this universe which encompasses us is one, and it is God; we are associates of God; we are his members. Our soul has capabilities, and is carried thither, if vices do not hold it down. Just as it is the nature of our bodies to stand erect and look upward to the sky, so the soul, which may reach out as far as it will, was framed by nature to this end, that it should desire equality with the gods. And if it makes use of its powers and stretches upward into its proper region it is by no alien path that it struggles toward the heights. It would be a great task to journey heavenwards; the soul but returns thither. When once it has found the road, it boldly marches on, scornful of all things. It casts no backward glance at wealth; gold and silver—things which are fully worthy of the gloom in which they once lay—it values not by the sheen which smites the eyes of the ignorant, but by the mire of ancient days, whence our greed first detached and dug them out.

The soul, I affirm, knows that riches are stored elsewhere than in men's heaped-up treasure-houses; that it is the soul, and not the strong-box, which should be filled. It is the soul that men may set in dominion over all things, and may install as owner of the universe, so that it may limit its riches only by the boundaries of East and West, and, like the gods, may possess all things; and that it may, with its own vast resources, look down from on high upon the wealthy, no one of whom rejoices as much in his own wealth as he resents the wealth of another. When the soul has trans-ported itself to this lofty height, it regards the body also, since it is a burden which must be borne, not as a thing to love, but as a thing to oversee; nor is it subservient to that over which it is set in mastery. For no man is free who is a slave to his body. Indeed, omitting all the other masters which are brought into being by excessive care for the body, the sway which the body itself exercises is captious and fastidious. Forth from this body the soul issues, now with unruffled spirit, now with exultation, and, when once it has gone forth, asks not what shall be the end of the deserted day. No; just as we do not take thought for the clippings of the hair and the beard, even so that divine soul, when it is about to issue forth from the mortal man, regards the destination of its earthly vessel—whether it be consumed by fire, or shut in by a stone, or buried in the earth, or torn by wild beasts—as being of no more concern to itself than is the afterbirth to a child just born. And whether this body shall be cast out and plucked to pieces by birds, or devoured when thrown to the sea-dogs as prey,

how does that concern him who is nothing? Nay, even when it is among the living, the soul fears nothing that may happen to the body after death; for though such things may have been threats, they were not enough to terrify the soul previous to the moment of death. It says: "I am not frightened by the executioner's hook, nor by the revolting mutilation of the corpse which is exposed to the scorn of those who would witness the spectacle. I ask no man to perform the last rites for me; I entrust my remains to none. Nature has made provision that none shall go unburied. Time will lay away one whom cruelty has cast forth." Those were eloquent words which Maecenas uttered:

I want no tomb; for Nature doth provide
For outcast bodies burial.

You would imagine that this was the saying of a man of strict principles. He was indeed a man of noble and robust native gifts, but in prosperity he impaired these gifts by laxness. Farewell.

XCIII. ON THE QUALITY, AS CONTRASTED WITH THE LENGTH, OF LIFE

———

WHILE READING THE LETTER IN WHICH YOU WERE LAMENTING the death of the philosopher Metronax as if he might have, and indeed ought to have, lived longer, I missed the spirit of fairness which abounds in all your discussions concerning men and things, but is lacking when you approach one single subject—as is indeed the case with us all. In other words, I have noticed many who deal fairly with their fellow-men, but none who deals fairly with the gods. We rail every day at Fate, saying "Why has A been carried off in the very middle of his career? Why is not B carried off instead? Why should he prolong his old age, which is a burden to himself as well as to others?"

But tell me, pray, do you consider it fairer that you should obey Nature, or that Nature should obey you? And what difference does it make how soon you depart from a place which you must depart from sooner or later? We should strive, not to live long, but to live rightly; for to achieve long life you have need of Fate only, but for right living you need the soul. A life is really long if it is a full life; but fullness is not attained until the soul has rendered to itself its proper Good, that is, until it has assumed control over itself. What benefit does this older man derive from the eighty years he has spent in idleness? A person like him has not lived; he has merely tarried awhile in life. Nor has he died late in life; he has simply been a long time dying. He has lived eighty years, has he? That depends upon the date from which you reckon his death! Your other friend, however, departed in the bloom of his manhood. But he had fulfilled all the duties of a good citizen, a good friend, a good son; in no respect had he fallen short. His age may have been incomplete, but his life was complete. The other man has lived eighty years, has he? Nay, he has existed eighty years, unless perchance you mean by "he has lived" what we mean when we say that a tree "lives."

Pray, let us see to it, my dear Lucilius, that our lives, like jewels of great price, be noteworthy not because of their width but because of their weight. Let us measure them by their performance, not by their duration. Would you know wherein lies the difference between this hardy man who, despising Fortune, has served through every campaign of life and has attained to life's Supreme Good, and that other person over whose head many years have passed? The former exists even after his death; the latter has died even before he was dead.

We should therefore praise, and number in the company of the blest, that man who has invested well the portion of time, however little, that has been allotted to him; for such a one has seen the true light. He has not been one of the common herd. He has not only lived, but flourished. Sometimes he enjoyed fair skies; sometimes, as often happens, it was only through the clouds that there flashed to him the radiance of the mighty star. Why do you ask: "How long did he live?" He still lives! At one bound he has passed over into posterity and has consigned himself to the guardianship of memory.

And yet I would not on that account decline for myself a few additional years;

> **Just as one of small stature can be a perfect man, so a life of small compass can be a perfect life**

although, if my life's space be shortened, I shall not say that I have lacked aught that is essential to a happy life. For I have not planned to live up to the very last day that my greedy hopes had promised me; nay, I have looked upon every day as if it were my last. Why ask the date of my birth, or whether I am still enrolled on the register of the younger men? What I have is my own. Just as one of small stature can be a perfect man, so a life of small compass can be a perfect life. Age ranks among the external things. How long I am to exist is not mine to decide, but how long I shall go on existing in my present way is in my own control. This is the only thing you have the right to require of me—that I shall cease to measure out an inglorious age as it were in darkness, and devote myself to living instead of being carried along past life.

And what, you ask, is the fullest span of life? It is living until you possess wisdom. He who has attained wisdom has reached, not the furthermost, but the most important, goal. Such a one may indeed exult boldly and give thanks to the gods—aye, and to himself also—and he may count himself Nature's creditor for having lived. He will indeed have the right to do so, for he has paid her back a better life than he has received. He has set up the pattern of a good man, showing the quality and the greatness of a good man. Had another year been added, it would merely have been like the past.

And yet how long are we to keep living? We have had the joy of learning the truth about the universe. We know from what beginnings Nature arises; how she orders the course of the heavens; by what successive changes she summons back the year; how she has brought to an end all things that ever have been, and has established herself as the only end of her own being. We know that the stars move by their own motion, and that nothing except the earth stands still, while all the other bodies run on with uninterrupted swiftness. We know how the moon outstrips the sun; why it is that the slower leaves the swifter behind; in what manner she receives her light, or loses it again; what brings on the night, and what brings back the day. To that place you must go where you are to have a closer view of all these things. "And yet," says the wise man, "I do not depart more valiantly because of this hope—because I judge the path lies clear before me to my own gods. I have indeed earned admission to their presence, and in fact have already been in their company; I have sent my soul to them as they had previously sent theirs to me. But suppose that I am utterly annihilated, and that after death nothing mortal remains; I have no less courage, even if, when I depart, my course leads—nowhere."

"But," you say, "he has not lived as many years as he might have lived." There are books which contain very few lines, admirable and useful in spite of their size; and there are also the *Annals of Tanusius*—you know how bulky the book is, and what men say of it. This is the case with the long life of certain persons—a state which resembles the *Annals of Tanusius*! Do you regard as more fortunate the fighter who is slain on the last day of the games than one who goes to his death in the middle of the festivities? Do you believe that anyone is so foolishly covetous of life that he would rather have his throat cut in the dressing-room than in the amphitheatre? It is by no longer an interval than this that we precede one another. Death visits each and all; the slayer soon follows the slain. It is an insignificant trifle, after all, that people discuss with so much concern. And anyhow, what does it matter for how long a time you avoid that which you cannot escape? Farewell.

XCVI. ON FACING HARDSHIPS

———

SPITE OF ALL DO YOU STILL CHAFE AND COMPLAIN, NOT UNDER-standing that, in all the evils to which you refer, there is really only one—the fact that you *do* chafe and complain? If you ask me, I think that for a *man* there is no misery unless there be something in the universe which he thinks miserable. I shall not endure myself on that day when I find anything unendurable.

I am ill; but that is a part of my lot. My slaves have fallen sick, my income has gone off, my house is rickety, I have been assailed by losses, accidents, toil, and fear; this is a common thing. Nay, that was an understatement; it was an inevitable thing. Such affairs come by order, and not by accident. If you will believe me, it is my inmost emotions that I am just now disclosing to you: when everything seems to go hard and uphill, I have trained myself not merely to obey God, but to agree with His decisions. I follow Him because my soul wills it, and not because I must. Nothing will ever happen to me that I shall receive with ill humor or with a wry face. I shall pay up all my taxes willingly. Now all the things which cause us to groan or recoil are part of the tax of life—things, my dear Lucilius, which you should never hope and never seek to escape.

It was disease of the bladder that made you apprehensive; downcast letters came from you; you were continually getting worse; I will touch the truth more closely, and say that you feared for your life. But come, did you not know, when you prayed for long life, that this was what you were praying for? A long life includes all these troubles, just as a long journey includes dust and mud and rain. "But," you cry, "I wished to live, and at the same time to be immune from all ills." Such a womanish cry does no credit to a man. Consider in what attitude you shall receive this prayer of mine (I offer it not only in a good, but in a noble spirit): "May gods and goddesses alike forbid that Fortune keep you in luxury!" Ask yourself voluntarily which you would choose if some god gave you the choice—a life in a café or life in a camp.

And yet life, Lucilius, is really a battle. For this reason those who are tossed about at sea, who proceed uphill and downhill over toilsome crags and heights, who go on campaigns that bring the greatest danger, are heroes and front-rank fighters; but persons who live in rotten luxury and ease while others toil are mere turtle-doves safe only because men despise them. Farewell.

XCVIII. ON THE FICKLENESS OF FORTUNE

YOU NEED NEVER BELIEVE THAT ANYONE WHO DEPENDS UPON HAPpiness is happy! It is a fragile support—this delight in adventitious things; the joy which entered from without will some day depart. But that joy which springs wholly from oneself is leal and sound; it increases and attends us to the last; while all other things which provoke the admiration of the crowd are but temporary Goods. You may reply: "What do you mean? Cannot such things serve both for utility and for delight?" Of course. But only if they depend on us, and not we on them. All things that Fortune looks upon become productive and pleasant, only if he who possesses them is in possession also of himself, and is not in the power of that which belongs to him. For men make a mistake, my dear Lucilius, if they hold that anything good, or evil either, is bestowed upon us by Fortune; it is simply the raw material of Goods and Ills that she gives to us—the sources of things which, in our keeping, will develop into good or ill. For the soul is more powerful than any sort of Fortune; by its own agency it guides its affairs in either direction, and of its own power it can produce a happy life, or a wretched one.

A bad man makes everything bad—even things which had come with the appearance of what is best; but the upright and honest man corrects the wrongs of Fortune, and softens hardship and bitterness because he knows how to endure them; he likewise accepts prosperity with appreciation and moderation, and stands up against trouble with steadiness and courage. Though a man be prudent, though he conduct all his interests with well-balanced judgment, though he attempt nothing beyond his strength, he will not attain the Good which is unalloyed and beyond the reach of threats, unless he is sure in dealing with that which is unsure. For whether you prefer to observe other men (and it is easier to make up one's mind when judging the affairs of others), or whether you observe yourself, with all prejudice laid aside, you will perceive and acknowledge that there is no utility in all these desirable and beloved things, unless you equip yourself in opposition to the fickleness of chance and its consequences, and unless you repeat to yourself often and uncomplainingly, at every mishap, the words: "Heaven decreed it otherwise!" Nay rather, to adopt a phrase which is braver and nearer the truth—one on which you may more safely prop your spirit—say to yourself, whenever things turn out contrary to your expectation: "Heaven decreed *better*!"

If you are thus poised, nothing will affect you and a man will be thus poised if he reflects on the possible ups and downs in human affairs before he feels their force, and if he comes to regard children, or wife, or property, with the idea that he will not necessarily possess them always and that he will not be any more wretched just because he ceases to possess them. It is tragic for the soul to be apprehensive of the future and wretched in anticipation of wretchedness, consumed with an anxious desire that the objects which give pleasure may remain in its possession to the very end. For such a soul will never be at rest; in waiting for the

There is no difference between grief for something lost and the fear of losing it

future it will lose the present blessings which it might enjoy. And there is no difference between grief for something lost and the fear of losing it.

But I do not for this reason advise you to be indifferent. Rather do you turn aside from you whatever may cause fear. Be sure to foresee whatever can be foreseen by planning. Observe and avoid, long before it happens, anything that is likely to do you harm. To effect this your best assistance will be a spirit of confidence and a mind strongly resolved to endure all things. He who can bear Fortune, can also beware of Fortune. At any rate, there is no dashing of billows when the sea is calm. And there is nothing more wretched or foolish than premature fear. What madness it is to anticipate one's troubles! In fine, to express my thoughts in brief compass and portray to you those busybodies and self-tormentors—they are as uncontrolled in the midst of their troubles as they are before them. He suffers more than is necessary, who suffers before it is necessary; such men do not weigh the amount of their suffering, by reason of the same failing which prevents them from being ready for it; and with the same lack of restraint they fondly imagine that their luck will last for ever, and fondly imagine that their gains are bound to increase as well as merely continue. They forget this spring-board on which mortal things are tossed, and they guarantee for themselves exclusively a steady continuance of the gifts of chance.

For this very reason I regard as excellent the saying of Metrodorus, in a letter of consolation to his sister on the loss of her son, a lad of great promise: "All the Good of mortals is mortal." He is referring to those Goods toward which men rush in shoals. For the real Good does not perish; it is certain and lasting and it consists of wisdom and virtue; it is the only immortal thing that falls to mortal lot. But men are so wayward, and so forgetful of their goal and of the point toward which every day jostles them, that they are surprised at losing anything, although some day they are bound to lose everything. Anything of which you are entitled the owner is in your possession but is not your own; for there is no strength in that which is weak, nor anything lasting and invincible in that which is frail. We must lose our lives as surely as we lose our property, and this, if we understand the truth, is itself a consolation. Lose it with equanimity; for you must lose your life also.

What resource do we find, then, in the face of these losses? Simply this—to keep in memory the things we have lost, and not to suffer the enjoyment which we have derived from them to pass away along with them. To have may be taken from us, to have had, never. A man is thankless in the highest degree if, after losing something, he feels no obligation for having received it. Chance robs us of the thing, but leaves us its use and its enjoyment—and we have lost this if we are so unfair as to regret. Just say to yourself: "Of all these experiences that seem so frightful, none is insuperable. Separate trials have been overcome by many: fire by Mucius, crucifixion by Regulus, poison by Socrates, exile by Rutilius, and a sword-inflicted death by Cato; therefore, let us also overcome something." Again, those objects which attract the crowd under the appearance of beauty and happiness, have been scorned by many men and on many occasions. Fabricius when he was general refused riches, and when he was censor branded them with disapproval. Tubero deemed poverty worthy both of himself and of the deity on the Capitol when, by the use of earthenware dishes at a public festival, he showed that man should be satisfied with that which the gods could still use. The elder Sextius rejected the honors of office; he was born with an obligation to take part in public affairs, and yet would not accept the broad stripe even when the deified Julius offered it to him. For he understood that what can be given can also be taken away.

Let us also, therefore, carry out some courageous act of our own accord; let us be included among the ideal types of history. Why have we been slack? Why do we lose heart? That which could be done, can be done, if only we purify our souls and follow Nature; for when one strays away from Nature one is compelled to crave, and fear, and be a slave to the things of chance. We may return to the true path; we may be restored to our proper state; let us therefore be so, in order that we may be able to endure pain, in whatever form it attacks our bodies, and say to Fortune: "You have to deal with a man; seek someone whom you can conquer!"

By these words, and words of a like kind, the malignity of the ulcer is quieted down; and I hope indeed that it can be reduced, and either cured or brought to a stop, and grow old along with the patient himself. I am, however, comfortable in my mind regarding him; what we are now discussing is our own loss—the taking-off of a most excellent old man. For he himself has lived a full life, and anything additional may be craved by him, not for his own sake, but for the sake of those who need his services. In continuing to live, he deals generously. Some other person might have put an end to these sufferings; but our friend considers it no less base to flee from death than to flee toward death. "But," comes the answer, "if circumstances warrant, shall he not take his departure?" Of course, if he can no longer be of service to anyone, if all his business will be to deal with pain. This, my dear Lucilius, is what we mean by studying philosophy while applying it, by practicing it on truth—note what courage a prudent man possesses against death, or against pain, when the one approaches and the other weighs heavily. What ought to be done must be learned from one who does it. Up to now we have dealt with arguments—whether any man can resist pain, or whether the approach of death can cast down even great souls. Why discuss it further? Here is an immediate fact for us to tackle—death does not make our friend braver to face pain, nor pain to face death. Rather does he trust himself in the face of both; he does not suffer with resignation because he hopes for death, nor does he die gladly because he is tired of suffering. Pain he endures, death he awaits. Farewell.

XCIX. ON CONSOLATION
TO THE BEREAVED

—

I ENCLOSE A COPY OF THE LETTER WHICH I WROTE TO MARULLUS AT the time when he had lost his little son and was reported to be rather womanish in his grief—a letter in which I have not observed the usual form of condolence: for I did not believe that he should be handled gently, since in my opinion he deserved criticism rather than consolation. When a man is stricken and is finding it most difficult to endure a grievous wound, one must humor him for a while; let him satisfy his grief or at any rate work off the first shock; but those who have assumed an indulgence in grief should be rebuked immediately, and should learn that there are certain follies even in tears.

"Is it solace that you look for? Let me give you a scolding instead! You are like a woman in the way you take your son's death; what would you do if you had lost an intimate friend? A son, a little child of unknown promise, is dead; a fragment of time has been lost. We hunt out excuses for grief; we would even utter unfair complaints about Fortune, as if Fortune would never give us just reason for complaining! But I had really thought that you possessed spirit enough to deal with concrete troubles, to say nothing of the shadowy troubles over which men make moan through force of habit. Had you lost a friend (which is the greatest blow of all), you would have had to endeavor rather to rejoice because you had possessed him than to mourn because you had lost him.

"But many men fail to count up how manifold their gains have been, how great their rejoicings. Grief like yours has this among other evils: it is not only useless, but thankless. Has it then all been for nothing that you have had such a friend? During so many years, amid such close associations, after such intimate communion of personal interests, has nothing been accomplished? Do you bury friendship along with a friend? And why lament having lost him, if it be of no avail to have possessed him? Believe me, a great part of those we have loved, though chance has removed their persons, still abides with us. The past is ours, and there is nothing more secure for us than that which has been. We are ungrateful for past gains, because we hope for the future, as if the future—if so be that any future is ours—will not be quickly blended with the past. People set a narrow limit to their enjoyments if they take pleasure only in the present; both the future and the past serve for our delight—the one with anticipation, and the other with memories but the one is contingent and may not come to pass, while the other must have been.

"What madness it is, therefore, to lose our grip on that which is the surest thing of all? Let us rest content with the pleasures we have quaffed in past days, if only, while we quaffed them, the soul was not pierced like a sieve, only to lose again whatever it had received. There are countless cases of men who have without tears buried sons in the prime of manhood—men who have returned from the funeral pyre to the Senate chamber, or to any other official duties, and have straightway busied themselves with something else. And rightly; for in the first place it is idle to grieve if you get no help from grief. In the second place, it is unfair to complain about what has happened to one man but is in store for all. Again, it is foolish to lament one's loss, when there is such a slight interval between the lost and the loser. Hence we should be more resigned in spirit, because we follow closely those whom we have lost.

"Note the rapidity of Time—that swiftest of things; consider the shortness of the course along which we hasten at top speed; mark this throng of humanity all straining toward the same point with briefest intervals between them—even when they seem longest; he whom you count as passed away has simply posted on ahead. And what is more irrational than to bewail your predecessor, when you yourself must travel on the same journey? Does a man bewail an event which he knew would take place? Or, if he did not think of death as man's lot, he has but cheated himself. Does a man bewail an event which he has been admitting to be unavoidable? Whoever complains about the death of anyone is complaining that he was a man. Everyone is bound by the same terms: he who is privileged to be born is destined to die. Periods of time separate us, but death levels us. The period which lies between our first day and our last is shifting and uncertain: if you reckon it by its troubles, it is long even to a lad, if by its speed, it is scanty even to a greybeard. Everything is slippery, treacherous, and more shifting than any weather. All things are tossed about and shift into their opposites at the bidding of Fortune; amid such a turmoil of mortal affairs nothing but death is surely in store for anyone. And yet all men complain about the one thing wherein none of them is deceived. "But he died in boyhood." I am not yet prepared to say that he who quickly comes to the end of his life has the better of the bargain; let us turn to consider the case of him who has grown to old age. How very little is he superior to the child! Place before your mind's eye the vast spread of time's abyss, and consider the universe; and then contrast our so-called human life with infinity: you will then see how scant is that for which we pray, and which we seek to lengthen. How much of this time is taken up with weeping, how much with worry! How much with prayers for death before death arrives, how much with our health, how much with our fears! How much is occupied by our years of inexperience or of useless endeavor! And half of all this time is wasted in sleeping. Add, besides, our toils, our griefs, our dangers—and you will comprehend that even in the longest life real living is the least portion thereof. Nevertheless, who will make such an admission as: "A man is not better off who is allowed to return home quickly, whose journey is accomplished before he is wearied out"? Life is neither a Good nor an Evil; it is simply the place where good and evil exist. Hence this little boy has lost nothing except a hazard where loss was more assured than gain. He might have turned out temperate and prudent; he might, with your fostering care, have been molded to a better standard; but (and this fear is more reasonable) he might have become just like the many. Note the youths of the noblest lineage whose extravagance has flung them into the arena; note those men who cater to the passions of themselves and others in mutual lust, whose days never pass without drunkenness or some signal act of shame; it will thus be clear to you that there was more to fear than to hope for.

"For this reason you ought not to invite excuses for grief or aggravate slight burdens by getting indignant. I am not exhorting you to make an effort and rise to great heights; for my opinion of you is not so low as to make me think that it is necessary for you to summon every bit of your virtue to face this trouble. Yours is not pain; it is a mere sting—and it is you yourself who are turning it into pain.

Tears fall, no matter how we try to check them, and by being shed they ease the soul

"Of a surety philosophy has done you much service if you can bear courageously the loss of a boy who was as yet better known to his nurse than to his father! And what, then? Now, at this time, am I advising you to be hard-hearted, desiring you to keep your countenance unmoved at the very funeral ceremony, and not allowing your soul even to feel the pinch of pain? By no means. That would mean lack of feeling rather than virtue—to behold the burial ceremonies of those near and dear to you with the same expression as you beheld their living forms, and to show no emotion over the first bereavement in your family. But suppose that I forbade you to show emotion; there are certain feelings which claim their own rights. Tears fall, no matter how we try to check them, and by being shed they ease the soul. What, then, shall we do? Let us allow them to fall, but let us not command them do so; let us according as emotion floods our eyes, but not as mere imitation shall demand. Let us, indeed, add nothing to natural grief, nor augment it by following the example of others. The display of grief makes more demands than grief itself: how few men are sad in their own company! They lament the louder for being heard; persons who are reserved and silent when alone are stirred to new paroxysms of tears when they behold others near them! At such times they lay violent hands upon their own persons—though they might have done this more easily if no one were present to check them; at such times they pray for death; at such times they toss themselves from their couches. But their grief slackens with the departure of onlookers. In this matter, as in others also, we are obsessed by this fault—conforming to the pattern of the many, and regarding convention rather than duty. We abandon nature and surrender to the mob—who are never good advisers in anything, and in this respect as in all others are most inconsistent. People see a man who bears his grief bravely: they call him undutiful and savage-hearted; they see a man who collapses and clings to his dead: they call him womanish and weak. Everything, therefore, should be referred to reason. But nothing is more foolish than to court a reputation for sadness and to sanction tears; for I hold that with a wise man some tears fall by consent, others by their own force.

"I shall explain the difference as follows: When the first news of some bitter loss has shocked us, when we embrace the form that will soon pass from our arms to the funeral flames—then tears are wrung from us by the necessity of Nature, and the life-force, smitten by the stroke of grief, shakes both the whole body, and the eyes also, from which it presses out and causes to flow the moisture that lies within. Tears like these fall by a forcing-out process, against our will; but different are the tears which we allow to escape when we muse in memory upon those whom we have lost. And there is in them a certain sweet sadness when we remember the sound of a pleasant voice, a genial conversation, and the busy duties of yore; at such a time the eyes are loosened, as it were, with joy. This sort of weeping we indulge; the former sort overcomes us.

"There is, then, no reason why, just because a group of persons is standing in your presence or sitting at your side, you should either check or pour forth your tears; whether restrained or outpoured, they are never

so disgraceful as when feigned. Let them flow naturally. But it is possible
for tears to flow from the eyes of those who are quiet and at peace. They
often flow without impairing the influence of the wise man—with such
restraint that they show no want either of feeling or of self-respect. We
may, I assure you, obey Nature and yet maintain our dignity. I have seen
men worthy of reverence, during the burial of those near and dear, with
countenances upon which love was written clear even after the whole appa-
ratus of mourning was removed, and who showed no other conduct than
that which was allowed to genuine emotion. There is a comeliness even
in grief. This should be cultivated by the wise man; even in tears, just as in
other matters also, there is a certain sufficiency; it is with the unwise that
sorrows, like joys, gush over.

"Accept in an unruffled spirit that which is inevitable. What can happen that is beyond belief? Or what that is new? How many men at this very
moment are making arrangements for funerals! How many are purchasing
grave-clothes! How many are mourning, when you yourself have finished
mourning! As often as you reflect that your boy has ceased to be, reflect
also upon man, who has no sure promise of anything, whom Fortune does
not inevitably escort to the confines of old age, but lets him go at whatever
point she sees fit. You may, however, speak often concerning the departed,
and cherish his memory to the extent of your power. This memory will
return to you all the more often if you welcome its coming without bitterness; for no man enjoys converse with one who is sorrowful, much less
with sorrow itself. And whatever words, whatever jests of his, no matter
how much of a child he was, may have given you pleasure to hear—these
I would have you recall again and again; assure yourself confidently that
he might have fulfilled the hopes which you, his father, had entertained.
Indeed, to forget the beloved dead, to bury their memory along with their
bodies, to bewail them bounteously and afterward think of them but
scantily—this is the mark of a soul below that of man. For that is the way
in which birds and beasts love their young; their affection is quickly roused
and almost reaches madness, but it cools away entirely when its object dies.
This quality does not befit a man of sense; he should continue to remember,

but should cease to mourn. And in no wise do I approve of the remark of Metrodorus—that there is a certain pleasure akin to sadness, and that one should give chase thereto at such times as these. I am quoting the actual words of Metrodorus. I have no doubt what your feelings will be in these matters; for what is baser than to "chase after" pleasure in the very midst of mourning—nay, rather by means of mourning—and even amid one's tears to hunt out that which will give pleasure? These are the men who accuse us of too great strictness, slandering our precepts because of sup- posed harshness—because (say they) we declare that grief should either not be given place in the soul at all, or else should be driven out immediately. But which is the more incredible or inhuman—to feel no grief at the loss of one's friend, or to go a-hawking after pleasure in the midst of grief? That which we Stoics advise is honorable; when emotion has prompted a moder- ate flow of tears, and has, so to speak, ceased to effervesce, the soul should not be surrendered to grief. But what do you mean, Metrodorus, by saying that with our very grief there should be a blending of pleasure? That is the sweetmeat method of pacifying children; that is the way we still the cries of infants, by pouring milk down their throats!

"Even at the moment when your son's body is on the pyre, or your friend breathing his last, will you not suffer your pleasure to cease, rather than tickle your very grief with pleasure? Which is the more honorable—to remove grief from your soul, or to admit pleasure even into the company of grief? Did I say "admit"? Nay, I mean "chase after," and from the hands, too, of grief itself. Metrodorus says: "There is a certain pleasure which is related to sadness." We Stoics may say that, but you may not. The only Good which you recognize is pleasure, and the only Evil, pain; and what relationship can there be between a Good and an Evil? But suppose that such a relationship does exist; now, of all times, is it to be rooted out? Shall we examine grief also, and see with what elements of delight and pleasure it is surrounded? Certain remedies, which are beneficial for some parts of the body, cannot be applied to other parts because these are, in a way, revolting and unfit; and that which in certain cases would work to a good purpose without any loss to one's self-respect may become unseemly because of the situation of the wound. Are you not, similarly, ashamed to cure sorrow by pleasure? No, this sore spot must be treated in a more drastic way. This is what you should preferably advise: that no sensation of evil can reach one who is dead; for if it can reach him, he is not dead. And I say that nothing can hurt him who is as naught; for if a man can be hurt, he is alive. Do you think him to be badly off because he is no more, or because he still exists as somebody? And yet no torment can come to him from the fact that he is no more—for what feeling can belong to one who does not exist?—nor from the fact that he exists; for he has escaped the greatest disadvantage that death has in it—namely, nonexistence.

"Let us say this also to him who mourns and misses the untimely dead: that all of us, whether young or old, live, in comparison with eternity, on the same level as regards our shortness of life. For out of all time there comes to us less than what anyone could call least, since "least" is at any rate some part; but this life of ours is next to nothing, and yet (fools that we are!), we marshal it in broad array!

"These words I have written to you, not with the idea that you should expect a cure from me at such a late date—for it is clear to me that you have told yourself everything that you will read in my letter—but with the idea that I should rebuke you even for the slight delay during which you lapsed from your true self, and should encourage you for the future, to rouse your spirit against Fortune and to be on the watch for all her missiles, not as if they might possibly come, but as if they were bound to come." Farewell.

CV. ON FACING
THE WORLD WITH
CONFIDENCE

———

I SHALL NOW TELL YOU CERTAIN THINGS TO WHICH YOU SHOULD PAY attention in order to live more safely. Do you however—such is my judgment—hearken to my precepts just as if I were counselling you to keep safe your health in your country-place at Ardea?

Reflect on the things which goad man into destroying man: you will find that they are hope, envy, hatred, fear, and contempt. Now, of all these, contempt is the least harmful, so much so that many have skulked behind it as a sort of cure. When a man despises you, he works you injury, to be sure, but he passes on; and no one persistently or of set purpose does hurt to a person whom he despises. Even in battle, prostrate soldiers are neglected: men fight with those who stand their ground. And you can avoid the envious hopes of the wicked so long as you have nothing which can stir the evil desires of others, and so long as you possess nothing remarkable. For people crave even little things, if these catch the attention or are of rare occurrence.

You will escape envy if you do not force yourself upon the public view, if you do not boast your possessions, if you understand how to enjoy things privately. Hatred comes either from running foul of others: and this can be avoided by never provoking anyone; or else it is uncalled for: and common sense will keep you safe from it. Yet it has been dangerous to many; some people have been hated without having had an enemy. As to not being feared, a moderate Fortune and an easy disposition will guarantee you that; men should know that you are the sort of person who can be offended without danger; and your reconciliation should be easy and sure. Moreover, it is as troublesome to be feared at home as abroad; it is as bad to be feared by a slave as by a gentleman. For every one has strength enough to do you some harm. Besides, he who is feared, fears also; no one has been able to arouse terror and live in peace of mind.

Contempt remains to be discussed. He who has made this quality an adjunct of his own personality, who is despised because he wishes to be despised and not because he *must* be despised, has the measure of contempt under his control. Any inconveniences in this respect can be dispelled by honorable occupations and by friendships with men who have influence with an influential person; with these men it will profit you to engage but not to entangle yourself, lest the cure may cost you more than the risk. Nothing, however, will help you so much as keeping still—talking very little with others, and as much as may be with yourself. For there is a sort of charm about conversation, something very subtle and coaxing, which, like intoxication or love, draws secrets from us. No man will keep to himself what he hears. No one will tell another only as much as he has heard. And he who tells tales will tell names, too. Everyone has someone to whom he entrusts exactly what has been entrusted to him. Though he checks his own garrulity, and is content with one hearer, he will bring about him a nation, if that which was a secret shortly before becomes common talk.

The most important contribution to peace of mind is never to do wrong. Those who lack self-control lead disturbed and tumultuous lives; their crimes are balanced by their fears, and they are never at ease. For they tremble after the deed, and they are embarrassed; their consciences do not allow them to busy themselves with other matters, and continually compel them to give an answer. Whoever expects punishment receives it, but whoever deserves it, expects it. Where there is an evil conscience some-thing may bring safety, but nothing can bring ease; for a man imagines that, even if he is not under arrest, he may soon be arrested. His sleep is troubled; when he speaks of another man's crime, he reflects upon his own, which seems to him not sufficiently blotted out, not sufficiently hidden from view. A wrongdoer sometimes has the luck to escape notice but never the assurance thereof. Farewell.

CIX. ON THE FELLOW-SHIP OF WISE MEN

YOU EXPRESSED A WISH TO KNOW WHETHER A WISE MAN CAN HELP a wise man. For we say that the wise man is completely endowed with every good, and has attained perfection; accordingly, the question arises how it is possible for anyone to help a person who possesses the Supreme Good.

Good men are mutually helpful; for each gives practice to the other's virtues and thus maintains wisdom at its proper level. Each needs someone with whom he may make comparisons and investigations. Skilled wrestlers are kept up to the mark by practice; a musician is stirred to action by one of equal proficiency. The wise man also needs to have his virtues kept in action; and as he prompts himself to do things, so is he prompted by another wise man. How can a wise man help another wise man? He can quicken his impulses, and point out to him opportunities for honorable action. Besides, he can develop some of his own ideas; he can impart what he has discovered. For even in the case of the wise man something will always remain to discover, something toward which his mind may make new ventures.

Evil men harm evil men; each debases the other by rousing his wrath, by approving his churlishness, and praising his pleasures; bad men are at their worst stage when their faults are most thoroughly intermingled, and their wickedness has been, so to speak, pooled in partnership. Conversely, therefore, a good man will help another good man. "How?" you ask. Because he will bring joy to the other, he will strengthen his faith, and from the contemplation of their mutual tranquility the delight of both will be increased. Moreover they will communicate to each other a knowledge of certain facts; for the wise man is not all-knowing. And even if he were all-knowing, someone might be able to devise and point out shortcuts, by which the whole matter is more readily disseminated. The wise will help the wise, not, mark you, because of his own strength merely, but because of the strength of the man whom he assists. The latter, it is true, can by himself develop his own parts; nevertheless, even one who is running well is helped by one who cheers him on.

"But the wise man does not really help the wise; he helps himself. Let me tell you this: strip the one of his special powers, and the other will accomplish nothing." You might as well, on that basis, say that sweetness is not in the honey: for it is the person himself who is to eat it, that is so equipped, as to tongue and palate, for tasting this kind of food that the special flavor appeals to him, and anything else displeases. For there are certain men so affected by disease that they regard honey as bitter. Both men should be in good health, that the one may be helpful and the other a proper subject for help. Again they say: "When the highest degree of heat has been attained, it is superfluous to apply more heat; and when the Supreme Good has been attained, it is superfluous to have a helper. Does a completely stocked farmer ask for further supplies from his neighbors? Does a soldier who is sufficiently armed for going well-equipped into action need any more weapons? Very well, neither does the wise man; for he is sufficiently equipped and sufficiently armed for life." My answer to this is, that when one is heated to the highest degree, one must have continued heat to maintain the highest temperature. And if it be objected that heat is self-maintaining, I say that there are great distinctions among the things that you are comparing; for heat is a single thing, but helpfulness is of many kinds. Again, heat is not helped by the addition of further heat, in order to be hot; but the wise man cannot maintain his mental standard without intercourse with friends of his own kind—with whom he may share his goodness. Moreover, there is a sort of mutual friendship among all the virtues. Thus, he who loves the virtues of certain among his peers, and in turn exhibits his own to be loved, is helpful. Like things give pleasure, especially when they are honorable and when men know that there is mutual approval. And besides, none but a wise man can prompt another wise man's soul in an intelligent way, just as man can be prompted in a rational way by man only. As, therefore, reason is necessary for the prompting of reason, so, in order to prompt perfect reason, there is need of perfect reason.

Some say that we are helped even by those who bestow on us the so-called indifferent benefits, such as money, influence, security, and all the other valued or essential aids to living. If we argue in this way, the veriest fool will be said to help a wise man. Helping, however, really means prompting the soul in accordance with Nature, both by the prompter's excellence and by the excellence of him who is thus prompted. And this cannot take place without advantage to the helper also. For in training the excellence of another, a man must necessarily train his own. But, to omit from discussion supreme goods or the things which produce them, wise men can nonetheless be mutually helpful. For the mere discovery of a sage by a sage is in itself a desirable event; since everything good is naturally dear to the good man, and for this reason one feels congenial with a good man as one feels congenial with oneself.

It is necessary for me to pass from this topic to another, in order to prove my point. For the question is asked, whether the wise man will weigh his opinions, or whether he will apply to others for advice. Now he is compelled to do this when he approaches state and home duties—everything, so to speak, that is mortal. He needs outside advice on such matters, as does the physician, the pilot, the attorney, or the pleader of cases. Hence, the wise will sometimes help the wise; for they will persuade each other. But in these matters of great import also—aye, of divine import, as I have termed them—the wise man can also be useful by discussing honorable things in common, and by contributing his thoughts and ideas. Moreover, it is in accordance with Nature to show affection for our friends, and to rejoice in their advancement as if it were absolutely our own. For if we have not done this, even virtue, which grows strong only through exercising our perceptions, will not abide with us. Now virtue advises us to arrange the present well, to take thought regarding the future, to deliberate and apply our minds; and one who takes a friend into council with him, can more easily apply his mind and think out his problem.

Therefore he will seek either the perfect wise man or one who has progressed to a point bordering on perfection. The perfect wise man, moreover, will help us if he aids our counsels with ordinary good sense. They say that men see farther in the affairs of others than in their own. A defect of character causes this in those who are blinded by self-love, and whose fear in the hour of peril takes away their clear view of that which is useful; it is when a man is more at ease and freed from fear that he will begin to be wise. Nevertheless, there are certain matters where even wise men see the facts more clearly in the case of others than in their own. Moreover, the wise man will, in company with his fellow sage, confirm the truth of that most sweet and honorable proverb—"always desiring and always refusing the same things": it will be a noble result when they draw the load "with equal yoke."

I have thus answered your demand, although it came under the head of subjects which I include in my volumes *On Moral Philosophy*. Reflect, as I am often wont to tell you, that there is nothing in such topics for us except mental gymnastics. For I return again and again to the thought: "What good does this do me? Make me more brave now, more just, more restrained! I have not yet the opportunity to make use of my training; for I still need the physician. Why do you ask of me a useless knowledge? You have promised great things; test me, watch me! You assured me that I should be unterrified though swords were flashing round me, though the point of the blade were grazing my throat; you assured me that I should be at ease though fires were blazing round me, or though a sudden whirlwind should snatch up my ship and carry it over all the sea. Now make good for me such a course of treatment that I may despise pleasure and glory. Thereafter you shall teach me to work out complicated problems, to settle doubtful points, to see through that which is not clear; teach me now what it is necessary for me to know!" Farewell.

CX. ON TRUE AND FALSE RICHES

———

FROM MY VILLA AT NOMENTUM I SEND YOU GREETING AND BID YOU keep a sound spirit within you—in other words, gain the blessing of all the gods, for he is assured of their grace and favor who has become a blessing to himself. Lay aside for the present the belief of certain persons—that a god is assigned to each one of us as a sort of attendant—not a god of regular rank, but one of a lower grade—one of those whom Ovid calls "plebeian gods." Yet, while laying aside this belief, I would have you remember that our ancestors, who followed such a creed, have become Stoics; for they have assigned a Genius or a Juno to every individual. Later on we shall investigate whether the gods have enough time on their hands to care for the concerns of private individuals; in the meantime, you must know that whether we are allotted to special guardians, or whether we are neglected and consigned to Fortune, you can curse a man with no heavier curse than to pray that he may be at enmity with himself.

There is no reason, however, why you should ask the gods to be hostile to anyone whom you regard as deserving of punishment; they *are* hostile to such a person, I maintain, even though he seems to be advanced by their favor. Apply careful investigation, considering how our affairs actually stand, and not what men say of them; you will then understand that evils are more likely to help us than to harm us. For how often has so-called affliction been the source and the beginning of happiness! How often have privileges which we welcomed with deep thanksgiving built steps for themselves to the top of a precipice, still uplifting men who were already distinguished—just as if they had previously stood in a position whence they could fall in safety! But this very fall has in it nothing evil, if you consider the end, after which nature lays no man lower. The universal limit is near; yes, there is near us the point where the prosperous man is upset, and the point where the unfortunate is set free. It is we ourselves that extend both these limits, lengthening them by our hopes and by our fears.

If, however, you are wise, measure all things according to the state of man; restrict at the same time both your joys and your fears. Moreover, it is worthwhile not to rejoice at anything for long, so that you may not fear anything for long. But why do I confine the scope of this evil? There is no reason why you should suppose that anything is to be feared. All these things which stir us and keep us a-flutter are empty things. None of us has sifted out the truth; we have passed fear on to one another; none has dared to approach the object which caused his dread, and to understand the nature of his fear—aye, the good behind it. That is why falsehood and vanity still gain credit—because they are not refuted. Let us account it worthwhile to look closely at the matter; then it will be clear how fleeting, how unsure, and how harmless are the things which we fear. The disturbance in our spirits is similar to that which Lucretius detected:

> Like boys who cower frightened in the dark,
> So grown-ups in the light of day feel fear.

What, then? Are we not more foolish than any child, we who "in the light of day feel fear"? But you were wrong, Lucretius; we are not afraid in the daylight; we have turned everything into a state of darkness. We see neither what injures nor what profits us; all our lives through we blunder along, neither stopping nor treading more carefully on this account. But you see what madness it is to rush ahead in the dark. Indeed, we are bent on getting ourselves called back from a greater distance; and though we do not know our goal, yet we hasten with wild speed in the direction whither we are straining.

The light, however, may begin to shine, provided we are willing. But such a result can come about only in one way—if we acquire by knowledge this familiarity with things divine and human, if we not only flood ourselves but steep ourselves therein, if a man reviews the same principles even though he understands them and applies them again and again to himself, if he has investigated what is good, what is evil, and what has falsely been so entitled; and, finally, if he has investigated honor and baseness, and Providence. The range of the human intelligence is not confined within these limits; it may also explore outside the universe its destination and its source, and the ruin toward which all nature hastens so rapidly. We have withdrawn the soul from this divine contemplation and dragged it into mean and lowly tasks, so that it might be a slave to greed, so that it might forsake the universe and its confines, and, under the command of masters who try all possible schemes, pry beneath the earth and seek what evil it can dig up therefrom—discontented with that which was freely offered to it.

Now God, who is the Father of us all, has placed ready to our hands those things which he intended for our own good; he did not wait for any search on our part, and he gave them to us voluntarily. But that which would be injurious, he buried deep in the earth. We can complain of nothing but ourselves; for we have brought to light the materials for our destruction, against the will of Nature, who hid them from us. We have bound over our souls to pleasure, whose service is the source of all evil; we have surrendered ourselves to self-seeking and reputation, and to other aims which are equally idle and useless.

What, then, do I now encourage you to do? Nothing new—we are not trying to find cures for new evils—but this first of all: namely, to see clearly for yourself what is necessary and what is superfluous. What is necessary will meet you everywhere; what is superfluous has always to be hunted-out—and with great endeavor. But there is no reason why you should flatter yourself over-much if you despise gilded couches and jeweled furniture. For what virtue lies in despising useless things? The time to admire your own conduct is when you have come to despise the necessities. You are doing no great thing if you can live without royal pomp, if you feel no craving for boars which weigh a thousand pounds, or for flamingo tongues, or for the other absurdities of a luxury that already wearies of game cooked whole, and chooses different bits from separate animals; I shall admire you only when you have learned to scorn even the common sort of bread, when you have made yourself believe that grass grows for the needs of men as well as of cattle, when you have found out that food from the treetop can fill the belly—into which we cram things of value as if it could keep what it has received. We should satisfy our stomachs without being over-nice. How does it matter what the stomach receives, since it must lose whatever it has received?—You enjoy the carefully arranged dainties which are caught on land and sea; some are more pleasing if they are brought fresh to the table, others, if after long feeding and forced fattening they almost melt and can hardly retain their own grease. You like the subtly devised flavor of these dishes. But I assure you that such carefully chosen and variously seasoned dishes, once they have entered the belly, will be overtaken alike by one and the same corruption. Would you despise the pleasures of eating? Then consider its result! I remember some words of Attalus, which elicited general applause:

"Riches long deceived me. I used to be dazed when I caught some gleam of them here and there. I used to think that their hidden influence matched their visible show. But once, at a certain elaborate entertainment, I saw embossed work in silver and gold equaling the wealth of a whole city, and colors and tapestry devised to match objects which surpassed the value of gold or of silver—brought not only from beyond our own borders, but from beyond the borders of our enemies; on one side were slave-boys notable for their training and beauty, on the other were throngs of slave-women, and all the other resources that a prosperous and mighty empire could offer after reviewing its possessions. What else is this, I said to myself, than a stirring-up of man's cravings, which are in themselves provocative of lust? What is the meaning of all this display of money? Did we gather merely to learn what greed was? For my own part I left the place with less craving than I had when I entered. I came to despise riches, not because of their uselessness, but because of their pettiness. Have you noticed how, inside a few hours, that program, however slow-moving and carefully arranged, was over and done? Has a business filled up this whole life of ours, which could not fill up a whole day?

"I had another thought also: the riches seemed to me to be as useless to the possessors as they were to the onlookers. Accordingly, I say to myself, whenever a show of that sort dazzles my eyes, whenever I see a splendid palace with a well-groomed corps of attendants and beautiful bearers carrying a litter: Why wonder? Why gape in astonishment? It is all show; such things are displayed, not possessed; while they please they pass away. Turn yourself rather to the true riches. Learn to be content with little, and cry out with courage and with greatness of soul: "We have water, we have porridge; let us compete in happiness with Jupiter himself." And why not, I pray thee, make this challenge even without porridge and water? For it is base to make the happy life depend upon silver and gold, and just as base to make it depend upon water and porridge. "But," some will say, "what could I do without such things?" Do you ask what is the cure for want? It is to make hunger satisfy hunger; for, all else being equal, what difference is there in the smallness or the largeness of the things that force you to be a slave? What matter how little it is that Fortune can refuse to you? Your very porridge and water can fall under another's jurisdiction; and besides, freedom comes, not to him over whom Fortune has slight power, but to him over whom she has no power at all. This is what I mean: you must crave nothing, if you would vie with Jupiter; for Jupiter craves nothing."

This is what Attalus told us. If you are willing to think often of these things, you will strive not to seem happy, but to be happy, and, in addition, to seem happy to yourself rather than to others. Farewell.

CXVI. ON SELF-CONTROL

—

THE QUESTION HAS OFTEN BEEN RAISED WHETHER IT IS BETTER TO have moderate emotions, or none at all. Philosophers of our school reject the emotions; the Peripatetics keep them in check. I, however, do not understand how any half-way disease can be either wholesome or helpful. Do not fear; I am not robbing you of any privileges which you are unwilling to lose! I shall be kindly and indulgent toward the objects for which you strive—those which you hold to be necessary to our existence, or useful, or pleasant; I shall simply strip away the vice. For after I have issued my prohibitions against the desires, I shall still allow you to wish that you may do the same things fearlessly and with greater accuracy of judgment, and to feel even the pleasures more than before; and how can these pleasures help coming more readily to your call, if you are their lord rather than their slave!

"But," you object, "it is natural for me to suffer when I am bereaved of a friend; grant some privileges to tears which have the right to flow! It is also natural to be affected by men's opinions and to be cast down when they are unfavorable; so why should you not allow me such an honorable aversion to bad opinion?"

There is no vice which lacks some plea; there is no vice that at the start is not modest and easily entreated; but afterward the trouble spreads more widely. If you allow it to begin, you cannot make sure of its ceasing. Every emotion at the start is weak. Afterward, it rouses itself and gains strength by progress; it is more easy to forestall it than to forgo it. Who does not admit that all the emotions flow as it were from a certain natural source? We are endowed by Nature with an interest in our own well-being; but this very interest, when overindulged, becomes a vice. Nature has intermingled pleasure with necessary things—not in order that we should seek pleasure, but in order that the addition of pleasure may make the indispensable means of existence attractive to our eyes. Should it claim rights of its own, it is luxury.

Let us therefore resist these faults when they are demanding entrance, because, as I have said, it is easier to deny them admittance than to make them depart. And if you cry: "One should be allowed a certain amount of grieving, and a certain amount of fear," I reply that the "certain amount" can be too long-drawn-out, and that it will refuse to stop short when you so desire. The wise man can safely control himself without becoming over-anxious; he can halt his tears and his pleasures at will; but in our case, because it is not easy to retrace our steps, it is best not to push ahead at all. I think that Panaetius gave a very neat answer to a certain youth who asked him whether the wise man should become a lover: "As to the wise man, we shall see later; but you and I, who are as yet far removed from wisdom, should not trust ourselves to fall into a state that is disordered, uncontrolled, enslaved to another, contemptible to itself. If our love be not spurned, we are excited by its kindness; if it be scorned, we are kindled by our pride. An easily won love hurts us as much as one which is difficult to win; we are captured by that which is compliant, and we struggle with that which is hard. Therefore, knowing our weakness, let us remain quiet. Let us not expose this unstable spirit to the temptations of drink, or beauty, or flattery, or anything that coaxes and allures."

The reason is unwillingness, the excuse, inability

Now that which Panaetius replied to the question about love may be applied, I believe, to all the emotions. In so far as we are able, let us step back from slippery places; even on dry ground it is hard enough to take a sturdy stand. At this

ENECA
oint, I know, you will confront me with that common complaint against the Stoics: "Your promises are too great, and your counsels too hard. We are mere manikins, unable to deny ourselves everything. We shall sorrow, but not to any great extent; we shall feel desires, but in moderation; we shall give way to anger, but we shall be appeased." And do you know why we have not the power to attain this Stoic ideal? It is because we refuse to believe in our power. Nay, of a surety, there is something else which plays a part: it is because we are in love with our vices; we uphold them and prefer to make excuses for them rather than shake them off. We mortals have been endowed with sufficient strength by nature, if only we use this strength, if only we concentrate our powers and rouse them all to help us or at least not to hinder us. The reason is unwillingness, the excuse, inability. Farewell.

CXVIII. ON THE VANITY
OF PLACE-SEEKING

——

YOU HAVE BEEN DEMANDING MORE FREQUENT LETTERS FROM ME. But if we compare the accounts, you will not be on the credit side. We had indeed made the agreement that your part came first, that you should write the first letters, and that I should answer. However, I shall not be disagreeable; I know that it is safe to trust you, so I shall pay in advance, and yet not do as the eloquent Cicero bids Atticus do: "Even if you have nothing to say, write whatever enters your head." For there will always be something for me to write about, even omitting all the kinds of news with which Cicero fills his correspondence: what candidate is in difficulties, who is striving on borrowed resources and who on his own; who is a candidate for the consulship relying on Caesar, or on Pompey, or on his own strongbox; what a merciless usurer is Caecilius, out of whom his friends cannot screw a penny for less than one percent each month.

But it is preferable to deal with one's own ills, rather than with another's—to sift oneself and see for how many vain things one is a candidate, and cast a vote for none of them. This, my dear Lucilius, is a noble thing, this brings peace and freedom to canvass for nothing, and to pass by all the elections of Fortune. How can you call it enjoyable, when the tribes are called together and the candidates are making offerings in their favorite temples—some of them promising money gifts and others doing business by means of an agent, or wearing down their hands with the kisses of those to whom they will refuse the least finger-touch after being elected—when all are excitedly awaiting the announcement of the herald, do you call it enjoyable, I say, to stand idle and look on at this Vanity Fair without either buying or selling? How much greater joy does one feel who looks without concern, not merely upon the election of a praetor or of a consul, but upon that great struggle in which some are seeking yearly honors, and others permanent power, and others the triumph and the prosperous outcome of war, and others riches, or marriage and offspring, or the welfare of themselves and their relatives! What a great-souled action it is to be the only person who is canvassing for nothing, offering prayers to no man, and saying: "Fortune, I have nothing to do with you. I am not at your service. I know that men like Cato are spurned by you, and men like Vatinius made by you. I ask no favors." This is the way to reduce Fortune to the ranks.

These, then, are the things about which we may write in turn, and this is the ever fresh material which we may dig out as we scan the restless multitudes of men, who, in order to attain something ruinous, struggle on through evil to evil, and seek that which they must presently shun or even find surfeiting. For who was ever satisfied, after attainment, with that which loomed up large as he prayed for it? Happiness is not, as men think, a greedy thing; it is a lowly thing; for that reason it never gluts a man's desire. You deem lofty the objects you seek, because you are on a low level and hence far away from them; but they are mean in the sight of him who has reached them. And I am very much mistaken if he does not desire to climb still higher; that which you regard as the top is merely a rung on the ladder. Now all men suffer from ignorance of the truth; deceived by common report, they make for these ends as if they were good, and then, after having won their wish, and suffered much, they find them evil, or empty, or less important than they had expected. Most men admire that which deceives them at a distance, and by the crowd good things are supposed to be big things.

Now, lest this happen also in our own case, let us ask what is the Good. It has been explained in various ways; different men have described it in different ways. Some define it in this way: "That which attracts and calls the spirit to itself is a Good." But the objection at once comes up— what if it does attract, but straight to ruin? You know how seductive many evils are. That which is true differs from that which looks like the truth; hence the Good is connected with the true, for it is not good unless it is also true. But that which attracts and allures is only *like* the truth; it steals your attention, demands your interest, and draws you to itself. Therefore, some have given this definition: "That is good which inspires desire for itself, or rouses toward itself the impulse of a struggling soul." There is the same objection to this idea; for many things rouse the soul's impulses, and yet the search for them is harmful to the seeker. The following definition is better: "That is good which rouses the soul's impulse toward itself in accordance with nature, and is worth seeking only when it begins to be thoroughly worth seeking." It is by this time an honorable thing; for that is a thing completely worth seeking.

Happiness is not, as men think, a greedy thing; it is a lowly thing; for that reason it never gluts a man's desire

The present topic suggests that I state the difference between the Good and the honorable. Now they have a certain quality which blends with both and is inseparable from either: nothing can be good unless it contains an element of the honorable, and the honorable is necessarily good. What, then, is the difference between these two qualities? The honorable is the perfect Good, and the happy life is fulfilled thereby; through its influence other things also are rendered good. I mean something like this: there are certain things which are neither good nor bad—as military or diplomatic service, or the pronouncing of legal decisions. When such pursuits have been honorably conducted, they begin to be good, and they change over from the "indifferent" class into the Good. The Good results from partnership with the honorable, but the honorable is good in itself. The Good springs from the honorable, but the latter from itself. What is good might have been bad; what is honorable could never have been anything but good.

Some have defined it as follows: "That is good which is according to nature." Now attend to my own statement: that which is good is according to nature, but that which is according to nature does not also become immediately good; for many things harmonize with nature, but are so petty that it is not suitable to call them good. For they are unimportant and deserve to be despised. But there is no such thing as a very small and despicable good, for, as long as it is scanty, it is not good, and when it begins to be good, it ceases to be scanty. How, then, can the Good be recognized? Only if it is completely according to nature.

People say: "You admit that that which is good is according to nature; for this is its peculiar quality. You admit, too, that there are other things according to nature, which, however, are not good. How then can the former be good, and the latter not? How can there be an alteration in the peculiar quality of a thing, when each has, in common with the other, the special attribute of being in accord with nature?" Surely because of its magnitude. It is no new idea that certain objects change as they grow. A person, once a child, becomes a youth; his peculiar quality is transformed; for the child could not reason, but the youth possesses reason. Certain things not only grow in size as they develop, but grow into something else. Some reply: "But that which becomes greater does not necessarily become different. It matters not at all whether you pour wine into a flask or into a vat; the wine keeps its peculiar quality in both vessels. Small and large quantities of honey are not distinct in taste." But these are different cases which you mention; for wine and honey have a uniform quality; no matter how much the quantity is enlarged, the quality is the same. For some things endure according to their kind and their peculiar qualities, even when they are enlarged.

There are others, however, which, after many increments, are altered by the last addition; there is stamped upon them a new character, different from that of yore. One stone makes an archway—the stone which wedges the leaning sides and holds the arch together by its position in the middle. And why does the last addition, although very slight, make a great deal of difference? Because it does not increase; it fills up. Some things, through development, put off their former shape and are altered into a new figure. When the mind has for a long time developed some idea, and in the attempt to grasp its magnitude has become weary, that thing begins to be called "infinite." And then this has become something far different from what it was when it seemed great but finite. In the same way we have thought of something as difficult to divide; at the very end, as the task grows more and more hard, the thing is found to be "indivisible." Similarly, from that which could scarcely or with difficulty be moved we have advanced on and on—until we reach the "immovable." By the same reasoning a certain thing was according to nature; its greatness has altered it into some other peculiar quality and has rendered it a Good. Farewell.

CXXIII. ON THE CON-FLICT BETWEEN PLEA-SURE
AND VIRTUE

———

WEARIED WITH THE DISCOMFORT RATHER THAN WITH THE length of my journey, I have reached my Alban villa late at night, and I find nothing in readiness except myself. So I am getting rid of fatigue at my writing table: I derive some good from this tardiness on the part of my cook and my baker. For I am communing with myself on this very topic—that nothing is heavy if one accepts it with a light heart, and that nothing need provoke one's anger if one does not add to one's pile of troubles by getting angry. My baker is out of bread; but the overseer, or the house-steward, or one of my tenants can supply me therewith. "Bad bread!" you say. But just wait for it; it will become good. Hunger will make even such bread delicate and of the finest flavor. For that reason I must not eat until hunger bids me; so I shall wait and shall not eat until I can either get good bread or else cease to be squeamish about it. It is necessary that one grow accustomed to slender fare: because there are many problems of time and place which will cross the path even of the rich man and one equipped for pleasure, and bring him up with a round turn. To have whatsoever he wishes is in no man's power; it is in his power not to wish for what he has not, but cheerfully to employ what comes to him. A great step toward independence is a good-humored stomach, one that is willing to endure rough treatment.

You cannot imagine how much pleasure I derive from the fact that my weariness is becoming reconciled to itself; I am asking for no slaves to rub me down, no bath, and no other restorative except time. For that which toil has accumulated, rest can lighten. This repast, whatever it may be, will give me more pleasure than an inaugural banquet. For I have made trial of my spirit on a sudden—a simpler and a truer test. Indeed, when a man has made preparations and given himself a formal summons to be patient, it is not equally clear just how much real strength of mind he possesses; the surest proofs are those which one exhibits off-hand, viewing one's own troubles not only fairly but calmly, not flying into fits of temper or wordy wranglings, supplying one's own needs by not craving something which was really due, and reflecting that our habits may be unsatisfied, but never our own real selves. How many things are superfluous we fail to realize until they begin to be wanting; we merely used them not because we needed them but because we had them. And how much do we acquire simply because our neighbors have acquired such things, or because most men possess them! Many of our troubles may be explained from the fact that we live according to a pattern, and, instead of arranging our lives according to reason, are led astray by convention.

There are things which, if done by the few, we should refuse to imitate; yet when the majority have begun to do them, we follow along—just as if anything were more honorable because it is more frequent! Furthermore, wrong views, when they have become prevalent, reach, in our eyes, the standard of righteousness. Everyone now travels with Numidian outriders preceding him, with a troop of slave-runners to clear the way; we deem it disgraceful to have no attendants who will elbow crowds from the road, or will prove, by a great cloud of dust, that a high dignitary is approaching! Everyone now possesses mules that are laden with crystal and murrine cups carved by skilled artists of great renown; it is disgraceful for all your baggage to be made up of that which can be rattled along without danger.

Everyone has pages who ride along with ointment-covered faces so that the heat or the cold will not harm their tender complexions; it is disgraceful that none of your attendant slave-boys should show a healthy cheek, not covered with cosmetics.

You should avoid conversation with all such persons: they are the sort that communicate and engraft their bad habits from one to another. We used to think that the very worst variety of these men were those who vaunted their words; but there are certain men who vaunt their wickedness. Their talk is very harmful; for even though it is not at once convincing, yet they leave the seeds of trouble in the soul, and the evil which is sure to spring into new strength follows us about even when we have parted from them. Just as those who have attended a concert carry about in their heads the melodies and the charm of the songs they have heard—a proceeding which interferes with their thinking and does not allow them to concentrate upon serious subjects—even so the speech of flatterers and enthusiasts over that which is depraved sticks in our minds long after we have heard them talk. It is not easy to rid the memory of a catching tune; it stays with us, lasts on, and comes back from time to time. Accordingly, you should close your ears against evil talk, and right at the outset, too; for when such talk has gained an entrance and the words are admitted and are in our minds, they become more shameless. And then we begin to speak as follows: "Virtue, Philosophy, Justice—this is a jargon of empty words. The only way to be happy is to do yourself well. To eat, drink, and spend your money is the only real life, the only way to remind yourself that you are mortal. Our days flow on, and life—which we cannot restore—hastens away from us. Why hesitate to come to our senses? This life of ours will not always admit pleasures; meantime, while it can do so, while it clamors for them, what profit lies in imposing thereupon frugality? Therefore get ahead of death, and let anything that death will filch from you be squandered now upon yourself. You have no mistress, no favorite slave to make your mistress envious; you are sober when you make your daily appearance in public; you dine as if you had to show your account-book to 'Papa'; but *that* is not living, it is merely going shares in someone else's existence. And what madness it is to be looking out for the interests of your heir, and to deny yourself everything, with the result that you turn friends into enemies by the vast amount of the Fortune you intend to leave! For the more the heir is to get from you, the more he will rejoice in your taking-off! All those sour fellows who criticize other men's lives in a spirit of priggishness and are real enemies to their own lives, playing schoolmaster to the world—you should not consider them as worth a farthing, nor should you hesitate to prefer good living to a good reputation."

These are voices which you ought to shun just as Ulysses did; he would not sail past them until he was lashed to the mast. They are no less potent; they lure men from country, parents, friends, and virtuous ways; and by a hope that, if not base, is ill-starred, they wreck them upon a life of baseness. How much better to follow a straight course and attain a goal where the words "pleasant" and "honorable" have the same meaning! This end will be possible for us if we understand that there are two classes of objects which either attract us or repel us. We are attracted by such things as riches, pleasures, beauty, ambition, and other such coaxing and pleasing objects; we are repelled by toil, death, pain, disgrace, or lives of greater frugality. We ought therefore to train ourselves so that we may avoid a fear of the one or a desire for the other. Let us fight in the opposite fashion: let us retreat from the objects that allure, and rouse ourselves to meet the objects that attack.

Do you not see how different is the method of descending a mountain from that employed in climbing upward? Men coming down a slope bend backward; men ascending a steep place lean forward. For, my dear Lucilius, to allow yourself to put your body's weight ahead when coming down, or, when climbing up, to throw it backward is to comply with vice. The pleasures take one downhill but one must work upward toward that which is rough and hard to climb; in the one case let us throw our bodies forward, in the others let us put the check-rein on them.

Do you believe me to be stating now that only those men bring ruin to our ears, who praise pleasure, who inspire us with fear of pain—that element which is in itself provocative of fear? I believe that we are also injured by those who masquerade under the disguise of the Stoic school and at the same time urge us on into vice. They boast that only the wise man and the learned is a lover. "He alone has wisdom in this art; the wise man too is best skilled in drinking and feasting. Our study ought to be this alone: up to what age the bloom of love can endure!" All this may be regarded as a concession to the ways of Greece; we ourselves should preferably turn our attention to words like these: "No man is good by chance. Virtue is something which must be learned. Pleasure is low, petty, to be deemed worthless, shared even by dumb animals—the tiniest and meanest of whom fly toward pleasure. Glory is an empty and fleeting thing, lighter than air. Poverty is an evil to no man unless he kick against the goads. Death is not an evil; why need you ask? Death alone is the equal privilege of mankind. Superstition is the misguided idea of a lunatic; it fears those whom it ought to love; it is an outrage upon those whom it worships. For what difference is there between denying the gods and dishonoring them?"

You should learn such principles as these, nay, rather you should learn them by heart; philosophy ought not to try to explain away vice. For a sick man, when his physician bids him live recklessly, is doomed beyond recall. Farewell.

CXXIV. ON THE TRUE GOOD AS ATTAINED BY REASON

Full many an ancient precept could I give,
Didst your not shrink, and feel it shame to learn
Such lowly duties.

Bᴜᴛ ʏᴏᴜ ᴅᴏ ɴᴏᴛ sʜʀɪɴᴋ, ɴᴏʀ ᴀʀᴇ ʏᴏᴜ ᴅᴇᴛᴇʀʀᴇᴅ ʙʏ ᴀɴʏ sᴜʙᴛʟᴇ-ties of study. For your cultivated mind is not wont to investigate such important subjects in a free-and-easy manner. I approve your method in that you make everything count toward a certain degree of progress, and in that you are disgruntled only when nothing can be accomplished by the greatest degree of subtlety. And I shall take pains to show that this is the case now also. Our question is, whether the Good is grasped by the senses or by the understanding; and the corollary thereto is that it does not exist in dumb animals or little children.

Those who rate pleasure as the supreme ideal hold that the Good is a matter of the senses; but we Stoics maintain that it is a matter of the understanding, and we assign it to the mind. If the senses were to pass judgment on what is good, we should never reject any pleasure; for there is no pleasure that does not attract, no pleasure that does not please. Conversely, we should undergo no pain voluntarily; for there is no pain that does not clash with the senses. Besides, those who are too fond of pleasure and those who fear pain to the greatest degree would in that case not deserve reproof. But we condemn men who are slaves to their appetites and their lusts, and we scorn men who, through fear of pain, will dare no manly deed. But what wrong could such men be committing if they looked merely to the senses as arbiters of good and evil? For it is to the senses that you and yours have entrusted the test of things to be sought and things to be avoided!

Reason, however, is surely the governing element in such a matter as this; as reason has made the decision concerning the happy life, and concerning virtue and honor also, so she has made the decision with regard to good and evil. For with them the vilest part is allowed to give sentence about the better, so that the senses—dense as they are, and dull, and even more sluggish in man than in the other animals—pass judgment on the Good. Just suppose that one should desire to distinguish tiny objects by the touch rather than by the eyesight! There is no special faculty more subtle and acute than the eye, that would enable us to distinguish between good and evil. You see, therefore, in what ignorance of truth a man spends his days and how abjectly he has overthrown lofty and divine ideals, if he thinks that the sense of touch can pass judgment upon the nature of the Supreme Good and the Supreme Evil! He says: "Just as every science and every art should possess an element that is palpable and capable of being grasped by the senses (their source of origin and growth), even so the happy life derives its foundation and its beginnings from things that are palpable, and from that which falls within the scope of the senses. Surely you admit that the happy life takes its beginnings from things palpable to the senses." But we define as "happy" those things that are in accord with Nature. And that which is in accord with Nature is obvious and can be seen at once—just as easily as that which is complete. That which is according to Nature, that which is given us as a gift immediately at our birth, is, I maintain, not a Good, but the beginning of a Good. You, however, assign the Supreme Good, pleasure, to mere babies, so that the child at its birth begins at the point whither the perfected man arrives. You are placing the treetop where the root ought to be. If anyone should say that the child, hidden in its mother's womb, of unknown sex too, delicate, unformed, and shapeless—if one should say that this child is already in a state of goodness, he would clearly seem to be astray in his ideas. And yet how little difference is there between one who has just lately received the gift of life, and one who is still a hidden burden in the bowels of the mother! They are equally developed, as far as their understanding of good or evil is concerned; and a child is as yet no more capable of comprehending the Good than is a tree or any dumb beast.

But why is the Good nonexistent in a tree or in a dumb beast? Because there is no reason there, either. For the same cause, then, the Good is non-existent in a child, for the child also has no reason; the child will reach the Good only when he reaches reason. There are animals without rea-son, there are animals not yet endowed with reason, and there are animals who possess reason, but only incompletely; in none of these does the Good exist, for it is reason that brings the Good in its company. What, then, is the distinction between the classes which I have mentioned? In that which does not possess reason, the Good will never exist. In that which is not yet endowed with reason, the Good cannot be existent at the time. And in that which possesses reason but only incompletely, the Good is capable of exist-ing, but does not yet exist. This is what I mean, Lucilius: the Good cannot be discovered in any random person, or at any random age; and it is as far removed from infancy as last is from first, or as that which is complete from that which has just sprung into being. Therefore, it cannot exist in the delicate body, when the little frame has only just begun to knit together. Of course not—no more than in the seed. Granting the truth of this, we understand that there is a certain kind of Good in a tree or a plant; but this is not true of its first growth, when the plant has just begun to spring forth out of the ground. There is a certain Good of wheat: it is not yet existent, however, in the swelling stalk, nor when the soft ear is pushing itself out of the husk, but only when summer days and its appointed maturity have ripened the wheat. Just as Nature in general does not produce her Good until she is brought to perfection, even so man's Good does not exist in man until both reason and man are perfected. And what is this Good? I shall tell you: it is a free mind, an upright mind, subjecting other things to itself and itself to nothing. So far is infancy from admitting this Good that boyhood has no hope of it, and even young manhood cherishes the hope without justification; even our old age is very fortunate if it has reached this Good after long and concentrated study. If this, then, is the Good, the good is a matter of the understanding.

"But," comes the retort, "you admitted that there is a certain Good of trees and of grass; then surely there can be a certain Good of a child also." But the true Good is not found in trees or in dumb animals; the Good which exists in them is called good only by courtesy. "Then what is it?" you say. Simply that which is in accord with the nature of each. The real Good cannot find a place in dumb animals—not by any means; its nature is more blest and is of a higher class. And where there is no place for reason, the Good does not exist. There are four natures which we should mention here: of the tree, animal, man, and God. The last two, having reasoning power, are of the same nature, distinct only by virtue of the immortality of the one and the mortality of the other. Of one of these, then—to wit God—it is Nature that perfects the Good; of the other—to wit man—pains and study do so. All other things are perfect only in their particular nature, and not truly perfect, since they lack reason.

Indeed, to sum up, that alone is perfect which is perfect according to nature as a whole, and nature as a whole is possessed of reason. Other things can be perfect according to their kind. That which cannot contain the happy life cannot contain that which produces the happy life; and the happy life is produced by Goods alone. In dumb animals there is not a trace of the happy life, nor of the means whereby the happy life is produced; in dumb animals the Good does not exist. The dumb animal comprehends the present world about him through his senses alone. He remembers the past only by meeting with something which reminds his senses; a horse, for example, remembers the right road only when he is placed at the starting point. In his stall, however, he has no memory of the road, no matter how often he may have stepped along it. The third state—the future—does not come within the ken of dumb beasts.

How, then, can we regard as perfect the nature of those who have no experience of time in its perfection? For time is three-fold—past, present, and future. Animals perceive only the time which is of greatest moment to them within the limits of their coming and going—the present. Rarely do they recollect the past—and that only when they are confronted with present reminders. Therefore the Good of a perfect nature cannot exist in an imperfect nature; for if the latter sort of nature should possess the Good, so also would mere vegetation. I do not indeed deny that dumb animals have strong and swift impulses toward actions which seem according to nature, but such impulses are confused and disordered. The Good, however, is never confused or disordered.

"What!" you say, "do dumb animals move in disturbed and ill-ordered fashion?" I should say that they moved in disturbed and ill-ordered fashion, if their nature admitted of order; as it is, they move in accordance with their nature. For that is said to be "disturbed" which can also at some other time be "not disturbed"; so, too, that is said to be in a state of trouble which can be in a state of peace. No man is vicious except one who has the capacity of virtue; in the case of dumb animals their motion is such as results from their nature. But, not to weary you, a certain sort of good will be found in a dumb animal, and a certain sort of virtue, and a certain sort of perfection—but neither the Good, nor virtue, nor perfection in the absolute sense. For this is the privilege of reasoning beings alone, who are permitted to know the cause, the degree, and the means. Therefore, good can exist only in that which possesses reason.

Good can exist only in that which possesses reason

Do you ask now whither our argument is tending, and of what benefit it will be to your mind? I will tell you: it exercises and sharpens the mind, and ensures, by occupying it honorably, that it will accomplish some sort of good. And even that is beneficial which holds men back when they are hurrying into wickedness. However, I will say this also: I can be of no greater benefit to you than by revealing the Good that is rightly yours, by taking you out of the class of dumb animals, and by placing you on a level with God. Why, pray, do you foster and practice your bodily strength? Nature has granted strength in greater degree to cattle and wild beasts. Why cultivate your beauty? After all your efforts, dumb animals surpass you in comeliness. Why dress your hair with such unending attention? Though you let it down in Parthian fashion, or tie it up in the German style, or, as the Scythians do, let it flow wild—yet you will see a mane of greater thickness tossing upon any horse you choose, and a mane of greater beauty bristling upon the neck of any lion. And even after training yourself for speed, you will be no match for the hare. Are you not willing to abandon all these details—wherein you must acknowledge defeat, striving as you are for something that is not your own and come back to the Good that is really yours?

And what is this Good? It is a clear and flawless mind, which rivals that of God, raised far above mortal concerns, and counting nothing of its own to be outside itself. You are a reasoning animal. What Good, then, lies within you? Perfect reason. Are you willing to develop this to its farthest limits—to its greatest degree of increase? Only consider yourself happy when all your joys are born of reason, and when—having marked all the objects which men clutch at, or pray for, or watch over—you find nothing which you will desire; mind, I do not say *prefer*. Here is a short rule by which to measure yourself, and by the test of which you may feel that you have reached perfection: "You will come to your own when you shall understand that those whom the world calls fortunate are really the most unfortunate of all." Farewell.

The
Enchiridion

—

EPICTETUS

Translated by William Abbott Oldfather

THE ENCHIRIDION

———

1 SOME THINGS ARE UNDER OUR CONTROL, WHILE OTHERS ARE NOT under our control. Under our control are conception, choice, desire, aversion, and, in a word, everything that is our own doing; not under our control are our body, our property, reputation, office, and, in a word, everything that is not our own doing. Furthermore, the things under our control are by nature free, unhindered, and unimpeded; while the things not under our control are weak, servile, subject to hindrance, and not our own. Remember, therefore, that if what is naturally slavish you think to be free, and what is not your own to be your own, you will be hampered, will grieve, will be in turmoil, and will blame both gods and men; while if you think only what is your own to be your own, and what is not your own to be, as it really is, not your own, then no one will ever be able to exert compulsion upon you, no one will hinder you, you will blame no one, will find fault with no one, will do absolutely nothing against your will, you will have no personal enemy, no one will harm you, for neither is there any harm that can touch you.

With such high aims, therefore, remember that you must bestir yourself with no slight effort to lay hold of them, but you will have to give up some things entirely, and defer others for the time being. But if you wish for these things also, and at the same time for both office and wealth, it may be that you will not get even these latter, because you aim also at the former, and certainly you will fail to get the former, which alone bring freedom and happiness.

Make it, therefore, your study at the very outset to say to every harsh external impression, "You are an external impression and not at all what you appear to be." After that examine it and test it by these rules which you have, the first and most important of which is this: Whether the impression has to do with the things which are under our control, or with those which are not under our control; and, if it has to do with some one of the things not under our control, have ready to hand the answer, "It is nothing to me."

2. Remember that the promise of desire is the attainment of what you desire, that of aversion is not to fall into what is avoided, and that he who fails in his desire is unfortunate, while he who falls into what he would avoid experiences misfortune. If, then, you avoid only what is unnatural among those things which are under your control, you will fall into none of the things which you avoid; but if you try to avoid disease, or death, or poverty, you will experience misfortune. Withdraw, therefore, your aversion from all the matters that are not under our control, and transfer it to what is unnatural among those which are under our control. But for the time being remove utterly your desire; for if you desire some one of the things that are not under our control you are bound to be unfortunate; and, at the same time, not one of the things that are under our control, which it would be excellent for you to desire, is within your grasp. But employ only choice and refusal, and these too but lightly, and with reservations, and without straining.

But for the time being remove utterly your desire

3. With everything which entertains you, is useful, or of which you are fond, remember to say to yourself, beginning with the very least things, "What is its nature?" If you are fond of a jug, say, "I am fond of a jug"; for when it is broken you will not be disturbed. If you kiss your own child or wife, say to yourself that you are kissing a human being; for when it dies you will not be disturbed.

4. When you are on the point of putting your hand to some undertaking, remind yourself what the nature of that undertaking is. If you are going out of the house to bathe, put before your mind what happens at a public bath—those who splash you with water, those who jostle against you, those who vilify you and rob you. And thus you will set about your undertaking more securely if at the outset you say to yourself, "I want to take a bath, and, at the same time, to keep my moral purpose in harmony with nature." And so do in every undertaking. For thus, if anything happens to hinder you in your bathing, you will be ready to say, "Oh, well, this was not the only thing that I wanted, but I wanted also to keep my moral purpose in harmony with nature; and I shall not so keep it if I am vexed at what is going on."

5. It is not the things themselves that disturb men, but their judgements about these things. For example, death is nothing dreadful, or else Socrates too would have thought so, but the judgment that death is dreadful, *this* is the dreadful thing. When, therefore, we are hindered, or disturbed, or grieved, let us never blame anyone but ourselves, that means, our own judgments. It is the part of an uneducated person to blame others where he himself fares ill; to blame himself is the part of one whose education has begun; to blame neither another nor his own self is the part of one whose education is already complete.

6. Be not elated at any excellence which is not your own. If the horse in his elation were to say, "I am beautiful," it could be endured; but when you say in your elation, "I have a beautiful horse," rest assured that you are elated at something good which belongs to a horse. What, then, is your own? The use of external impressions. Therefore, when you are in harmony with nature in the use of external

> **It is not the things themselves that disturb men, but their judgements about these things**

impressions, then be elated; for then it will be some good of your own at which you will be elated.

7. Just as on a voyage, when your ship has anchored, if you should go on shore to get fresh water, you may pick up a small shellfish or little bulb on the way, but you have to keep your attention fixed on the ship, and turn about frequently for fear lest the captain should call; and if he calls, you must give up all these things, if you would escape being thrown on board all tied up like the sheep. So it is also in life: If there be given you, instead of a little bulb and a small shellfish, a little wife and child, there will be no objection to that; only, if the Captain calls, give up all these things and run to the ship, without even turning around to look back. And if you are an old man, never even get very far away from the ship, for fear that when He calls you may be missing.

8. Do not seek to have everything that happens happen as you wish, but wish for everything to happen as it actually does happen, and your life will be serene.

9. Disease is an impediment to the body, but not to the moral purpose, unless that consents. Lameness is an impediment to the leg, but not to the moral purpose. And say this to yourself at each thing that befalls you; for you will find the thing to be an impediment to something else, but not to yourself.

10. In the case of everything that befalls you, remember to turn to yourself and see what faculty you have to deal with it. If you see a handsome lad or woman, you will find continence the faculty to employ here; if hard labor is laid upon you, you will find endurance; if reviling, you will find patience to bear evil. And if you habituate yourself in this fashion, your external impressions will not run away with you.

11. Never say about anything, "I have lost it," but only "I have given it back." Is your child dead? It has been given back. Is your wife dead? She has been given back. "I have had my farm taken away." Very well, this too has been given back. "Yet it was a rascal who took it away." But what concern is it of yours by whose instrumentality the Giver called for its return?

So long as He gives it you, take care of it as of a thing that is not your own, as travelers treat their inn.

12. If you wish to make progress, dismiss all reasoning of this sort: "If I neglect my affairs, I shall have nothing to live on." "If I do not punish my slave-boy he will turn out bad." For it is better to die of hunger, but in a state of freedom from grief and fear, than to live in plenty, but troubled in mind. And it is better for your slave-boy to be bad than for you to be unhappy. Begin, therefore, with the little things. Your paltry oil gets spilled, your miserable wine stolen; say to yourself, "This is the price paid for a calm spirit, this the price for peace of mind." Nothing is got without a price. And when you call your slave-boy, bear in mind that it is possible he may not heed you, and again, that even if he does heed, he may not do what you want done. But he is not in so happy a condition that your peace of mind depends upon him.

> **Never say about anything, "I have lost it," but only "I have given it back."**

13. If you wish to make progress, then be content to appear senseless and foolish in externals, do not make it your wish to give the appearance of knowing anything; and if some people think you to be an important personage, distrust yourself. For be assured that it is no easy matter to keep your moral purpose in a state of conformity with nature, and, at the same time, to keep externals; but the man who devotes his attention to one of these two things must inevitably neglect the other.

14. If you make it your will that your children and your wife and your friends should live forever, you are silly; for you are making it your will that things not under your control should be under your control, and that what is not your own should be your own. In the same way, too, if you make it your will that your slave-boy be free from faults, you are a fool; for you are making it your will that vice be not vice, but something else. If, however, it

is your will not to fail in what you desire, this is in your power. Wherefore, exercise yourself in that which is in your power. Each man's master is the person who has the authority over what the man wishes or does not wish, so as to secure it, or take it away. Whoever, therefore, wants to be free, let him neither wish for anything, nor avoid anything, that is under the control of others; or else he is necessarily a slave.

15. Remember that you ought to behave in life as you would at a banquet. As something is being passed around it comes to you; stretch out your hand and take a portion of it politely. It passes on; do not detain it. Or it has not come to you yet; do not project your desire to meet it, but wait until it comes in front of you. So act toward children, so toward a wife, so toward office, so toward wealth; and then some day you will be worthy of the banquets of the gods. But if you do not take these things even when they are set before you, but despise them, then you will not only share the banquet of the gods, but share also their rule. For it was by so doing that Diogenes and Heracleitus, and men like them, were deservedly divine and deservedly so called.

16. When you see someone weeping in sorrow, either because a child has gone on a journey, or because he has lost his property, beware that you be not carried away by the impression that the man is in the midst of external ills, but straightway keep before you this thought: "It is not what has happened that distresses this man (for it does not distress another), but his judgment about it." Do not, however, hesitate to sympathize with him so far as words go, and, if occasion offers, even to groan with him; but be careful not to groan also in the center of your being.

For this is your business, to play admirably the role assigned you; but the selection of that role is Another's

17. Remember that you are an actor in a play, the character of which is determined by the Playwright: if He wishes the

play to be short, it is short; if long, it is long; if He wishes you to play the part of a beggar, remember to act even this role adroitly; and so if your role be that of a cripple, an official, or a layman. For this is your business, to play admirably the role assigned you; but the selection of that role is Another's.

18. When a raven croaks inauspiciously, let not the external impression carry you away, but straightway draw a distinction in your own mind, and say, "None of these portents are for me, but either for my paltry body, or my paltry estate, or my paltry opinion, or my children, or my wife. But for me every portent is favorable, if I so wish; for whatever be the outcome, it is within my power to derive benefit from it."

19. You can be invincible if you never enter a contest in which victory is not under your control. Beware lest, when you see some person preferred to you in honor, or possessing great power, or otherwise enjoying high repute, you are ever carried away by the external impression, and deem him happy. For if the true nature of the good is one of the things that are under our control, there is no place for either envy or jealousy; and you yourself will not wish to be a praetor, or a senator, or a consul, but a free man. Now there is but one way that leads to this, and that is to despise the things that are not under our control.

20. Bear in mind that it is not the man who reviles or strikes you that insults you, but it is your judgment that these men are insulting you. Therefore, when someone irritates you, be assured that it is your own opinion which has irritated you. And so make it your first endeavor not to be carried away by the external impression; for if once you gain time and delay, you will more easily become master of yourself.

21. Keep before your eyes day by day death and exile, and everything that seems terrible, but most of all death; and

You can be invincible if you never enter a contest in which victory is not under your control

then you will never have any abject thought, nor will you yearn for anything beyond measure.

22. If you yearn for philosophy, prepare at once to be met with ridicule, to have many people jeer at you, and say, "Here he is again, turned philosopher all of a sudden," and "Where do you suppose he got that high brow?" But do you not put on a high brow, and do you so hold fast to the things which to you seem best, as a man who has been assigned by God to this post; and remember that if you abide by the same principles, those who formerly used to laugh at you will later come to admire you, but if you are worsted by them, you will get the laugh on yourself twice.

23. If it should ever happen to you that you turn to externals with a view to pleasing someone, rest assured that you have lost your plan of life. Be content, therefore, in everything to *be* a philosopher, and if you wish also to be taken for one, show to yourself that you are one, and you will be able to accomplish it.

24. Let not these reflections oppress you: "I shall live without honor, and be nobody anywhere." For, if lack of honor is an evil, you cannot be in evil through the instrumentality of some other person, any more than you can be in shame. It is not your business, is it, to get office, or to be invited to a dinner-party? Certainly not. How, then, can this be any longer a lack of honor? And how is it that you will be "nobody anywhere," when you ought to be somebody only in those things which are under your control, wherein you are privileged to be a man of the very greatest honor? But your friends will be without assistance? What do you mean by being "without assistance"? They will not have paltry coin from you, and you will not make them Roman citizens. Well, who told you that these are some of the matters under our control, and not rather things which others do? And who is able to give another what he does not himself have? "Get money, then," says some friend, "in order that we too may have it." If I can get money and at the same time keep myself self-respecting, and faithful, and high-minded, show me the way and I will get it. But if you require me to lose the good things that belong to me, in order that you may acquire the things that are not good, you can see for yourselves how

unfair and inconsiderate you are. And which do you really prefer? Money, or a faithful and self-respecting friend? Help me, therefore, rather to this end, and do not require me to do those things which will make me lose these qualities.

"But my country," says he, "so far as lies in me, will be without assistance." Again I ask, what kind of assistance do you mean? It will not have loggias or baths of your providing. And what does that signify? For neither does it have shoes provided by the blacksmith, nor has it arms provided by the cobbler; but it is sufficient if each man fulfill his own proper function. And if you secured for it another faithful and self-respecting citizen, would you not be doing it any good? "Yes." Very well, and then you also would not be useless to it. "What place, then, shall I have in the State?" says he. Whatever place you can have, and at the same time maintain the man of fidelity and self-respect that is in you. But if, through your desire to help the State, you lose these qualities, of what good would you become to it, when in the end you turned out to be shameless and unfaithful?

25. Has someone been honored above you at a dinner-party, or in salutation, or in being called in to give advice? Now if these matters are good, you ought to be happy that he got them; but if evil, be not distressed because you did not get them; and bear in mind that, if you do not act the same way that others do, with a view to getting things which are not under our control, you cannot be considered worthy to receive an equal share with others. Why, how is it possible for a person who does not haunt some man's door, to have equal shares with the man who does? For the man who does not do escort duty, with the man who does? For the man who does not praise, with the man who does? You will be unjust, therefore, and insatiable, if, while refusing to pay the price for which such things are bought, you want to obtain them for nothing. Well, what is the price for heads of lettuce? An obol, perhaps. If, then, somebody gives up his obol and gets his heads of lettuce, while you do not give your obol, and do not get them, do not imagine that you are worse off than the man who gets his lettuce. For as he has his heads of lettuce, so you have your obol which you have not given away.

Now it is the same way also in life. You have not been invited to some-body's dinner-party? Of course not; for you didn't give the host the price at which he sells his dinner. He sells it for praise; he sells it for personal atten-tion. Give him the price, then, for which it is sold, if it is to your interest. But if you wish both not to give up the one and yet to get the other, you are insatiable and a simpleton. Have you, then, nothing in place of the dinner? Indeed you have; you have not had to praise the man you did not want to praise; you have not had to put up with the insolence of his doorkeepers.

26. What the will of nature is may be learned from a consideration of the points in which we do not differ from one another. For example, when some other person's slave-boy breaks his drinking cup, you are instantly ready to say, "That's one of the things which happen." Rest assured, then, that when your own drinking cup gets broken, you ought to behave in the same way that you do when the other man's cup is broken. Apply now the same principle to the matters of greater importance. Some other person's child or wife has died; no one but would say, "Such is the fate of man." Yet when a man's own child dies, immediately the cry is, "Alas! Woe is me!" But we ought to remember how we feel when we hear of the same misfor-tune befalling others.

27. Just as a mark is not set up in order to be missed, so neither does the nature of evil arise in the universe.

28. If someone handed over your body to any person who met you, you would be vexed; but that you hand over your mind to any person that comes along, so that, if he reviles you, it is disturbed and troubled—are you not ashamed of that?

29. In each separate thing that you do, consider the matters which come first and those which follow after, and only then approach the thing itself. Otherwise, at the start you will come to it enthusiastically, because you have never reflected upon any of the subsequent steps, but later on, when some difficulties appear, you will give up disgracefully. Do you wish to win an Olympic victory? So do I, by the gods! for it is a fine thing. But consider the matters which come before that, and those which follow after, and only when you have done that, put your hand to the task. You have to submit to

discipline, follow a strict diet, give up sweet cakes, train under compulsion, at a fixed hour, in heat or in cold; you must not drink cold water, nor wine just whenever you feel like it; you must have turned yourself over to your trainer precisely as you would to a physician. Then when the contest comes on, you have to "dig in" beside your opponent, and sometimes dislocate your wrist, sprain your ankle, swallow quantities of sand, sometimes take a scourging, and along with all that get beaten. After you have considered all these points, go on into the games, if you still wish to do so; otherwise, you will be turning back like children. Sometimes they play wrestlers, again gladiators, again they blow trumpets, and then act a play. So you too are now an athlete, now a gladiator, then a rhetorician, then a philosopher, yet with your whole soul nothing; but like an ape you imitate whatever you see, and one thing after another strikes your fancy. For you have never gone out after anything with circumspection, nor after you had examined it all over, but you act at haphazard and half-heartedly.

Consider first the nature of the business, and then learn your own natural ability

In the same way, when some people have seen a philosopher and have heard someone speaking like Euphrates (though, indeed, who can speak like him?), they wish to be philosophers themselves. Man, consider first the nature of the business, and then learn your own natural ability, if you are able to bear it. Do you wish to be a contender in the pentathlon, or a wrestler? Look to your arms, your thighs, see what your loins are like. For one man has a natural talent for one thing, another for another. Do you suppose that you can eat in the same fashion, drink in the same fashion, give way to impulse and to irritation, just as you do now? You must keep vigils, work hard, abandon your own people, be despised by a paltry slave, be laughed to scorn by those who meet you, in everything get the worst of it, in honor, in office, in court, in every paltry affair. Look these drawbacks over carefully, if you are willing at the price of these things to secure tranquility, freedom and calm. Otherwise, do not approach philosophy; don't act like a child—now a philosopher, later on a tax-gatherer, then a rhetorician, then a procurator of Caesar. These things do not go together. You must be one person, either good or bad; you must labor to improve either your own governing principle or externals; you must work hard either on the inner man, or on things outside; that is, play either the role of a philosopher or else that of a layman.

30. Our duties are in general measured by our social relationships. He is a father. One is called upon to take care of him, to give way to him in all things, to submit when he reviles or strikes you. "But he is a bad father." Did nature, then, bring you into relationship with a *good* father? No, but simply with a father. "My brother does me wrong." Very well, then, maintain the relation that you have toward him; and do not consider what he is doing, but what you will have to do, if your moral purpose is to be in harmony with nature. For no one will harm you without your consent; you will have been harmed only when you think you are harmed. In this way, therefore, you will discover what duty to expect of your neighbor, your citizen, your commanding officer, if you acquire the habit of looking at your social relations with them.

31. In piety toward the gods, I would have you know, the chief element is this, to have right opinions about them—as existing and as administering the universe well and justly—and to have set yourself to obey them and to submit to everything that happens, and to follow it voluntarily, in the belief that it is being fulfilled by the highest intelligence. For if you act in this way, you will never blame the gods, nor find fault with them for neglecting you. But this result cannot be secured in any other way than by withdrawing your idea of the good and the evil from the things which are not under our control, and placing it in those which are under our control, and in those alone. Because, if you think any of those former things to be good or evil, then, when you fail to get what you want and fall into what you do not want, it is altogether inevitable that you will blame and hate those who are responsible for these results. For this is the nature of every

living creature, to flee from and to turn aside from the things that appear harmful, and all that produces them, and to pursue after and to admire the things that are helpful, and all that produces them. Therefore, it is impossible for a man who thinks that he is being hurt to take pleasure in that which he thinks is hurting him, just as it is also impossible for him to take pleasure in the hurt itself. Hence it follows that even a father is reviled by a son when he does not give his child some share in the things that seem to be good; and this it was which made Polyneices and Eteocles enemies of one another, the thought that the royal power was a good thing. That is why the farmer reviles the gods, and so also the sailor, and the merchant, and those who have lost their wives and their children. For where a man's interest lies, there is also his piety. Wherefore, whoever is careful to exercise desire and aversion as he should, is at the same time careful also about piety. But it is always appropriate to make libations, and sacrifices, and to give of the first fruits after the manner of our fathers, and to do all this with purity, and not in a slovenly or careless fashion, nor, indeed, in a miserly way, nor yet beyond our means.

32. When you have recourse to divination, remember that you do not know what the issue is going to be, but that you have come in order to find this out from the diviner; yet if you are indeed a philosopher, you know, when you arrive, what the nature of it is. For if it is one of the things which are not under our control, it is altogether necessary that what is going to take place is neither good nor evil. Do not, therefore, bring to the diviner desire or aversion, and do not approach him with trembling, but having first made up your mind that every issue is indifferent and nothing to you, but that, whatever it may be, it will be possible for you to turn it to good use, and that no one will prevent this. Go, then, with confidence to the gods as to counselors; and after that, when some counsel has been given you, remember whom you have taken as counselors, and whom you will be disregarding if you disobey. But go to divination as Socrates thought that men should go, that is, in cases where the whole inquiry has reference to the outcome, and where neither from reason nor from any other technical art are means vouchsafed for discovering the matter in question. Hence,

when it is your duty to share the danger of a friend or of your country, do not ask of the diviner whether you ought to share that danger. For if the diviner forewarns you that the omens of sacrifice have been unfavorable, it is clear that death is portended, or the injury of some member of your body, or exile; yet reason requires that even at this risk you are to stand by your friend, and share the danger with your country. Wherefore, give heed to the greater diviner, the Pythian Apollo, who cast out of his temple the man who had not helped his friend when he was being murdered.

33. Lay down for yourself, at the outset, a certain stamp and type of character for yourself, which you are to maintain whether you are by yourself or are meeting with people. And be silent for the most part, or else make only the most necessary remarks, and express these in few words. But rarely, and when occasion requires you to talk, talk, indeed, but about no ordinary topics. Do not talk about gladiators, or horse races, or athletes, or things to eat or drink—topics that arise on all occasions; but above all, do not talk about people, either blaming, or praising, or comparing them. If, then, you can, by your own conversation bring over that of your companions to what is seemly. But if you happen to be left alone in the presence of aliens, keep silence.

> **Above all, do not talk about people, either blaming, or praising, or comparing them**

Do not laugh much, nor at many things, nor boisterously.

Refuse, if you can, to take an oath at all, but if that is impossible, refuse as far as circumstances allow.

Avoid entertainments given by outsiders and by persons ignorant of philosophy; but if an appropriate occasion arises for you to attend, be on the alert to avoid lapsing into the behavior of such laymen. For you may rest assured, that, if a man's companion be dirty, the person who keeps close company with him must of necessity get a share of his dirt, even though he himself happens to be clean.

In things that pertain to the body take only as much as your bare need requires, I mean such things as food, drink, clothing, shelter, and household slaves; but cut down everything which is for outward show or luxury.

In your sex-life preserve purity, as far as you can, before marriage, and, if you indulge, take only those privileges which are lawful. However, do not make yourself offensive, or censorious, to those who do indulge, and do not make frequent mention of the fact that you do not yourself indulge.

If someone brings you word that So-and-so is speaking ill of you, do not defend yourself against what has been said, but answer, "Yes, indeed, for he did not know the rest of the faults that attach to me; if he had, these would not have been the only ones he mentioned."

It is not necessary, for the most part, to go to the public shows. If, however, a suitable occasion ever arises, show that your principal concern is for none other than yourself, which means, wish only for that to happen which does happen, and for him only to win who does win; for so you will suffer no hindrance. But refrain utterly from shouting, or laughter at anyone, or great excitement. And after you have left, do not talk a great deal about what took place, except in so far as it contributes to your own improvement; for such behavior indicates that the spectacle has aroused your admiration.

Do not go rashly or readily to people's public readings, but when you do go, maintain your own dignity and gravity, and at the same time be careful not to make yourself disagreeable.

When you are about to meet somebody, in particular when it is one of those men who are held in very high esteem, propose to yourself the question, "What would Socrates or Zeno have done under these circumstances?" and then you will not be at a loss to make proper use of the occasion. When you go to see one of those men who have great power, propose to yourself the thought, that you will not find him at home, that you will be shut out, that the door will be slammed in your face, that he will pay no attention to you. And if, despite all this, it is your duty to go, go and take what comes, and never say to yourself, "It was not worth all the trouble." For this is characteristic of the layman, that is, a man who is vexed at externals.

In your conversation avoid making mention at great length and excessively of your own deeds or dangers, because it is not as pleasant for others to hear about your adventures, as it is for you to call to mind your own dangers.

Avoid also raising a laugh, for this is a kind of behavior that slips easily into vulgarity, and at the same time is calculated to lessen the respect which your neighbors have of you. It is dangerous also to lapse into foul language. When, therefore, anything of the sort occurs, if the occasion be suitable, go even so far as to reprove the person who has made such a lapse; if, however, the occasion does not arise, at all events show by keeping silence, and blushing, and frowning, that you are displeased by what has been said.

34. When you get an external impression of some pleasure, guard yourself, as with impressions in general, against being carried away by it; nay, let the matter wait upon *your* leisure, and give yourself a little delay. Next think of the two periods of time, first, that in which you will enjoy your pleasure, and second, that in which, after the enjoyment is over, you will later repent and revile your own self; and set over against these two periods of time how much joy and self-satisfaction you will get if you refrain. However, if you feel that a suitable occasion has arisen to do the deed, be careful not to allow its enticement, and sweetness, and attractiveness to overcome you; but set over against all this the thought, how much better is the consciousness of having won a victory over it.

35. When you do a thing which you have made up your mind ought to be done, never try not to be seen doing it, even though most people are likely to think unfavorably about it. If, however, what you are doing is not right, avoid the deed itself altogether; but if it is right, why fear those who are going to rebuke you wrongly?

36. Just as the propositions, "It is day," and "It is night," are full of meaning when separated, but meaningless if united; so also, granted that

for you to take the larger share at a dinner is good for your body, still, it is bad for the maintenance of the proper kind of social feeling. When, therefore, you are eating with another person, remember to regard, not merely the value for your body of what lies before you, but also to maintain your respect for your host.

37. If you undertake a role which is beyond your powers, you both disgrace yourself in that one, and at the same time neglect the role which you might have filled with success.

38. Just as you are careful, in walking about, not to step on a nail or to sprain your ankle, so be careful also not to hurt your governing principle. And if we observe this rule in every action, we shall be more secure in setting about it.

39. Each man's body is a measure for his property, just as the foot is a measure for his shoe. If, then, you abide by this principle, you will maintain the proper measure, but if you go beyond it, you cannot help but fall headlong over a precipice, as it were, in the end. So also in the case of your shoe; if once you go beyond the foot, you get first a gilded shoe, then a purple one, then an embroidered one. For once you go beyond the measure there is no limit.

If it is right, why fear those who are going to rebuke you wrongly?

40. Immediately after they are fourteen, women are called "ladies" by men. And so when they see that they have nothing else but only to be the bedfellows of men, they begin to beautify themselves, and put all their hopes in that. It is worthwhile for us to take pains, therefore, to make them understand that they are honored for nothing else but only for appearing modest and self-respecting.

41. It is a mark of an ungifted man to spend a great deal of time in what concerns his body, as in much exercise, much eating, much drinking, much evacuating of the bowels, much copulating. But these things

are to be done in passing; and let your whole attention be devoted to the mind.

42. When someone treats you ill or speaks ill of you, remember that he acts or speaks thus because he thinks it is incumbent upon him. That being the case, it is impossible for him to follow what appears good to you, but what appears good to himself; whence it follows, that, if he gets a wrong view of things, the man that suffers is the man that has been deceived. For if a person thinks a true composite judgement to be false, the composite judgement does not suffer, but the person who has been deceived. If, therefore, you start from this point of view, you will be gentle with the man who reviles you. For you should say on each occasion, "He thought that way about it."

43. Everything has two handles, by one of which it ought to be carried and by the other not. If your brother wrongs you, do not lay hold of the matter by the handle of the wrong that he is doing, because this is the handle by which the matter ought not to be carried; but rather by the other handle—that he is your brother, that you were brought up together, and then you will be laying hold of the matter by the handle by which it ought to be carried.

44. The following statements constitute a *non sequitur*: "I am richer than you are, therefore I am superior to you"; or, "I am more eloquent than you are, therefore I am superior to you." But the following conclusions are better: "I am richer than you are, therefore my property is superior to yours"; or, "I am more eloquent than you are, therefore my elocution is superior to yours." But *you* are neither property nor elocution.

45. Somebody is hasty about bathing; do not say that he bathes badly, but that he is hasty about bathing. Somebody drinks a good deal of wine; do not say that he drinks badly, but that he drinks a good deal. For until you have decided what judgment prompts him, how do you know that what he is doing is bad? And thus the final result will not be that you receive convincing sense-impressions of some things, but give your assent to others.

46. On no occasion call yourself a philosopher, and do not, for the most part, talk among laymen about your philosophic principles, but do what follows from your principles. For example, at a banquet do not say how people ought to eat, but eat as a man ought. For remember how Socrates had so completely eliminated the thought of ostentation, that people came to him when they wanted him to introduce them to philosophers, and he used to bring them along. So well did he submit to being overlooked. And if talk about some philosophic principle arises among laymen, keep silence for the most part, for there is great danger that you will spew up immediately what you have not digested. So when a man tells you that you know nothing, and you, like Socrates, are not hurt, then rest assured that you are making a beginning with the business you have undertaken. For sheep, too, do not bring their fodder to the shepherds and show how much they have eaten, but they digest their food within them, and on the outside produce wool and milk. And so do you, therefore, make no display to the laymen of your philosophical principles, but let them see the results which come from these principles when digested.

47. When you have become adjusted to simple living in regard to your bodily wants, do not preen yourself about the accomplishment; and so likewise, if you are a water-drinker, do not on every occasion say that you are a water-drinker. And if ever you want to train to develop physical endurance, do it by yourself and not for outsiders to behold; do not throw your arms around statues, but on occasion, when you are very thirsty, take cold water into your mouth, and then spit it out, without telling anybody.

48. This is the position and character of a layman: he never looks for either help or harm from himself, but only from externals. This is the position and character of the philosopher: he looks for all his help or harm from himself.

Signs of one who is making progress are: he censures no one, praises no one, blames no one, finds fault with no one, says nothing about himself as though he were somebody or knew something. When he is hampered or prevented, he blames himself. And if anyone compliments him, he smiles to himself at the person complimenting; while if anyone censures him, he makes no defense. He goes about like an invalid, being careful not to disturb, before it has grown firm, any part which is getting well. He has put away from himself his every desire, and has transferred his aversion to those things only, of what is under our control, which are contrary to nature. He exercises no pronounced choice in regard to anything. If he gives the appearance of being foolish or ignorant he does not care. In a word, he keeps guard against himself as though he were his own enemy lying in wait.

49. When a person gives himself airs because he can understand and interpret the books of Chrysippus, say to yourself, "If Chrysippus had not written obscurely, this man would have nothing about which to give himself airs."

But what is it I want? To learn nature and to follow her. I seek, therefore, someone to interpret her; and having heard that Chrysippus does so, I go to him. But I do not understand what he has written; I seek, therefore, the person who interprets Chrysippus. And down to this point there is nothing to justify pride. But when I find the interpreter, what remains is to put his precepts into practice; this is the only thing to be proud about. If, however, I admire the mere act of interpretation, what have I done but turned into a grammarian instead of a philosopher? The only difference, indeed, is that I interpret Chrysippus instead of Homer. Far from being proud, therefore, when somebody says to me, "Read me Chrysippus," I blush the rather, when I am unable to show him such deeds as match and harmonize with his words.

50. Whatever principles are set before you, stand fast by these like laws, feeling that it would be impiety for you to transgress them. But pay no attention to what somebody says about you, for this is, at length, not under your control.

51. How long will you still wait to think yourself worthy of the best things, and in nothing to transgress against the distinctions set up by the

reason? You have received the philosophical principles which you ought to accept, and you have accepted them. What sort of a teacher, then, do you still wait for, that you should put off reforming yourself until he arrives? You are no longer a lad, but already a full-grown man. If you are now neglectful and easy-going, and always making one delay after another, and fixing first one day and then another, after which you will pay attention to yourself, then without realizing it you will make no progress, but, living and dying, will continue to be a layman throughout. Make up your mind, therefore, before it is too late, that the fitting thing for you to do is to live as a mature man who is making progress, and let everything which seems to you to be best be for you a law that must not be transgressed. And if you meet anything that is laborious, or sweet, or held in high repute, or in no repute, remember that now is the contest, and here before you are the Olympic games, and that it is impossible to delay any longer, and that it depends on a single day and a single action, whether progress is lost or saved. This is the way Socrates became what he was, by paying attention to nothing but his reason in everything that he encountered. And even if you are not yet a Socrates, still you ought to live as one who wishes to be a Socrates.

52. The first and most necessary division in philosophy is that which has to do with the application of the principles, as, for example, Do not lie. The second deals with the demonstrations, as, for example, How comes it that we ought not to lie? The third confirms and discriminates between these processes, as, for example, How does it come that this is a proof? For what is a proof, what is logical consequence, what contradiction, what truth, what falsehood? Therefore, the third division is necessary because of the second, and the second because of the first; while the most necessary of all, and the one in which we ought to rest, is the first. But we do the opposite; for we spend our time in the third division, and all our zeal is devoted to it, while we utterly neglect the first. Wherefore, we lie, indeed, but are ready with the arguments which prove that one ought not to lie.

53. Upon every occasion we ought to have the following thoughts at our command:

> *Lead thou me on, O Zeus, and Destiny,*
> *To that goal long ago to me assigned.*
> *I'll follow and not falter; if my will*
> *Prove weak and craven, still I'll follow on.*
> *"Whoso has rightly with necessity complied,*
> *We count him wise, and skilled in things divine."*
> *"Well, O Crito, if so it is pleasing to the gods, so let it be."*
> *"Anytus and Meletus can kill me, but they cannot hurt me."*

NOTES

NOTES TO *LETTERS FROM A STOIC*

141 **offered his own throat to Chaerea:** A reference to the murder of Caligula, on the l'alatine, AD 41.

142 **whither you are already being led:** i.e., to death.

142 **is culled from another man's Garden:** The Garden of Epicurus.

143 **aside and it is pure murder:** During the luncheon interval, condemned criminals were often driven into the arena and compelled to fight for the amusement of those spectators who remained throughout the day.

144 **Come now; do you:** The remark is addressed to the brutalized spectators.

147 **for he is outward bound:** A jesting allusion to the Roman funeral: the corpse's feet pointed to the door.

147 **burial some other man's dead:** His former owner should have kept him and buried him.

147 **you used to bring me little images:** Small figures, generally of terracotta, were frequently given to children as presents at the Saturnalia.

147 **his teeth are just dropping out:** i.e., the old slave resembles a child in that he is losing his teeth (but for the second time).

154 **now it is a year:** i.e., the whole year is a Saturnalia.

154 **we should be neither like the liberty-capped:** The *pilleus* was worn by newly freed slaves and by the Roman populace on festal occasions.

156 **practice our strokes on the "dummy":** The post gladiators used when preparing themselves for combats in the arena.

160 **old amid the worries of procuratorships:** The procurator did the work of a quaestor in an imperial province. Positions in Rome to which Lucilius might succeed were such as *praefectus annonae*, in charge of the grain supply, or *praefectus urbi*, director of public safety, and others.

160 **when he stood on the very summit:** And therefore could speak with authority on this point.

160 **a style so debauched as that:** Seneca whimsically pretends to assume that eccentric literary style and high political positions go hand in hand.

160 **those whom your slave-secretary:** A slave kept by every prominent Roman to identify the master's friends and dependants.

166 **He who ponders these things:** Death, poverty, temptation, and suffering.

169 **tell you about Cato, how he read Plato's:** The *Phaedo,* on the immortality of the soul.

169 **the good Fortune to save:** i.e., to save and bring back to Rome as a prisoner.

170 **which fate gave to the Scipios in Africa:** Scipio Africanus defeated Hannibal at Zama in 202 BC. Scipio Aemilianus, also surnamed Africanus, was by adoption the grandson of Hannibal's conqueror. He captured Carthage in the Third Punic War, 146 BC. The Scipio mentioned by Seneca died in 46 BC.

183 **and without the art:** i.e., philosophy.

183 **cross the Pennine or Graian:** The Great St. Bernard and the Little St. Bernard routes over the Alps.

183 **traverse the Candavian:** A mountain in Illyria, over which the *Via Egnatia* ran.

183 **or face the Syrtes:** Dangerous quicksands along the north coast of Africa.

183 **Your bordered robe:** The *toga praetezta*, badge of the official position of Lucilius.

194 **according to this part of the world**: i.e., Rome.

194 **So you in your province:** Lucilius was at this time imperial procurator in Sicily.

200 **You over there have Etna:** Etna was of especial interest to Lucilius. Besides being a governor in Sicily, he may have written the poem *Aetna.*

200 **I have had to be satisfied with Baiae:** Not far from Naples, and across the bay from Puteoli. It was a fashionable and dissolute watering place.

200 **he will not select Canopus:** Situated at the mouth of the westernmost branch of the Nile, and proverbial in Latin literature for the laxity of its morals.

205 **when our friend Chrysippus:** It is nowhere else related of the famous Stoic philosopher Chrysippus that he objected to the salutations of his friends; and, besides, the morning salutation was a Roman, not a Greek, custom.

208 **full fate of an athlete; the anointing:** i.e., an "anointing" with mud.

208 **sand-sprinkle in the Naples tunnel:** A characteristic figure. After anointing, the wrestler was sprinkled with sand, so that the opponent's hand might not slip. The Naples tunnel furnished a shortcut to those who, like Seneca in this letter, did not wish to take the time to travel by the shore route along the promontory of Pausilipum.

220   **For, as my friend Attalus:** The teacher of Seneca, often mentioned by him.

221   **dear friend Annaeus Serenus:** An intimate friend of Seneca, probably a relative, who died in the year 63 from eating poisoned mushrooms. Seneca dedicated to Serenus several of his philosophical essays.

240   **summit and is full of confidence:** In which case, he would be completely superior to her.

241   **race that lies beyond the Dahae:** A nomad Scythian tribe east of the Caspian Sea.

243   **wholly concerned with cleverness:** Eloquence and the other arts please mainly by their cleverness; nor does philosophy abjure such cleverness as style; but here in these letters, wherein we are discussing the soul, the graces of speech are of no concern.

269   **the famous Roman general:** Calpurnius, in Sicily, during the first Punic war.

269   **It is not the Three Hundred:** The soldiers of Leonidas.

270   **not be wounded even by "Pythius":** A nickname for an especially large machine for assaulting walls.

299   **to him the radiance of the mighty star:** i.e., the Sun.

300   **on the register of the younger men:** Men between the ages of seventeen and forty-six.

300   **Age ranks among the external things:** As riches, health, etc.

315   **The only Good which you:** i.e., the Epicureans.

315   **is it to be rooted out?:** i.e., grief should not be replaced by pleasure; otherwise grief will cease to exist.

322   **mutual friendship among all the virtues:** In other words, Wisdom, Justice, Courage, and Self-Restraint, together with other qualities of simplicity, kindness, etc., being "avatars" of Virtue herself, are interrelated.

322   **we are helped even by those:** i.e., certain of the Peripatetic school.

325   **Genius or a Juno to every individual:** Every man had his Genius, and every woman her Juno. In the case of the Stoics, God dwelt in every soul.

339   **pleasure than an inaugural banquet:** i.e., a dinner given by an official when he entered upon his office.

342   **wise man and the learned is a lover:** Meaning, in line with the Stoic paradoxes, that only the sage knows how to be rightly in love.

344   **For with them:** i.e., the Epicureans.

344   **Supreme Good and the Supreme Evil! He:** i.e., the advocate of the "touch" theory.

345   **Good only when he reaches reason:** According to the Stoics (and other schools also), the "innate notions," or groundwork of knowledge, begin to be subject to reason after the attainment of a child's seventh year.

345   **possess reason, but only incompletely:** i.e., they are limited to "practical judgment."

348   **which rivals that of God:** One of the most conspicuous Stoic paradoxes maintained that "the wise man is God."

NOTES TO *THE ENCHIRIDION*

354   **But for the time being:** The remark, as many others of the admonitions, is addressed to a student or a beginner.

354   **but lightly, and with reservations:** See M. Aurelius, 1, 4, where Mr. Haines (in *L.C.L.*) suggests that the reference is to some such reservations as recommended in James iv. 15: "For that ye ought to say is, If the Lord will, we shall live, and do this, or that."

356   **may pick up a small shellfish or little bulb:** The Greeks ate a good many different bulbous plants, as we use a variety of different plants for "greens."

357   **that your peace of mind depends upon him:** That is, the slave-boy
would be in a remarkable position of advantage if his master's peace of
mind depended, not upon the master himself, but upon the actions of
his slave-boy.

358   **but the selection of that role is Another's:** A reverent designation for
God. See I. 25, 13.

360   **any more than you can be in shame:** That is, every man is exclusively
responsible for his own good or evil. But honor and the lack of it
are things which are obviously not under a man's control, since they
depend upon the action of other people. It follows, therefore, that lack
of honor cannot be an evil, but must be something indifferent.

361   **An obol:** See note on frag. 11.

362   **the nature of evil arise in the universe:** That is, it is inconceivable
that the universe should exist in order that some things may go wrong;
hence, nothing natural is evil, and nothing that is by nature evil can
arise.—Thus in effect Simplicius, and correctly, it seems.

362   **In each separate thing that you do:** This chapter is practically word
for word identical with III. 15. Since it was omitted in Par., and not
commented on by Simplicius, it may have been added in some second
edition, whether by Arrian or not.

363   **you must not drink cold water:** That is, *cold* water not at all; while
wine may be drunk, but only at certain times, i.e., probably with one's
meals. Such prohibitions are still common in Europe, particularly in
popular therapeutics.

366   **helped his friend when he was being murdered:** A few more
unimportant details are given by Aelian, *Varia Historia*, 3, 44; and
Simplicius in his commentary on this passage, p. 258 c ff. (Heinsius),
or p. 411 (Schweighäuser). The point of the story is that a man does
not need to go to a diviner in order to learn whether he should defend
his country or his friends. That question was long ago settled by the
greatest of diviners, Apollo at Delphi, who ordered to be cast out of
his temple an inquirer that had once failed to defend his own friend.

367   **readily to people's public readings:** A favorite way of introducing a new work of literature to the reading public, somewhat like our modern musical recitals, or artists' exhibitions.

368   **by keeping silence, and blushing:** The ordinary person, to be sure, can no more call up a blush off-hand than he can a sneeze or a hiccup, and the observation of nature implied by the command is, therefore, imperfect. But all Epictetus means is that one should make no effort to conceal any natural expression of moral resentment under such circumstances.

369   **Each man's body is a measure for his property:** That is, property, which is of use only for the body, should be adjusted to a man's actual bodily needs, just as a shoe is (or at least should be) adjusted to the actual needs of a man's foot. The comparison seems to have been a commonplace; see Demophilus, *Similitudines*, 20 (Mullach); Horace, *Epist.* I. 7, 98 and 10, 42 f.

370   **Somebody is hasty about bathing:** The implication must be that a hurried bath, like a hurried shave, is apt to leave something to be desired.

371   **do not throw your arms around statues:** That is, in cold weather, because this takes a person out of doors where people can see him.

374   **and skilled in things divine:** Euripides, frag. 965 Nauck.

374   **it is pleasing to the gods, so let it be:** Plato, *Crito*, 43 D (slightly modified).

374   **but they cannot hurt me:** Plato, *Apology*, 30 C–D (somewhat modified).

ABOUT THE AUTHORS

——

Marcus Aurelius was Roman Emperor from 161 to 180 AD. He was the last emperor during the Pax Romana, a time of peace and stability for the Roman Empire. He wrote *Meditations,* one of the key texts of Stoic philosophy, while on campaign, as a way to foster his own self-improvement.

Seneca was a Stoic philosopher, statesman, and playwright. He was the tutor and advisor of Emperor Nero before he was forced to drink poison for allegedly having aided in an assassination attempt against the emperor. He is best known for his letters and essay on moral issues as well as his tragedies, including *Medea* and *Phaedra.*

Epictetus was born into slavery but gained his freedom and became one of the primary thinkers in the Stoic tradition. The only record of his teachings comes via Arrian, his pupil, who recorded much of his philosophy and reasoning.

Massimo Pigliucci is an author, blogger, and podcaster, as well as the K.D. Irani Professor of Philosophy at the City College of New York. His academic work is in evolutionary biology, philosophy of science, the nature of pseudoscience, and practical philosophy. Massimo publishes regular columns in *Skeptical Inquirer* and in *Philosophy Now.* His books include *How to Be a Stoic: Using Ancient Philosophy to Live a Modern Life* (Basic Books) and *Nonsense on Stilts: How to Tell Science from Bunk* (University of Chicago Press). Massimo's latest book is *The Quest for Character: What the Story of Socrates and Alcibiades Teaches Us about Our Search for Good Leaders* (Basic Books). More by Massimo at https://massimo pigliucci.org.